Disrupting White Mindfulness

Manchester University Press

Disrupting White Mindfulness

Race and Racism in the Wellbeing Industry

Cathy-Mae Karelse

MANCHESTER UNIVERSITY PRESS

The right of Cathy-Mae Karelse to be identified as the
author of this work has been asserted in accordance with the
Copyright, Designs and Patents Act 1988.

Published by Manchester University Press
Oxford Road, Manchester M13 9PL

www.manchesteruniversitypress.co.uk

British Library Cataloguing-in-Publication Data
A catalogue record for this book is available from the British
Library

ISBN 978 1 5261 6206 9 hardback
ISBN 978 1 5261 7626 4 paperback

First published 2023

The publisher has no responsibility for the persistence or
accuracy of URLs for any external or third-party internet
websites referred to in this book, and does not guarantee
that any content on such websites is, or will remain, accurate
or appropriate.

Typeset by Newgen Publishing UK

Printed and bound in Great Britain by
TJ Books Limited, Padstow, Cornwall

For Ché and Ruth
who clear the path and create untold joy

It is always important to see things as they are, not the masks that other people portray them to be – Akwaeke Emezi

Contents

Contents

Tables

Acknowledgements

There are countless people who have supported me in different ways on this journey. Their encouragement and constancy have added significantly to completion of this book. At many times it has felt more like a collaboration than a sole venture, which has enriched the process and filled it with a sense of connection.

I could start with any number of people, but will begin with Heidi Mirza whose conversation is always stimulating and fills me with so many ideas, possibilities, and delight. Her accompaniment into uncharted territory always feels uplifting and explorative and leaves me with a sense of growth and possibility. But there is also deep guidance and reassurance and focus that arises for which I am so grateful.

For her engaging dialogue and shared interest, Jaime Kucinskas reminds me just by virtue of her nature to adopt a wide-open perspective to this work that can feel very focused and intense. I have so much appreciation for her deep interest in my writing and her enthusiasm for the different perspective I bring. This connection is enriching and has helped me value my work and think more deeply about it.

I am grateful to Stephen Stanley for his early read, comments, and enthusiasm for my project that buoyed me at times when the content has felt isolating. I also thank those who read very early drafts of my writing: Ulrich Pagel and Sian Hawthorne provided helpful insight when I was first forming ideas and spurred me on as I started this journey. Jo Gillibrand willingly gave time to help me shape initial ideas, as did Masato Kato, Thando Njovane, and many others who dipped into different aspects of my work and boosted my vision. Dima Chami always offered stimulating engagement and connection, as have Juliette Liebi, Meera Patel, Gillian Marcelle, Shireen Badat, Rachel Lilley, Bernadette Carelse, Pauline Gibbs, Byron Lee, Barbara Reid, Aesha Frances, Dean Frances, Tracey Cramond, and Tarik Dervish.

I am also thankful to many colleagues for their time and willingness to enter challenging conversations that diversity and decolonisation raise. Despite the discomfort the topic can bring, they remained faithful to a commitment to change. The office staff at various organisations who fielded my questions, I realise, remain nameless, but I am most grateful for their quiet facilitation and the time taken to deliver and verify information. This provided a tremendous steer and helped me navigate the field.

Gratitude to my editors at Manchester University Press, Tom Dark, Laura Swift, and Emma Brennan, for clear guidance and patience as I produced this book. They made the journey a pleasure. My gratitude also to the reader/s at Manchester University Press of the initial proposal, and any external readers whose supportive feedback helped guide my writing and improved the final piece.

Deep appreciation to my circle of friends and family who've shown interest in my work, checked in on me regularly, and taken time to acquaint themselves with my field. My wonderful South African roots have been nourished through rich collaborations with Lucille Meyer and Shafika Isaacs. Our collective political, practical thought and work is always inspirational and bridges many worlds of ethics and transformation, filling me with a sense of possibility and imagination.

My spirit is always nurtured by Lama Rod, whose felt presence elevates my being and reminds me to consciously cultivate joy, gratitude, and tenderness.

I am ever grateful to my amazing family. Thank you for your love, devotion, and backing. Charli, thank you for your careful reading and encouragement and your ever helpful feedback. B, the many conversations continue to stimulate and set me in new directions. Joseph, you are my muse, thank you for the many laughs, the wonderful company, and Motown Wednesdays, all of which have kept me on form. Lynne and Mark, thank you for all your care and amity. Finally, Ché and Ruth, I am constantly inspired by you. You continue to amaze me and grow my heart and I am unceasingly grateful for the relationship you share with one another. You bring me infinite joy.

Abbreviations

BAME	Black, Asian and Minority Ethnic
BGR	Buddhist Global Relief
BIPOC	Black, Indigenous, People of Colour
BLM	Black Lives Matter
BME	Black and Minority Ethnic
CfM	Centre for Mindfulness
DEI	Diversity, equity, and inclusion
EBMC	East Bay Meditation Centre
EDI	Equity, diversity, and inclusion
EHRC	Equality and Human Rights Commission
GM	Global Majority
MBCT	Mindfulness-Based Cognitive Therapy
MBI:TAC	Mindfulness-Based Interventions: Teaching Assessment Criteria
MBSR	Mindfulness-Based Stress Reduction
NHS	National Health Service, UK
PGM	People of the Global Majority
TAC	Mindfulness-Based Interventions: Teaching Assessment Criteria
TT	Teacher training
TTP	Teacher training programme

Introduction: encountering the world of White Mindfulness

[A]nyone who saw [your name] before meeting you would assume you are a white man. One day you will have to apply for jobs. We just wanted to make sure you could make it to the interview.

Austin Channing Brown (2018: 15)

What might a decolonised mindfulness look like? Is it possible even to imagine a justice-infused mindfulness responsive to the needs of the many? The wellness industry, now worth US$4 trillion, has enveloped therapies and wellbeing methods that individualise and privatise health (Hill, 2019). Mindfulness, one such approach, has exploded onto the Western wellbeing scene over the last decade. A form of meditation increasingly popularised in the West since the early 1980s, mindfulness itself has developed into a multibillion-dollar industry (Patricio, 2018), comprising seemingly endless commodities such as apps, podcasts, trainings, and colouring-in books. Unravelling the tapestry of how the industry formed reveals a Western mindfulness trajectory enmeshed in the socio-political settings in which it takes root. In the context of late capitalism, its upsurge is indicative of growing levels of ill health, the loss of workdays, and a desire for meaning among those dissatisfied with the realities of living in perilous conditions. Yet, as is glaringly evident, the Mindfulness Industry[1] is also mostly White and, given its usual price tag, mindfulness is a predominantly middle- or upper-class consumable. Its popularisation, it seems, comes at the cost of being accessible to everyone. Such inequality is particularly conspicuous in an industry that makes claims to 'common humanity' and 'universality'.

A term I use, Western mindfulness, might be understood in various ways. It might refer to the mindfulness gifted through Buddhist lineages and cosmologies as they are engaged with and practiced in the West, interpretations of these teachings that integrate personal and social liberation, or Western secularised mindfulness with its hyper-focus on the individual. The categories are of course non-exclusive and permeable; their porous borders bleed into one another, allowing practitioners to move between them with some ease. Hardening their edges is convenient for purposes of comparison, but it belies the multiple voices found within any of the above groupings. Classical teachings of mindfulness are broad-ranging and not one thing. Different Buddhist traditions subscribe to their own philosophies and customs. Similarly, the broad rubric of 'secular mindfulness' collapses wide-ranging interpretations, some of which focus on refining the self while others emphasise social change. My work on White Mindfulness,[2] which commonly calls itself secular mindfulness, focuses on dominant discourses and trends among leading organisations in Britain and the US. I home in on the story of Western mindfulness' racialised trajectory to consider what an alternative might look like. In writing this book, I am acutely aware that I am a part of the systems I critique. My commentary does not in any way suggest that my worldview is unbiased. In fact, my position as a Black feminist researcher within the wellness space is the starting point from which I grapple with forging futures of belonging for all. Although multiple intersectional factors create exclusions, I emphasise race and, to a lesser extent, gender. By adopting a critical lens, I am asking something more of mindfulness, at a time when social justice is an imperative in the world of our making.

For me, mindfulness cannot generate individual stability in isolation from social stability. That is like taking a fish out of water and suggesting it try just a little bit harder to swim. Certainly, mindfulness can reduce anxiety and stress as much as other community-focused activities. Without a radical transformation agenda, though, White Mindfulness all too easily individualises problems that are socially induced. In doing so, it creates an individualised response to social and systemic harms. I argue that the rush to create individual stability in isolation from collective, social, and global stability perpetuates a problem for which mindfulness all too easily becomes a mere balm or quick fix.

Born in apartheid South Africa, into a family legally classified 'Coloured' by the apartheid regime, I started my journey into yoga and meditation at an early age, via the influences of Venketesananda Saraswati, who travelled to South Africa in 1962 to spread the teachings of his teacher, Swami Sivananda. Despite the limitations imposed by apartheid structures, that world opened possibilities beyond formal religion and expanded my community. Yet in the context of South Africa, I was aware of how yoga and Buddhism increasingly became the enclave of White South Africans. Decades later, as I ventured formally into the world of mindfulness, I was struck anew by its predominance in whiteness.[3] We can see whiteness as not merely a racial marker, but an invisibilised mode of social power built on living histories of oppressions, exclusions, discriminations, and vulnerabilities. As an ideology it preserves social norms that sustain White supremacy and privilege. My attention was captured by the irony of teachings of liberation, espoused by long-standing traditions, being infused with inequalities in the settings in which they evolve. I was curious to understand how industrialised mindfulness, which emphasises noticing and awareness, comes to embody and mirror whiteness as if unaware. Mindfulness can appear to reflect the water in which it swims, uncritically. In fact, in its popularisation and commercialisation, mindfulness becomes intrinsically tied to endemic forms of oppression and, in effect, to whiteness. This trend of mindfulness is what I term White Mindfulness. Considering whiteness and its interplay with mindfulness, this book unpacks the complexity of White Mindfulness and prospects for transformation. It underlines the ferocity and tenacity of race as a social construct in our everyday worlds and social spaces.

In her 2018 book *I'm Still Here: Black Dignity in a World Made for Whiteness*, Austin Channing Brown explains why her parents gave her the name Austin. In the epigraph to this introduction, Brown's parents explain how her naming was intended to improve her access to opportunities that would usually be denied to Black[4] people. Brown confirms that this is indeed how her world unfolded. She would find herself in situations in which her face-to-face interviewers were stunned by their irreconciliation of her name and the reality of her Black, female body. In the world of these interviewers, upon recognising her given name, they commonly expect to meet a White, male person. Brown's experience speaks to the long-standing histories of designed social inequities in which even a name sets in motion denial to work, education, justice, housing, and other human rights. Her story tells of the waters Western mindfulness inhabits. It speaks to the social norms writ large in Western societies steeped in historic, well-worn injustices. White Mindfulness, like a sizeable white ship, navigates these waters that are apparently fluid on the surface, yet thick with obstructions, currents, and tides that inhibit change. Its captains and most of its crew remain oblivious to the depths of injustices in which they cruise. Habits of White privilege, so deeply ingrained, operate in plain sight in social structures, yet remain invisible to those whom they benefit. So steeped are the murky waters in social forces of whiteness that, like the Greenwich Meridian, they function as a natural, unquestioned given; a default from which the world navigates. Inhabiting the world of White Mindfulness requires, it seems, Brown's parents' manoeuvres: adopting its names, customs, and practices.

The apartheid regime discriminated against its citizens on the basis of difference, most notably race. The system of racial capitalism created a society in which the vast majority of citizens, 87 per cent, were marginalised and stripped of political and socio-economic power.[5] Unlike the US and UK, South Africa has a majority Black population. Like many of my generation, I was actively involved in the South African anti-apartheid struggle and in nation-building. After moving from South Africa to the UK, with my critical faculties intact and a heart open to the prospect of social change, my career shifted in a direction of wellness studies. I was keen to integrate wellness and social justice. To qualify as a mindfulness teacher, I entered the world of mindfulness training. I looked at what was fast becoming mainstream training and chose what I, at the time, considered the best route. Interestingly, the formal channels of qualification were not the Buddhist temples and centres spread across the US and UK. Instead, a secularised form of mindfulness that kept a foot in the Buddhist world but positioned itself in medicine, psychology, science, and academia stood out. At the time, drawn by the attraction of teachings that were booming, I travelled to the US to receive my training, hopeful about how a contemplative, transformation-based practice could serve people. I stepped into the training excited that it was accredited and led by Jon Kabat-Zinn – founder of the rapidly expanding Mindfulness-Based Stress Reduction (MBSR) programme. The trainings I attended did not disappoint and it was clear from the deep investment of teachers like Kabat-Zinn, Florence Meleo-Meyer, Melissa Blacker, and Saki Santorelli that they were intended to plumb the depths and width of a mindfulness that could serve growing numbers of people experiencing stress. And there is no doubt that these early versions of 'secular mindfulness' supported and continue to support many people through crises and challenges. However, it is also true that the field mushroomed and that those championing what has become White Mindfulness did not read the signs of how its disconnect from social justice issues led to its assimilation by neoliberalism and whiteness.

Overcome by a blend of awe, openness, and trust in a common agenda, it was only upon reflection that I registered the fallout of these trainings. How could anyone not merge mindfulness and social liberation? Although I entered with Audre Lorde's famous 'the master's tools will never dismantle the master's house' quote in hand, I showed up hopeful (Lorde, 2007b).[6] The power of these spaces is compelling; they offer highly valued certificates and qualifications that, despite their shortcomings, open worlds. I used the teachings personally and qualified to teach mindfulness to others with my own integration of social justice teachings. Over time, through immersion in the field, I came to realise that the training spaces I occupied are mostly blind to their own whiteness: their exclusivity is unknown to those in power. With profound insight, Lorde writes of how when we enter these spaces with Black bodies, we must learn not only the course material but enough of the social norms to navigate these spaces comfortably, undetected, to blend in, not be a thorn in the side nor cause trouble. As little as a decade ago, the training space was different to what it is now. The mood of disruption and decoloniality had not yet become commonplace. Subversive voices within these White spaces were considered interesting, contraire, angry, and were often met with a 'yes, but'.

From 2006 I followed the Centre for Mindfulness (CfM) Teacher Training Pathway (TTP) attaining CfM's 'platinum'

Certified Teacher status in 2015. I ascribe this descriptor as the qualification was, at the time, the highest qualification one could attain from the CfM to round off years of immersion in courses and other forms of study. At the same time, in 2010 I became a Mindfulness-Based Cognitive Therapy (MBCT) trainer. In addition, I attended annual and often bi-annual teacher-led silent retreats, fulfilling CfM's teaching requirements. Immersing myself in the field, I also undertook training in the supervision and assessment of secular mindfulness teachers. By all accounts, I ticked all the boxes to become a secular mindfulness trainer and eventually a teacher trainer. Entering the field in this way aided my understanding of the Western mindfulness project and sensitised me to the sector's inclusionary efforts and exclusionary patterns. During my mindfulness training, all my teachers, whether in training or meditation halls, were White. Blending in required that I avoid the texture of the water and pay no attention to race, class, or other characteristics of difference. The trainings in fact promised to transcend these obstacles by treating us all as 'equals' who shared a common purpose of noticing and overcoming personal patterns as a pathway to changing society. Interpretations of mindfulness encouraged us not to see difference and to treat one another as the same. That 'sameness' was forged along the lines of normative whiteness: we were trained in the image of our teachers, who encouraged us to navigate our own individual suffering without becoming 'bogged down' in 'the story' of our conditioning.

As a politically active Black South African woman conditioned in systemic apartheid, a race-gender-class lens is intrinsic to my worldview. It seems imperative to consider how difference is manipulated to entrench dominant power and discourses, and conversely to leverage difference to create a world of collective belonging. Patricia Hill Collins names this ambiguous positioning, in which we are inside situations but also on the outside looking in, an 'outsider-within' (Hill Collins, 1997; 1986). This of course comes with its own complexities and confusions: working with the cruise ship metaphor it relates to remaining on board yet knowing how to swim, knowing the ropes but never becoming captain, all the while remembering how to walk on land. As an 'outsider-within' the world of White Mindfulness, I became increasingly curious about whether what I was seeing correlated with other Black experiences within the field and whether the view changes depending on who's looking and where we are looking from. I was drawn increasingly to Lorde's consideration of smart subversion strategies such as organising in small identity-based groups. I wondered about my role within the Mindfulness Industry and what, as a teacher, I was training others to do and to become. My interest in the mutual entrapment of Western secular mindfulness and whiteness grew in tandem with a spotlight being shone by secular mindfulness critics on its inherent racialised exclusions (see Hsu, 2014; 2016; Magee, 2016; 2018; Sylvia, 2016; williams *et al.*, 2016; Black, 2017; Gleig, 2019; Yancy and McRae, 2019). I wanted to probe further into this complex web of Western mindfulness' socio-political fabric to investigate Lorde's master's tools claims. This would allow me to learn whether it is possible to get the White cruise ship to change course without upsetting management.

As my own interest in the exclusive nature of the Mindfulness Industry grew, so did the momentum of discerning voices. A growing number of conversations about and critiques of the racialised, exclusive nature of the wellness industry shone a light on its lack of diversity and its blindness to difference. These investigations went further than talk of exclusions. They dived into the engine room of the cruise ship to uncover the mechanisms and structures that keep the ship afloat. This book joins these compelling contributions that seek to build more just societies. Highlights include a 2015 public dialogue between Angela Davis – a long-standing Black feminist academic meditator and radical activist of note – and Jon Kabat-Zinn on mindfulness and social justice. In the same year, Reverend angel Kyodo williams, Lama Rod Owens, and Jasmine Syedullah conceptualised *Radical Dharma*, offering a framework for reimagining social justice through a Buddhist lens. At the time, Jaweed Kameel also covered Global Majority (GM) groups springing up in Buddhist settings to offset predominantly White meditation gatherings. In the following year, Funie Hsu published *We've Been Here All Along*, telling the story of the exclusion of Asian Americans from US Buddhist developments. Concurrently, Christopher Raiche described the active use of Buddhist teachings to deny and downplay difference through selective interpretations of human 'sameness'. In 2017, Angela Black commented on the whiteness of the mindfulness sector. There have since been numerous

critiques of the racialised nature of the Mindfulness Industry such
as *The Mindful Elite* (Kucinskas, 2019), *Buddhism and Whiteness*
(Yancy and McCrae, 2019), and *McMindfulness* (Purser, 2019),
all showing the ease with which spirituality is commodified. Most
recently, during the final stages of writing this book, *Beyond White
Mindfulness* (Fleming *et al.*, 2022), an edited collection under-
scoring the urgency of diverse narratives and the importance of
the mindfulness-social justice relationship, was released. These
rich interventions have helped me unpack the muddiness of White
Mindfulness.

Toni Morrison's notion of framing tells us how multiple
ingredients shape perception. Together with Stuart Hall's thought
that ingredients coalesce to create political conjunctures, we can see
how the Mindfulness Industry comes to embody the complex interplay of neoliberalism, postracialism, and whiteness as ideologies of
advanced capitalism. Working alongside whiteness, postracialism
and neoliberalism comprise the waters that shape White Mindfulness.
The former refuses the construct of race, thereby denying its use
to oppress, appropriate, and sow division (Goldberg, 2015). The
latter has become a collective term to denote, among other things,
a form of advanced capitalism in which a shrinking state promotes
free markets and privatisation while commodifying even the 'self'.
These ideologies, which I discuss in greater detail in the first part of
this book, work hand in glove to maintain dominance. The idea of
individual, indivisible entities intrinsic to these worldviews isolates
persons from their communities to create an atomised, privatised
'self'. Moreover, they engulf White Mindfulness to the extent that
its popular social media image regurgitates systemic whiteness.

The 2014 *Time* cover of a slim, White blonde woman in seated
meditation selling mindfulness is reminiscent of tropes of sexualised
women associated with boxing and Formula 1 marketing (Pickert,
2014). But such sexist marketisation is merely one face of cultural
appropriation. In 2015, shortly after *Time*'s coverage, Google held a
Wisdom 2.0 event to promote mindfulness as a pathway to living a
fuller and more compassionate life. The proceedings were interrupted
by demonstrators campaigning against rent increases in Silicon Valley
(Healey, 2015). Ironically, while the chair encouraged the audience
to 'roll out the welcome mat' to pay attention to what they were
feeling in their bodies, Google evicted the campaigners who were

local residents. This act of removing what is undesirable reveals the selective intentionality that White Mindfulness encourages. Noticing and acting against injustices appears not to be included in mindfulness' ambit of paying attention and expanding awareness. Instead of engaging the protestors or turning towards them, as mindfulness usually suggests when approaching difficulty, the activists were banished. The Mindfulness Industry dismisses *Time*'s front cover and the Google 2.0 eviction as unrepresentative detractions from a revolution being started from the inside out. In many respects, this book poses a different interpretation of these events as marking White Mindfulness' absorption into systems of inequality.

In a lesser known 2008 UK exposé, tenants forcibly evicted from their Heygate homes in London with the promise of social housing that didn't materialise were offered life skills to cope. While the authorities created an impression of care by enlisting The Happiness Project to provide the dispossessed residents with emotional regulation training, their new homes were sold to foreign investors.[7] Targeting the individual to cultivate inner resilience in response to rising stress levels is a distraction that discharges officials from social responsibility. In this example, it obscures the direct link between the residents' distress and the socio-economic disruption of their lives. Such acts privatise stress, ignore the direct causes of mental illness, and prove cost-inefficient compared to addressing inequalities directly (O'Brien, 2019). In this scenario, mindfulness adds to the incessant cruelties of systemic whiteness by expecting residents to weather injustices.

As patterns that showcase mindfulness' complicity in discrimination emerged, critique escalated and its immersion in whiteness became better known. To compound matters, the intersecting pandemics of 2020 – COVID-19, racism, and collapsing economies – exposed the increased vulnerabilities of Black people to institutional racism. Following George Floyd's murder, the expansion of the Black Lives Matter (BLM) movement placed the whiteness of the Mindfulness Industry centre stage, shifting the debate on inclusion beyond morality towards an imperative to secure its future. This prompted a scramble for Black bodies to change the face of the Mindfulness Industry. Yet the concepts of diversity and inclusion are themselves questionable. What is it that a greater diversity of people is included into? Does power change in these organisations, and do newcomers feel a sense of belonging and ownership? As is increasingly apparent, to forge futures of belonging for all, there is a need to understand why histories of coloniality and empire remain alive and durable today and to grapple with how difference continues to be exploited or ignored rather than leveraged. It is worth reiterating that whiteness itself is about far more than race; it comprises multiple intersecting factors, such as race, class, gender, sexuality, faith, disability, and age, that create systemic exclusions from jobs, education, mortgages, health, and justice.

Diving more deeply into the waters of secular mindfulness, it becomes clear that when the Mindfulness Industry uses the concept of embodiment, it fails to mention the many ways in which it is forged in the wake of age-old injustices that are normalised to such an extent that they go unquestioned. The aspiration to embody mindfulness belies the industry's embodiment of whiteness. Austin Channing Brown's parents note that one plays the system in order to excel in it. Yet as Brown herself says, being inside the system in no way guarantees an easy ride. In fact, the same systemic obstacles used to marginalise people function at every level, whether in the boardroom or the classroom. Given its colonial roots, the Mindfulness Industry is not only inextricable from the socio-political and economic fabric that shapes it, it also has little immunity against it. Like many uncritical education systems, it does the work of neoliberalism and postracialism, emphasising individual noticing, coping, and resilience while de-emphasising context and structure.

In my experience, entering the mindfulness space required me to leave my 'baggage', critique, and justice agenda at the door. Real-world narratives, like those of the Silicon Valley protestors and Heygate residents, are seen to detract from cultivating presence and diving deeper into a realisation of one's humanity. What I chose to do with mindfulness once I left the classroom was considered my private affair. Whether I chose to become a mindful sniper, or a social justice activist depended on my own conscience.[8] In this way, White Mindfulness refuses any political stand. It batted liberally for all teams until, like many organisations steeped in whiteness, it met the BLM movement with performative statements of support. Yet the Mindfulness Industry is unable to cast off a history that is not based in social justice. The choice to ostensibly flatten inequalities by treating everyone as the same fosters elites, as Kucinskas (2019) tells us, who remain distant from inequalities. At the same time, the precariat is taught coping skills to endure adverse conditions, and activists are encouraged to take refuge in mindful self-care without necessarily addressing why they are fatigued. In contrast, for socially engaged Buddhists,[9] such as the *Radical Dharma* authors and communities like the Buddhist Peace Fellowship, suffering is concomitantly individual and social (williams *et al.*, 2016). Rooted in the interrelation of Buddhist doctrine and political justice, mindfulness and social justice are inseparable. These movements 'agitate' for those who align with their ethics and values to generate and bring about social change, not merely to support it. They highlight agency to end the suffering of all beings and emphasise the creation of conditions for 'human flourishing'. This is a far cry from my training as a mindfulness teacher, during which politics was navigated with dis-ease. Yet it is in these very spaces that whiteness and neoliberalism produce new economies such as the Mindfulness Industry tasked to ensure the everyday survival and mental wellbeing of workers living socially fragmented, dislocated, undervalued lives.

This is not to say that the Mindfulness Industry doesn't help people or bring relief. Indeed, in the early days of mindfulness being popularised in the West, it primarily gained a foothold in response to rising levels of stress. Jon Kabat-Zinn's MBSR programme seeded a cross-sectoral industry in hospitals, boardrooms, sports arenas, and civil society. Early studies touted mindfulness for effective stress relief. Favourable media coverage of the 'right kind of efficient mindfulness' – an eight-week programme – parachuted it to fame and fortune. But in adopting 'stress' as a contemporary moniker for the Buddhist notion of suffering, it absorbed into its solution both individualisation and privatisation.

Because of these developments, the mindfulness community increasingly faces questions regarding its socially engaged purpose (Thompson, 2017; Duerr, 2015; Forbes, 2016). Arguments for an explicitly pro-justice, community-engaged function challenge individualised mindfulness models that emphasise inner liberation as a necessary and sufficient first step towards social justice. In her dialogue with Kabat-Zinn in 2015, Davis underscores the politicised nature of mindfulness and its potential role and re-contextualisation in accordance with social justice values (Davis and Kabat-Zinn, 2015). In the context of her decades-long work on decarceration, in which she argues for the abolition of the racialised prison industrial complex, Davis enquires into how mindfulness can be of service to the project of prison abolition and to incarcerated people. Taking account that the calming influences of mindfulness can turn into placation and sedation, she asks how helpful these qualities are when systems must be changed. Davis challenges the notion of an 'apolitical' mindfulness that considers itself impartial to the disproportionate number of young Black men, and growing number of Black women, who are interned. She calls on a mindfulness that does not separate the politics of the school-to-prison pipeline and institutional racism from a practice of freedom. Her argument leads us to question the uses of power when the Mindfulness Industry declares itself neutral and her challenge remains unanswered. Although not necessarily in direct response to Davis's queries, engaged mindfulness advocates identify the importance of both inner and outer practice and foreground 'scholarly enquiry, spiritual practice and social activism' as a foundation of transformation (Ng, 2014). This still-unfolding debate pushes the boundaries of mindfulness beyond the comfort zone of 'individual noticing' towards political transformation. It suggests that mindfulness is never neutral, or without an agenda, and that claims of 'impartiality' are themselves political.

In support of Davis's challenges, the premise of this book is that the proliferation of mindfulness in the West is politically, conceptually, and contextually contentious. Discord relates in part to ethical disputes surrounding commodification, inaccessibility, and elitism, not to mention deployment in the military and Fortune 500 corporations (Eaton, 2014; Myers, 2015; Caring-Lobel, 2016). The mindful soldier who can shoot with greater precision collides with the ethics of non-harming and compassion that are fundamental to Buddhist traditions. Similarly, mindfulness purposed for profit to benefit the 1 per cent by making workers more focused, productive, and resilient rubs up against values of a world that leaves no one behind, as advocated by the United Nation's Sustainable Development Goals.[10] Added to this, mindfulness' reconceptualisation to reduce stress is seen as simultaneously skilful in bringing it into popular discourses, and opportunistic in performing 'attention policing'. Similarly, its recontextualisation is contested on the grounds of secularisation and assimilation (see McMahan, 2012; Sun, 2014). Secularisation is, after all, a politically informed, non-neutral process that selectively absorbs traditions into dominant Western cultures. Prolific as it is, the Mindfulness Industry seems beset by these complex fault lines that repeatedly favour the status quo. There is nothing in the commercialisation of mindfulness that upsets dominant discourses. On the contrary, the very industrialisation of mindfulness rests on interpretations that make it suitable, pliable, and adaptable to ideology.

The story of White Mindfulness

As an outsider-within, in this book I unravel why the industry evolves as it does, how its choices and actions reinforce its position, and how it could look and be different. Lorde's master's tools metaphor frames my inquiry. I use her guidance to tell the story of White Mindfulness using the metaphor of a white cruise ship reluctant to change course despite tempestuous seas. In this context, becoming crew to rechart a course is a brave and potentially foolhardy, suffocating act.

Disrupting White Mindfulness investigates the Western trajectory of the Mindfulness Industry in three parts. The first of these, 'The roots of exclusion and Othering', lays out the theoretical components on which my critique of White Mindfulness rests. The second part, 'Wrapping mindfulness in whiteness', discusses the status and methods of White Mindfulness, drawing on three significant organisations. The final part, 'Embodying justice, changing worlds', addresses an emergent movement that combines mindfulness with embodied liberation and social justice.

Part I explores how deep histories of exclusion in Western societies commonly escape those they privilege, to the extent that norms such as Othering – a concept I discuss in Chapter 1 – go unseen and unnamed. When cultures blinkered to exclusions dominate, the problem persists. In this context, the very descriptor 'secular mindfulness' masks the inherently political nature of secularisation. To explain how power today is rooted in histories of coloniality, Chapter 1 draws on Edward Said's 1978 ground-breaking text, *Orientalism*. Said's framework explains how seamlessly Othering shapes both the extraction of mindfulness from its Buddhist origins in Southeast Asia, and the context into which it arrives in the twenty-first-century West. I also bring in subversive voices that trouble hegemonic discourses including Toni Morrison, bell hooks, and Homi Bhabha to reveal the depths of dominant narratives and to emphasise alternative ones. Chapter 2 expands on the socio-political and economic contexts in which the Mindfulness Industry evolves, showing how racialised neoliberal forces shape an industry intricately interwoven with and almost inseparable from whiteness. The waters that shape White Mindfulness, the seas in which it freely swims, reveal unquestioned forces that are embedded in its making. Chapter 3 sketches brief histories of Buddhism and mindfulness' integration in the West to show the perpetuity of Othering in an uninterrupted distribution of power. Here I outline the origins of secular mindfulness as a hiding place that conceals the whiteness of Westernised mindfulness. In this part, I question what the concepts of universality and inclusion mean in White Western organisations rooted in historic sites of colonial exclusion and marginalisation of the Black and Orientalised Other. This framing allows me to reflect on the use of diversity. I draw on the work of the pre-eminent intellectual, Sara Ahmed, to argue that diversity offers a convenient distraction from the bedrock of intersectional inequalities and can all too often result in window dressings that make us feel good about 'doing diversity' without making any changes.

Through detailed case studies of British and United States mindfulness organisations which pledge to make mindfulness accessible to all, Part II considers why organisations take certain forms and whether claims of universalism can be realised through their philosophies and chosen pedagogical architectures. Chapter 4 reveals how these institutions mirror asymmetrical power structures prevalent in the West. Drilling down into demographic profiles exposes institutional leadership and decision-making roles that reinforce, recycle, and secure White dominance of the industry, mirrored in White, middle-class, mainly women staff, with White men in positions of leadership. Expanding White Mindfulness beyond White, middle-class locations shows how the burden of wellness and the responsibility for distress is placed on marginalised groups themselves rather than on those structures that generate the injustices they face, or those who benefit from the injustices. A key concern here is that adding diversity onto White Mindfulness as an afterthought – what I call adjunctive strategies – serves to reinforce the industry's white-washing mantra: 'we are all the same and belong to a common humanity'. In the Mindfulness Industry, these narratives of 'sameness' obscure racial and other differences and the systemic exploitation of these differences to reinforce and further create social divisions. Chapter 5 discusses the mechanisms, including pedagogy, through which White Mindfulness reinvents itself. It shows the significant role education plays in normalising, instrumentalising, and institutionalising whiteness. This investigation allows me to query how the refrain of inclusion functions in a wealthy, White-led sector reluctant to embrace real, messy, uncomfortable 'difference' of a racialised GM. Looking closely at how White Mindfulness shapes the sector, it considers the impact of whiteness on bodies and what becomes embodied in a world that appears to selectively forget positionality and context. In Chapter 6, I show how the industry's educational programmes serve to reproduce ideological frameworks that selectively interpret competence and experiential learning. A focus on audit culture exposes everyday unquestioned mechanisms that reinforce White privilege and selective ways of knowing and teaching that result in exclusions. I make the case that such educational cultures and instruments parade as standards yet augment and cement racialised divisions.

In Part III, *Disrupting White Mindfulness* turns its attention to an industry that talks the talk of social change but is divested of true social justice aspirations. I explore the undoing of a rapidly growing industry that sees itself as a force for good yet is oblivious to its role in individualisation and universalism. I contend that the industry in effect generates the very stress it sets out to relieve and that to work in the service of social justice, the White Mindfulness Industry requires meaningful transformation beyond the symbolic politics of 'performing diversity'. Chapter 7 engages decolonisation and considers why decolonial praxis is on the increase. It questions the very premise of White Mindfulness and revisits Jon Kabat-Zinn's 'second Renaissance' idea. Continuing this investigation, Chapter 8 upends White Mindfulness' fixation with 'the present moment' and 'nowness'. It draws on queer and global South notions of temporality to probe into what might be forgotten with an insistence on the primacy of the present moment. Questioning what is eclipsed as we engage with ideas of 'noticing', I consider why dominant narratives are so easily assumed as given while marginalised voices are suppressed. This chapter wonders what might be imagined as communities take root in their own inter-pretations and narratives and contemplate their own power. In a similar fashion, Chapter 9 complicates White Mindfulness' ideas of emotion and affect by drawing on Sara Ahmed's *The Cultural Politics of Emotion*. White Mindfulness' emphasis on 'sameness' is swapped here for more complex understandings of difference which, when leveraged, generate far richer possibilities for worldmaking. Engaging with diversity in a more meaningful way places prospects of justice in all its forms back on the table. Commonplace notions like embodiment and compassion are complicated by the circu-lation of dominant emotional artefacts that dictate how society is forged. Claims to compassion and empathy are upturned by narratives rooted in the realities of most of the world's population. Chapter 10 discusses the unlikelihood that social and racial justice can be achieved in the White Mindfulness Industry without fun-damental root and branch decolonisation. What such a process might look like is revealed in an uncompromising challenge to the sector to acknowledge the implications of its Orientalist origins and its neoliberal, postracial complexities as the pandemic of racism remains centre stage. In keeping with the call for subversion and disruption from a growing intersectional movement for justice, it explores different radical interpretations of mindfulness. It draws on current examples to argue for contemplative practices embedded in visionary, community-driven transformation projects and initiatives in the service of social justice. I discuss projects already in the making that leverage difference, acknowledge the continued legacies of historical appropriations and injustices, and present decolonised agendas, architectures, and futures. This final part seeks to look beyond decolonisation as curriculum change, engaging instead concepts of liberation and embodied justice as cornerstones that shift the landscape of power. The Mindfulness Industry is urged to rethink its apolitical edicts, pedagogy, and practices to be fit for a post-COVID, politically informed millennial generation of critical consumers who demand an antiracist, respectful world of belonging. In conclusion, Danai Mupotsa's poem 'Justice' declares the imperative of embodying justice and creating liberation partly through disrupting the very constructs we use in this work to dis-cuss institutionalised whiteness and mostly through embodying the very freedoms we seek. While this critical appraisal contributes to more honest understandings of the prospects of social mindfulness, it is but a foundation from which new imaginings can join practices of freedom and embodying liberation already underway.

Talking about 'race' and gender

This book grapples with race and difference, asking challenging questions about how bodies come to be marked in the ways they are and how the Mindfulness Industry becomes embroiled in divided and racialised societies. Acknowledging that race, gender, class, and disability are constructs, it considers how these come to reside in bodies, shaping real experiences. But talking about race and racism is not straightforward because in doing so, it gives credence to and can reduce our lives to constructs. To overcome some of these challenges, I use critical race theory which helps identify race as a construct and shows how the construct nonetheless marks minoritised communities and has real deleterious effects on people's lives. Nonetheless, I am aware that all characteristics, including race, can homogenise groups, and as Audre Lorde reminds us, we are complex beings who do not live single-issue lives.

Historically, racial categorisations use the construct of race to exploit people. As Toni Morrison says: 'definitions belong to the definers, not the defined'. This is not to undermine the use of political Blackness to subvert systemic racism. It is to acknowledge histories of empire and coloniality based largely on the construct of race. I use race to critique White Mindfulness and explain why the industry is racialised. In doing so, I am cautious not to recentre whiteness by foregrounding the movements that cultivate joy and freedom, not in reaction or response to systemic whiteness, but as a call to liberation.

Today the messiness of definitions and the clumsy groupings of people can deny differences within groups that are collectively marked. The UK markers Black and Minority Ethnic (BME) and Black, Asian and Minority Ethnic (BAME), for example, are problematic in that they collapse differences between people who share the fact that they are not White. The differences between and within the various communities that fall within these categories include the fact that many people don't neatly fall into a single category of ethnicity. Also, different ethnic groups are marginalised in different ways while privileges of class, gender, sexuality, religion, and colour deepen chasms within perceived ethnic groups. Still, the descriptor allows insight into its intersection with other exploited characteristics of difference to critique systems and structures that perpetuate injustices.

Such a critique and the use of critical race theory threatens the status quo; it has been banned in some US states with efforts to do the same in the UK (Rashawn and Gibbons, 2021; Trilling, 2020). Despite measures to quell critique, social movements for justice continue to grapple with the exploitation of people based on race and further characteristics of difference. Currently, Black, Indigenous, and People of Colour (BIPOC) brings together diverse communities marked by similar experiences of dispossession in the US. For some critics, the US categorisation People of Colour used increasingly in the UK still centres whiteness – whoever does not fall into the default category of White is, by default, perceived to be 'of colour'. In the UK, Black and Brown is being used as a generic term to a similar effect, to bring together people systemically racialised. These are intended as inclusive terms at a time when Blackness, difference, and identity are being claimed as strengths.

In this book, I mostly use the descriptors People of the Global Majority (PGM), Global Majority (GM), or Black, which includes multiple ethnic and cultural identities, as generic terms. I recognise that the term Black, deriving from social conditions rooted in segregation, can obscure the multiple histories and cultures it aims to represent and can deny the privileges that come with lighter-skinned and white-assumed appearance. The PGM/GM descriptor establishes itself beyond the context of whiteness to embrace Black, Brown, and Asian people as well as those who have been racialised as 'ethnic minorities' (Campbell-Stephens, 2020). The term recognises that the GM comprise 80 per cent of the world's population compared to a 20 per cent global minority of White people. This statistic serves to highlight the racialised nature of power and economic control in US and UK contexts. It also moves beyond the concept of minorities, which can be used dismissively or to diminish people and their histories in comparison to 'the main population'. Because GM does not employ racial markers, it allows people to self-identify using as many intersectional signifiers of difference as they choose to. When people self-identify and choose to come together in relation to common causes, this usually changes the power dynamic of naming. Still, on a cautionary note, White power and privilege can remain the default from which issues like access are measured. The decolonial project involves undoing such normativity.

The terminology of PGM/GM does a lot more than group together people who are not White. Shifting the perspective on identity to a global level, it acknowledges the role of empire and coloniality, spear-headed by a global minority, in shaping race and creating borders. As a global term, GM aims to accommodate multiple identities and cultures, not all of which are defined by whiteness in parts of the world where White supremacy is not the dominant discourse. In recognition that the terms I use are racial markers, I capitalise words referencing racial difference.

As a cis-gender woman, I am also cognisant of the default gender binaries I use in the book. These binaries exclude trans, gender non-conforming, non-binary, and gender diverse people. The respondents with whom I spoke in my studies while gathering data between 2015 and 2018 only declared 'male' and 'female' gender markers. None self-identified as non-binary, and none disclosed that they were trans. The inclusion of binary and cis-gender perspectives only is a shortcoming of the research. Figures I use, particularly of organisational board members, were usually gathered from websites and not from interviews. In these cases, I was unable to check gender designations with board members themselves. Still, the use of male and female markers on their own, in this book, is therefore not intended to indicate that there are no other genders. In the same way that the Greenwich Meridian sets an international measure, and White acts as an unraced default to normalise whiteness, categories that fall outside gender binaries can easily be construed deviant or less 'real' than 'male' and 'female'. Since my central concern is disrupting whiteness in the sector, troubling gender within the dominant Western mindfulness world is as important in revealing the underpinnings of gender-normative whiteness and must be a crucial component of decolonising White Mindfulness.

Dismantling unhelpful dichotomies

In segregated societies, it is easy to adopt dichotomies when interrupting colonialism and whiteness and to apportion blame and punishment for the histories that engineered our current power structures and relationships. This is very different to reparation and acknowledgement of who benefits from inequalities. When punishment is emphasised rather than repair, it becomes easier to exclude potential allies rather than call out acts of racism, sexism, classism, homo-, and transphobia.

I write this book in the understanding that justice is not a fixed notion with a set look and feel. It is something that is created in societies by those committed to building just landscapes, in which all have the means to enjoy equal access to freedoms. Justice is a 'doing word'. Justice requires inner, outer, inter, and in-between work that considers the entangled nature of our interrelatedness and the connective tissue that glues, unites, and combines communities and bridges oppositional communities. A challenge in this work is that it's easier to see justice as something to be given by someone else. Yet for many of us committed to justice, our current challenge includes reconnecting with our 'power-within' and our communal power or 'power-with others' (Wallerstein, 2006). As we build communities and movements of transformation, our inclusive spaces disrupt a world forged on inequalities. Social justice comes through the ways we show up in community and the ways we collectively disrupt and dismantle arrangements that deny so many of us a sense of belonging. Subversion allows us to dismantle not only outer structures but also the embodied effects of oppressions and injustices that eclipse our power. Through embodied justice – toppling our internal statues and statutes of oppression – we can bring the dream of freedom into reality. The work of becoming free is intra- and interpersonal, collective, and social. It is not done in isolation; it takes place in community, through witnessing and supporting one another, sharing visions and dreams as we build a new evolving reality. Justice is work we do to create the microcosms, in our communities, of the structures we wish to see in our societies.

A reflective journal

Even if it is found intellectually interesting, a book of this nature risks failing to effect change. To make the material more relevant, and to honour the traditions of critique that emphasise inquiry, agency, and transformation, I encourage you to consider how this knowledge applies to you as an insider, outsider, or an outsider-within the Mindfulness Industry or White systems. Questions posed throughout are intended to uphold the tradition of applying knowledge to real-life contexts. In this way, the book invites conversation and inquiry into change.

Notes

1 The concept Mindfulness Industry is capitalised to indicate an industry premised on White Mindfulness.

2 Following the work of Nell Irvin Painter, author of *The History of White People* (2011) and 'Why White Should be Capitalised Too' (2020), I capitalise White denoting that it too is a construct and not a default. This brings the category White on par with Black, showing that both constructs are ways of perpetuating racialised inequalities. While the US National Association of Black Journalists (2020) have called for White to be capitalised so that it does not appear as a default, the Associated Press (2020) continues to debate the issue. I also capitalise White Mindfulness to denote its construction in whiteness, distinct from multiple forms of mindfulness practiced in various global traditions.

3 Whiteness comprises an arrangement of structural conditions related to racial power and privilege. It functions to produce racialised Others and to reproduce the economic and political power and interests of dominant groups. The study of whiteness makes it visible so as to deconstruct and redistribute power. Yet Ahmed (2004a) cautions that such investigation can become a narcissistic exercise that serves to reinforce rather than dismantle power. Unless critical whiteness studies can guarantee an undoing of the power relations that protect whiteness, it amounts to what Ahmed calls a 'politics of declaration' and inaction.

4 While I use the terms Black and People of the Global Majority (PGM) or Global Majority (GM) interchangeably in this book, I acknowledge race as a construct. Later in this introduction I explain my preference for these terms over and above 'Black and Minority Ethnic' (BME) and 'Black, Asian, and Minority Ethnic' (BAME), or the US terms People of Colour (POC) and Black, Indigenous, People of Colour (BIPOC).

5 A concept that originated in apartheid South Africa, racial capitalism signifies the interrelation and mutual dependence of racism and capital. Drawing on various sources and realities, Arun Kundnani describes racial capitalism as a 'bridging of the economic and the cultural, of the class struggle and the struggle against [W]hite supremacy, allowing us to understand police and plantation violence as linked to capital accumulation' (Kundnani, 2020).

6 Lorde's full quote reads: 'For the master's tools will never dismantle the master's house. They may allow us temporarily to beat him at his own game, but they will never enable us to bring about genuine change.'

7 The Happiness Project, founded by Robert Holden (1994), runs an eight-week course titled, 'Be Happy'. The programme focuses on personal happiness as a pathway to success; it unlinks happiness and the structural causes of stress and power.

8 The concept 'mindful sniper' is based on US military training in mindfulness, with objections from some that, due to its harmful nature, this is not mindfulness. Matthieu Ricard, the famous French monk, explains that unwholesome deeds, like killing, performed outside an ethical framework, do not comply with the Buddhist notion of mindfulness (Krznaric, 2017).

9 Socially engaged Buddhism is well documented. There is discrepancy as to its origins, commonly ascribed to the Vietnamese Buddhist monk Thich Nhat Hanh (Yarnell, 2003: 286). Batchelor, for instance, argues that it emerged among Vietnamese monks in the 1930s in resistance to colonial oppression (Batchelor, 1994: 360). It is not my intention to explore this movement in this work. It is cited to acknowledge and highlight the actively engaged aspect of Buddhism regarded by many practitioners an inherent part of Buddhism and mindfulness. These practitioners denounce the need for the descriptor 'engaged' in the first instance, insisting that Buddhist practice necessarily spans inner and outer worlds (Bell, 2000: 413).

10 The 17 Sustainable Development Goals, adopted by the United Nations' member states in 2015, are part of its 2030 agenda to create peace and prosperity for people and planet.

Part I

The roots of exclusion and Othering

1

Othering: the roots of colonisation and Orientalism

The smallest incidents of our social life contain all the moral and political values of society, all its structures of domination and power, all its mechanisms of oppression.

Augusto Boal (1994: 40)

The 2015 Centre for Mindfulness Conference included a panel of Black mindfulness practitioners comprising academics, scientists, and teachers who spoke of their experiences working within the White Mindfulness world. They addressed one another rather than the audience in a conversation about their practice and work. All of them expressed feeling Othered and a sense of not belonging. The audience were silent, presumably uncomfortable by these frank accounts of what being part of a predominantly White Mindfulness space felt like, both at the conference and in their workplaces. The panel were giving voice to broader systems like the apartheid regime that mark people and their bodies in ways that endure long beyond the formalities of apartheid. Their experiences of discrimination underscored the porous borders between the world of Western mindfulness and the broader society. Societies and cultures, after all, live deep within individual and collective bodies – as Augusto Boal notes in the epigraph. In *Playing in the Dark*, Toni Morrison talks of the institutional, normative frames that shape us: institutions and values that imprint themselves upon our psyches and bodies. As Steve Biko, a South African political leader assassinated by the apartheid regime, famously stated, '[t]he most potent weapon in the hands of the oppressor is the mind of the oppressed' (Biko, 1978: 19). Yet it is people, most often collectively, who transcend such conditioning to bring about change.

Legacies of racial capitalism prevalent as much in the US and UK as in South Africa continue to marginalise the same communities through lack of access to employment, education, and work. In other words, Othering is not simply a 'light touch', it is deeply rooted in enduring systems of discrimination and exploitation that exclude groups based on multiple intersecting oppressions. When legislated, such exploitation of difference presents as *de jure* apartheid which criminalises people based on difference. But even where legislation is absent, oppressions meted out by dominant powers are normalised as de facto features in many societies. Discriminatory social tenets entrench disregard and disrespect for life and reinforce it daily. They impose social barriers, glass ceilings, and normalise insidious and explicit forms of Othering. Such discriminatory norms are prevalent in most colonising, colonised, and colonial-settler societies and commonly produce racialised democracies.

The US is no stranger to the strong imprint of Othering, exploitations, and exclusions. In May 2020, George Floyd's publicly screened murder sparked a resurgence of the intercontinental Black Lives Matter (BLM) Global Network. Global BLM protests once again shone a light on institutionalised racism of police forces and systemic racism in multiple countries. In the US, home to the BLM movement, structural inequalities are evident in disproportionate rates of incarceration and killings of Black, Asian, Latinx, and Indigenous people, as well as patterns of racialised inaccess to housing, education, work, justice, and the franchise. Solidarity action in the UK renewed focus on the 1999 MacPherson Report[1] of an institutionally racist police force and wider systemic racism. In March 2021, however, a UK government-commissioned report declared that there is no such thing as institutional or structural racism in the UK (Sewell *et al.*, 2021). It claimed that the UK offers an antiracism model for the rest of the world. At the same time, the report stoked divisions between people of Black African and Black Caribbean heritage, saying the latter group should try to behave more like the former.

The report of the UK Commission on Race and Ethnic Disparities drew wide-ranging criticism from all walks of society including academics, journalists, the health sector, charities, and educational authorities. Critics exposed the British government's denialism as a far cry from the realities of structural racism and the lived experience of the majority of Black Britons. Disproportionate levels of 'stop and search' and incarceration, unequal pay in corporate and public sectors, academic attainment gaps, and staff retention augment the structural inequalities found in White supremacist societies (Runnymede Trust, 2021). Such normalised institutionalised racism and systemic injustices reverberate throughout the US and UK. Bodies that don't fit the norm of whiteness become marked as 'Other', as misfits, as not belonging. De facto apartheid operates largely unhindered in both societies.

Systemic racism entrenches Othering. Found in laws, policies, socio-economic structures, and services, de facto racism legitimises discrimination which is then dismissed as banter or episodic. In her 2020 book, *Subtle Acts of Exclusion*, Tiffany Jana sets out to rebrand microaggressions 'subtle acts of exclusion', which they say is less value-loaded. Jana says we all commit these acts in everyday life, a common one being the use of 'hi guys', which, much as it can be claimed as a gender-neutral term, can be offensive to gender nonconforming, nonbinary people, and women. Through these subtle, daily acts, systemic discriminations and defaults reproduce themselves. Prevalent throughout societies, they are found as much in White Mindfulness as elsewhere. They of course also occur on a grander scale as macroaggressions.

Recognition of systemic racism at the highest level of government fails to guarantee the dismantling of structures built on apartheid. Mass media, educational curricula, and skewed access to finances, work, and justice continue to bolster racialised societies on a daily basis. Still, when Joe Biden makes a presidential statement about systemic racism at his inauguration, this at least opens up a questioning of where racialised Othering and power come from. How does race come to intersect all signifiers of difference – be it class, gender, faith, disability, age, sexuality – and why does it remain a characteristic of difference exploited in the West?

Following Morrison, practices of Othering prevalent in the US, UK, and South Africa offer practical insight into how these everyday cultures frame and bleed into White Mindfulness. To further understand Othering, this chapter locates its roots in coloniality and Orientalism. For this purpose, I draw on the pioneering work of the pre-eminent intellectual Edward Said, founder of postcolonial studies. His discussion of Orientalism and latent Orientalism explains how the West asserted its dominance not only structurally but in cultural and literary respects to exercise control over colonised lands and people. His seminal work, *Orientalism*, explains that the migration of knowledges from the imagined Orient (the East) to the Occident (the West) creates the very Othering we find today in White Mindfulness.[2] Considering power from colonial, subversive, and innovative perspectives opens up the discussion of how Othering persists and is challenged. As an example of its constancy, I discuss the ways in which White Mindfulness normalises itself through the medical industrial complex. But this is not a one-way street. As evidence of a counter-narrative to cultural appropriation and Othering, I also review forms of protest and subversion that expose the ongoing extraction of knowledges by the West. Funie Hsu's *We've Been Here All Along* and Dedunu Sylvia's contribution to *5 Responses to the Awkwardly Titled 'New Face of Buddhism'* constitute challenges to persistent forms of Othering and knowledge appropriation. Capturing current modes of disruption, this chapter recounts new organisations, movements, and innovations such as the Radical Dharma pro-freedom movement including Rod Owens' invocation of Ru Paul in the halls of a convert Buddhist retreat space. According to Lorde's thesis, these subversive acts, responsive to the political moment and need, occur outside the master's house.

Said's *Orientalism* and mindfulness' Othering problem

European colonisation spanned at least five centuries starting in the fourteenth century in the Balkans and extending to the Scramble for Africa in the nineteenth century. Britain's East India Company established trade and slave routes from the seventeenth to the nineteenth century. But it was not only spices and materials that were commodified. This era enabled the enslavement of people, indentured labour, and slave routes. People were bought and sold, and differences based on faith and traditions were exploited to enrich colonial powers. In these settings, it is more than force and resistance through which the world is shaped during this period of pillage. Dominant narratives and worldviews took root.

In 1978, in what was to become a canonical text titled *Orientalism*, Edward Said proposed that the process of colonisation used not only brute force but more subtle methods of control to gain dominion over lands, economies, people, minds, cultures, and traditions. Said explains that the Orient and Occident, much like race, are constructs built on condescending, patronising attitudes that the West holds about the East. When the West studied the Orient, sometimes to learn, and sometimes as part of empire, it recycled these attitudes.

Orientalism explains how the West created an idea of an idolatrous, backward, homologous East that had to be saved by a cultured, scientific, rational West. Prejudicial constructs reinforced disparaging attitudes and derogatory outsider interpretations of the East by scholars of the Orient including eugenicists, novelists, benevolent missionaries, and colonial officials set to 'save' the inhabitants of heathen lands (Said, 2003: 205). The colonial lens facilitated and justified European imperialism, colonisation, and dominance. Power over the East perpetuates the ongoing extraction of knowledge, labour, and wealth. It enables 'the political, economic, cultural and social domination of the West, not just during colonial times, but also in the present' (Said, 1978: 357).

Said's concept of latent Orientalism refers to the power, superiority, and supremacy colonisers claimed (Said, 1978: 50). In other words, Orientalism is not limited to geography but practiced latently through mental constructs. In Biko's words, it oppresses minds and is conveyed by embedding the colonial gaze through documentation, exposition, education, and scholarship.[3] Latent Orientalism suggests that mental models of Western superiority inevitably influenced works which are prominent in both the West and the East. Today it is seen in ongoing racism against Asian Westerners and generally against People of the Global Majority (PGM).

The construct of the Orient is created for the express purpose of embedding interconnected processes of cultural repression and appropriation. In other words, the Orient serves the function of enriching the West spiritually and culturally while the West enforces its political and economic dominion. But processes of appropriation are nuanced. The works of the Orientalist scholars Thomas and Caroline Rhys Davids, for instance, form the basis on which the modern interpretation of mindfulness commonly rests.

Their examination and interpretation of Pāli texts – Pāli being the original language in which Buddhist teachings were recorded – still forms the basis of Western interpretations of Buddhism.[4]

Judith Snodgrass explains that under the guise of 'academic intrigue', the West maintained a firm hold over Asian translators involved in the production of English texts. When Asian translators disagreed with interpretations exposing the limitations of Western methodologies, their objections exposed skewed relations of power (Snodgrass, 2007: 196). Burmese scholar and translator Shwe Zan Aung explains that translation methods used by Westerners were inadequate. He says that the literal translation of terms often had for Buddhists 'no meaning whatever'.[5] Aung's testimony illuminates the Westerner's power in framing knowledge from the Orient. In fact, Caroline Rhys Davids – with whom Aung collaborated – excised certain of his translations on the basis that they were 'contaminated' by his cultural views (Snodgrass, 2007: 197; see Rhys Davids, 1910). This display of authority and ownership extends to the analytical apparatus used in numerous American, British, and European libraries and museums to categorise and curate Eastern experiences. Such classification systems condition the Western psyche and super-impose a European schema through which the Orient is cast and Othered. These mechanisms and technologies of Western engage-ment with Eastern traditions and people reinforce its sense of super-iority, stereotyping, racism, and distortions of difference. As Said reminds us: 'The Orient existed for the West, or so it seemed to countless Orientalists, whose attitude to what they worked on was either paternalistic or candidly condescending' (Said, 2003: 204).

Aung's account and experience helps us understand the workings of latent Orientalism. It elucidates the colonial gaze and ongoing forms of cultural appropriation, and roots Othering in systems of coloniality and Orientalism. To centre the Other, Orientalism invites us to rethink the externalised East–West dichotomy as symptom-atic of an internal Western divide (Prakash, 1995: 199). It suggests that the violent acts of colonisation and destruction found in both colonised lands and within the lands of colonisers stem from the West's own internal fragmentation and Othering. In other words, it is an inherently disintegrated West that externalises its interior fractures and generates an Orient in the first instance. Today these highly divided societies perpetuate the ideology of Othering through ongoing systems of White supremacy.

The politicised process of secularisation maps closely to the underpinnings of Orientalism, especially since colonisation by the West is part of 'the modernist project' (Smith, 1999: 59). Knowledges obtained 'for' the West by colonisers support agendas of domination and include subjugation on all levels of being human. Physical, mental, emotional, collective, and spiritual expressions of humanity are suppressed and repressed whether through systems of slavery, incarceration, murder, disenfranchisement, or the denial of human rights. But some forms of oppression are less explicit and more latent. Subtle acts of aggression include the creation of White spaces that cement dominant discourses and alienate people who are systemically marginalised. In White Mindfulness contexts, through the neo-colonial, White gaze, the hyper-individualised, modern citizen is stripped of difference and therefore, it is claimed, is not Othered. This feeds a postracial culture in which identity is erased and racism, whether overt or subtle acts of exclusion, is seen as 'episodic' and 'individualised'. In these settings, when people object to injustices, the complainant becomes the problem (Ahmed, 2012: 63).

Complicating Said's *Orientalism*

Postcolonial critics and conservative commentators alike engage Said's work. In his nuanced postcolonial appraisal of *Orientalism*, critical theorist Homi Bhabha counters what he reads as a dominant/oppressed (Occident/Orient) narrative in which sovereignty resides only with the coloniser. Although Said argues precisely against the view of a homologous Orient or Occident, and invites us to centre the Other, Bhabha takes this further, proposing that worlds are ambivalent and multifaceted, and that *Orientalism* offers an insufficient account of the voices of the 'subjugated'. He undoes the passivity of the 'Oriental' and centres their power and defiance of 'authority'.[6] In other words, while political processes of cultural appropriation reinforce dominant power structures, 'the colonised' can actively be subversive in ways other than through acts of defiance and resistance. Social movements can form around bodies that are Othered without recentring the mechanisms of whiteness or dominant power. In other words, social groups can be proactive, creative, and transformative rather than only ever reactive. The Radical Dharma movement serves as testimony to Bhabha's theory. But it is important to note that these bodies place themselves on the line and are marked as subversive.

Like Bhabha, Buddhist historian Judith Snodgrass rejects the dominant/subjugated binary that characterises colonialism and suggests instead an articulation of cultures. She cites the Pāli Text Society[7] as an example of cultural articulation that embraced Asian agency and participation. While she acknowledges colonialism, she recognises scholarly collaboration and complicity rather than appropriation. For Snodgrass, the master's tools approach can be effective in that a 'mutually generative power/knowledge nexus' functioning in the interests of marginalised groups can potentially unseat hegemonic power (Snodgrass, 2007: 201).

Snodgrass supposes a benevolent monopoly of power and a sense of mutuality and consensus which both Said and Bhabha dispute. For although Asian collaboration with Rhys Davids can be read as cultural articulation, Aung's experience disputes this. Snodgrass also refrains from differentiating which groups had agency within Asia, and whose interests they served. In other words, she implies that homogeneous Asian societies were wholly complicit with scholarly collaboration and that they resisted colonialism through textual challenges. Snodgrass further believed that Asians were only interested in derailing colonialism to present a modern Asia and a rational belief system. When she favours Asian 'modernity', she neglects to mention that it was framed in Western terms (Braun, 2013: 80). Her notion of 'subversion' is satisfied by battles in the field of literary translation as a sufficient avenue through which to challenge colonialism.

Further objections to Said's *Orientalism* include a few conservative critiques. Orientalist apologists Bernard Lewis and Bayly Winder accuse Said of 'word pollution' and declare that the term Orientalism was abandoned in the 1970s as outdated and unrepresentative of the interests and concerns of scholars (Lewis, 1982: 49; Winder, 1981: 617). Another conservative critic, Malcolm Kerr, takes issue with Said's views of literary intellectuals as prisoners of empire who are unable to defy racist stereotyping and who are interested only in advancing 'Western imperial domination of the East' (Kerr, 1980: 546–7). Kerr instead appeals, as does Snodgrass, to the 'individual goodwill of scholars', although, unlike her, he dismisses any association of their work with the Orientalist project. In other words, he reifies the scholar's ability to step outside positionalities and conditioning. For Kerr, scholars are capable of 'objectivity' and are untainted by power, privilege, and perspective.

Despite Said's assertion that colonialism and Orientalism inform *all* intellectual thought,[8] Kerr objects to his associating scholarship with politics, and rejects the notion that the individual scholar is unobjective. Given his reverence for scholars as universal authorities and bearers of objective truth, he claims that scholarship offers independent thought and functions outside the confines of political and cultural conditions. In making his case, Kerr inadvertently exemplifies Said's very critique of Orientalism as a 'discourse of power' that posits knowledge as universal and neutral. His denial that the scholar is shaped by their politics, conditioning, and exposure, protects people, especially those in positions of power, from declaring their positionalities. These problems pertain to White Mindfulness. They seed the idea that scholarship and 'good' people operate independently of social constructs and forces making positionality unimportant.

Breaking the colonial gaze by embodying justice

In Said's frame, even those who critique structural power are themselves always bound to some or other degree by the systems that forge and shape them/us. As a critic of White Mindfulness, I am subject to the same constrained agency as Kerr, even though our social construction and lenses bring us to divergent perspectives and insights. As a Black intersectional feminist, I will inevitably hold different views and outlooks to a White non-feminist. Yet as bell hooks, professor, author, feminist, and social activist, reminds us, the world is usually cast through the lens of a White, heteronormative, cis-gendered, often Christian man. However, this does not mean that all Black feminists hold the same views nor that my views form only in relation to dominant ideologies.

By being explicit about my positionality, though, I create clarity and accountability – it is clear how my politics are shaped, and I take responsibility for my non-static frame of reference.

hooks uses the oppositional gaze to defy the normative framing of the world. Drawing on cinema and the portrayal of Black women, she challenges the normative male gaze that reinforces the '[W]hite supremacist capitalist imperialist dominating gaze' (hooks, 1992) and reveals how the latter normative gaze objectifies and marks Black women's bodies as defiant and vulnerable. The oppositional gaze, while it is anti-discriminatory, derives its power from pride in Blackness, queerness, and Black joy, and restores embodied pride. Cultivating vigilance and somatic literacy of one's relationship to bodily vulnerability and power is a practice of embodying justice. Keen awareness of one's agency, as well as the body's limits, recognises the impact of politics and Othering on the body. It also creates space for collective bodies, community, celebration, and joy.

hooks reminds us that Othering occurs even when people are in the majority – like in South Africa – by robbing them of political and economic power. In other words, dominant power represents systemic control and ideological dominance. It cannot be Othered. Coming from a place of the oppositional gaze does more than offer an alternative perspective. It returns to the body as a site of power, agency, vulnerability, and joy. The cultivation of oppositional power denies neither state power nor the ongoing proclivities of marginalisation and Othering. It does, however, remember the rootedness of the body in power and justice and its exposure and vulnerability when in defiance. For when the marked body forms part of a social movement for freedom and for change, it is no longer dependent on White spaces for inclusion. Belonging is given and created in community with other bodies, giving expression to collective bodies that usually align around shared values. Yet, inevitably, when the marked body portrays power and knowledge that is unavailable to the coloniser or the state, it poses a threat to dominant power and becomes a site of repression and control.

In describing the colonial gaze, Said explains that Orientalism's 'inaugural heroes' select aspects of cultures deemed useful through their own gaze.[9] This pattern, so deeply hidden in Western appropriation, permeates secularisation processes. It camouflages the role 'heroes' play in extricating from traditions and cultures (of Others) what it desires. Commensurate with Nobel laureate Toni Morrison's 'White gaze', it depicts the assumed authority of travellers to Asia, translators of texts (Said, 2003: 94), and bearers of teachings, who narrate the secular. Morrison's 'White gaze' explains how easily Black authors tend to live in the shadow of society, consumed by the lens and default of social whiteness. When Black authors assume that their readers are White, they slip into narrative that distorts their own experience (Wagner-Martin, 2014: 22). Morrison speaks of the liberation of stepping outside the racialised gaze to write freely. Her 'White gaze' echoes the work of Said's 'inaugural heroes'. Orientalists write for White audiences; Black and Brown bodies are absent in their frame. As Said says, 'Every statement made by Orientalists or White Men (who are usually interchangeable) conveyed a sense of the irreducible distance separating White from Coloured, or Occidental from Oriental' (Said, 1978: 228).

The 'hero's' right to select what is regarded as consequential, and to elide that considered futile, is what generates an Orientalist outlook. When academic expertise is allocated to Orientalist works it gives them prestige and adds layers of authority. Even though written from a skewed perspective, the works come to present the realities they describe; they produce a discourse that regenerates itself. This is where White Mindfulness is implicated in cultural appropriation and policing, a term critical theorist Richard King uses to denote the cherry-picking, culling, and distortions underlying knowledge extraction.[10] These injustices reposition Western dominion as accommodating, rational, and superior. Latent Orientalism causes those using a neo-colonial or 'White gaze' to see nothing wrong and to regard their contributions as progress or modernisation. When White Mindfulness, detached from political context, sensibilities, and insights, selects what it regards as useful to 'reduce human suffering', it ironically participates in similar acts of injustice.

Knowledge acquisition or appropriation?

Identity and positionality highlight the complexity of the knowledge/power dialectic. To accommodate academic curiosity, Said provided a 'get out' clause saying that sometimes we seek 'knowledge of other people and other times [for] understanding, compassion, careful study and analysis ... for purposes of co-existence and humanistic enlargement of horizons'. He contrasts this with knowledge taken as 'part of an overall campaign of self-affirmation, belligerency and outright war ... and the will to dominate for the purposes of control and external dominion' (Said, 2003: xiv).

White Mindfulness leaders appeal to Said's benign category of knowledge acquisition: mindfulness is practiced to help them in their own lives and to help others. But it appears that this appeal is not quite so simple on at least three counts. First, when knowledge supposedly gained for personal interest is purposed to tackle global stress and depression without acknowledging the source of the knowledge, the innocence of academic or personal curiosity come into question. Second, when mindfulness is extracted to suit Western society's needs for stress reduction without attention to its underlying causes, what at first appears benign morphs into expediency. Third, the re-presentation of mindfulness as a universal, professionalised discourse that enables its resale in Asia as part of a 'collaboration' slips into Said's 'will to dominate'.

The dominant narrative of 'common humanity' and 'human flourishing' white-washes appropriation, paternalism, and Western professionalisation of non-US and -UK knowledges. In other words, without due consideration to context and histories of pillage, what may begin as a sincere curiosity and endeavour to foster peace can easily become part of histories of conquest and appropriation.

This is not to deny the multiple avenues through which mindfulness is delivered in the West. Indeed, many Asian and Southeast Asian teachers travelled to the US and UK precisely to teach their traditions. Among these, Chögyam Trungpa Rinpoche and Chöje Akong Tulku Rinpoche established Samye Ling in 1960s Scotland as one of the first Tibetan Buddhist centres in the West. Maintaining their Buddhist foundations, they articulated diverse cultures by allowing Westerners to experience monastic life for periods of time. In contrast, White Mindfulness commonly cherry-picks teachings like mindfulness from Buddhist doctrine which therefore lose their contextual meaning and purpose. Especially when this is done with good intention, perhaps it is important to recognise that this may no longer be mindfulness. It may simply be therapeutic coping or stress-reduction strategies.

This brings into focus the question, who owns and controls these knowledges? And, in the context of secularisation, how are the teachings and teachers linked to their origins and traditions? How do they honour the people, lands, and cultures from which these teachings hail?

Linda Tuhiwai Smith, scholar, professor, and leader in Indigenous education, argues that, from Indigenous perspectives, 'outsider' researchers commonly 'steal' knowledge from Others and then use it for the benefit of those who did the 'stealing'. She says, 'some [I]ndigenous and minority group researchers would call this simply racist'. It is 'imbued with an "attitude" and a "spirit" which assumes a certain ownership of the entire world, and which has established systems and forms of governance which embed that attitude in institutional practices' (Smith, 1999: 56).

Smith, like Said, argues that it is this Orientalist, colonialist framework that shapes cultural exchanges, unless marginalised groups dictate the terms and value of their involvement. However, inequitable power arrangements between Asian collaborators and Orientalists, or marginalised groups and hegemonic forces, favour those with decision-making authority, access to funding, and network capital. Power in these settings includes the implicit hidden power that is internalised and embodied in deeply held beliefs and performances. This is Said's latent Orientalism at play: the practices of Othering, privilege, and superiority escape those buoyed by the tides of discrimination, unless they consciously reveal them.

Subverting Othering

Postcolonialism addresses the aftermath of the mental imprint and infrastructural devastation left in the wake of empire. It improves the prospects of subversion by showing the links between coloniality and implicit forms of structural and institutional power. Ideologically, whiteness emerges through coloniality and slavery as a modern form of White supremacy. It perpetuates divides through strategies like the prison industrial complex, White male-centred policies, and institutionalised injustices. Together, frameworks of latent Orientalism and postcolonialism disclose the underlying Othering found in society in institutions and systems of injustice.

The Mindfulness Industry, not unlike what has come to be called the yoga industrial complex (Gandhi and Wolff, 2017), swims uncritically in these waters. Critics argue that the commercialised practice of yoga in the West comprises cultural appropriation and contributes to White supremacy. Stripped of yoga's history and the colonial history of India, the yoga industrial complex is seen to cement the tenets of US and UK societies. As such, it resembles White Mindfulness, blinkered and oblivious to its context, complicity, and positionality. Yet, as an established industry ingrained in late capitalism, it is unlikely to disrupt itself.

Adopting a postcolonial frame, transdisciplinary scholar Funie Hsu exposes White Mindfulness' disavowal of groups that remain racially Othered, marking its cultural appropriation as a cornerstone of neo-colonialism and latent Orientalism (Hsu, 2016: 374). In *We've Been Here All Along*, she narrates the pain caused by convert Buddhist erasure of Asian Buddhist teachers and initiatives. Although as many as half a million Asian migrants settled in the US between 1977 and 2000 (Cadge, 2005), the (largely White) convert Buddhist communities remained separate from traditional Buddhists. Hsu identifies enactments of whiteness and Othering in this disengagement with traditional Buddhist centres and Asian mindfulness practitioners (Hsu, 2017; 2016). In this way, White Mindfulness conforms to dominant practices of whiteness and feeds systems premised on inequalities, nationally and globally.

To add to this, critic Dedunu Sylvia lists the ways in which secular mindfulness colonises cultures demonstrating ongoing acts of racial alterity. Her appraisal echoes critics of the yoga industrial complex:

> Countless 'mindfulness' books and workshops and trainings at heavy costs. Glorified retreats for White, able-bodied, thin, cis, straight, and class-privileged peoples. Images and films focused almost exclusively on the attainment of nirvana by the White man. Histories of generational attachment to colonialism, slavery, genocide, and conquest, all unapologetically glossed over through exotified ventures to the 'third world.' All I can see is Buddhist practice – particularly 'mindfulness' and 'loving-kindness' ideals – used to placate resistance from marginalized populations. Upheld to weaponize model minority myths of Asian passivity in contrast to Black liberation. Exercised in the service of corporate, capitalist, and militarized agendas.
>
> (Sylvia, 2016)

In Sylvia's testament, everyday expressions of culture and ritual, which may not be regarded as religious by the bearers of such traditions, are removed from what comes to constitute White Mindfulness. Her work raises questions of whether what appears on her list is indeed mindfulness. Surely, ignoring histories of torture, pain, and appropriation that denude cultural practices of their traditions does not undo such histories. When colonialism and appropriation go unacknowledged, it creates false communities of practice or practice premised on falsehoods or half-truths.

In the formal trainings I received in the US and UK, my trainers sometimes acknowledged their teachers. However, there was no mention of the histories and pain inherent in the secularisation process, the positioning of Westerners as teachers and 'experts', nor the audiences who occupied teaching centres and meditation halls. In these ways, the depiction of Western mindfulness as a benevolent force camouflages hegemonic power. Through the resale of Mindfulness-Based Stress Reduction (MBSR) and Mindfulness-Based Cognitive Therapy (MBCT) in the East, Asian collaborators sometimes adopt Westernised versions of their own cultures. In the absence of the co-production of inclusive models, whether in Asia or the West, White Mindfulness establishes dominion over the traditions of colonised knowledges and sits uncomfortably close to coloniality and whiteness.

In recent years, subversion has taken more explicit form in the White Mindfulness world. My secular mindfulness training was predominantly White-led and shrouded in whiteness until Lama Rod Owens, American Tantric teacher, and co-author of *Radical Dharma*, disrupted Gaia House teachings by naming the living histories of ongoing dispossession as part of the teachings. Lama Rod's very presence in that traditionally White space marked a departure from the usual. Positioning himself as a Black, queer teacher trained in Tibetan Buddhism, he stepped beyond traditional Buddhism to embrace other parts of his identity. In conversation with meditation teacher Kate Johnson, Lama Rod explains the desire to 'practice Tantra within [his] cultural context … as a person who is descended from slaves … I have to be me … If we can't be ourselves then it's more than likely you're going to be a violent person' (Owens and Johnson, 2020).

It is through understanding and declaring our positionality that we become what Lama Rod calls 'authentic'. And by being authentic, he transformed the retreat space by introducing Audre Lorde and Ru Paul as modern-day teachers of transformation. This event offered a long-awaited exhalation for Black and queer communities who rallied after the retreat to perpetuate the spirit of collective freedom. This retreat blended Tibetan Buddhism with social justice and liberation while maintaining respect for both traditions. It acknowledged centuries of ongoing extraction and degradation of people, resources, and knowledges across all continents. But, of course, subversion does not undo systemic oppressions, let alone internalised latent colonialism, overnight. It requires its own gestation period and pathway to decentre hegemonic discourses. Social movements gather momentum over time and these seeds of the Radical Dharma movement are being nourished both in the US and UK. Along with the challenges coming from Hsu and Sylvia, this can be seen as disrupting the status quo.

The making of White Mindfulness through the medical-industrial complex

To gain a foothold, White Mindfulness used the pathways of medicalisation, healthism, privatisation, and scientification to change how we relate to wellness. The term medical industrial complex, coined in 1969, refers to wide-ranging corporatisation, privatisation, and the profit-seeking ethos of global health systems (Ehrenreich, 1970). Many aspects of healthcare systems are now run by for-profit companies who provide medical equipment and education to the medical establishment, thereby entrenching their power.

Within a for-profit framework, the Mindfulness Industry's wellness orientation turns away from the reasons for escalating levels of stress and depression in ever younger populations. Its version of stress reduction and human flourishing interprets wellness at an individual level and medicalises health. Medicalisation[11] classifies social disorders such as stress as medical conditions, an act that creates and expands medical social control. In practical terms, to deal with stress, I require therapeutic interventions that commonly lock me into a 'disease-therapy cycle' (Barker, 2014). In this setting, mindfulness becomes such a therapeutic modality – a twenty-first-century Valium – to subdue distress. And while mindfulness may indeed bring relief, the industry attends to symptoms and not to causes. But there is another side to this that does not look like medicalisation. When the Mindfulness Industry offers coping strategies that build the patient's independence, it fosters self-management encouraging individuals to oversee their wellbeing. In a turn of phrase, trainees are encouraged to believe that they are responsible citizens 'able to respond' to life's stressors. While these sentiments are meant to place power with patients, they also create a sense of failure when patients are repeatedly re-exposed to the socio-political causes of distress. When mindfulness encourages self-regulation and the constant monitoring of attention, it exacerbates cultures of social atomisation, fear, and blame (Honey, 2014).

In keeping with medicalisation, healthism explains that since everyday life is now medicalised, the moral responsibility for wellness resides with individuals (Crawford, 1980). Health privatisation, common beyond the US and UK, reinforces this message. Those who become ill and who cannot afford treatment are blamed for incompetence, non-compliance, and poor self-governance. They are seen as a drain on the taxpayer. To exacerbate matters, uncritical therapisation of mindfulness accentuates personal responsibility for mental wellbeing. In contrast, community and critical psychologists emphasise socio-political awareness and transformation as a pathway to reducing and combatting mental illness (Arthington, 2016).

Scientification is yet another pathway through which late-stage capitalism assimilates White Mindfulness. Western science is seen as a gateway to popularise mindfulness. In a two-step process, Buddhism is presented as a science rather than a religion. In this guise, mindfulness appears rational, logical, and perfectly acceptable to a society built on eighteenth-century Enlightenment principles that subordinated religion to science. Second, neuroscience and randomised control trials produce an evidence base to legitimise mindfulness. Even though researchers active in the mindfulness community caution against the objectification of science, the field finds itself in the grip of the 'power of a scientific narrative'. Cautions from scientists that research studies lack rigour and that side effects aren't sufficiently investigated (see Thompson, 2016; Britton, 2014; Kerr, 2014) remain fringe to mindfulness' popularisation. Instead, a dominant scientific paradigm which favours rationality over tradition absorbs casualties and losses. Gold-standard trainings further endorse these limited research findings in their quest to 'professionalise' the field and protect the public from charlatans (Crane *et al.*, 2016). Yet popular training models are by their nature exclusive, raising questions around which public is being protected from what and by whom.

Ideological shifts that position mindfulness as part of the medical industrial complex undermine communal wellbeing. As a therapeutic modality, White Mindfulness is booming in a context of government austerities and self-governance agendas. Added to this, when White Mindfulness banishes protesters, it acts as an arbiter that decides what constitutes legitimate anger and action against injustices, what peace looks like, whether it's related to freedom and whom it serves. Talk of an inner revolution in the absence of social change places White Mindfulness dangerously close to the waters of neoliberalism.

The undoing of this trajectory must shift beyond statements of support for the BLM movement; it calls for a reckoning with race and how White Mindfulness addresses the causes of stress. It requires a re-examination of ethos, framework, and purpose.

When White Mindfulness works in corporate settings to improve focus and productivity, or in military settings to hone sniper efficiency, or when it trains resilience in people losing their homes, it repeats systemic violence at the cost of humanity. In White spaces, PGM have to work harder, blend in, navigate, not offend or cause harm, adjust, adapt, and toe the line. If the master's tools are the control and repression of humanity, adopting them to turn the scales of power are defeatist and antithetical to justice. This raises questions for decolonisation: is it possible to decolonise institutions forged on the de facto premise of Othering, even where this was unintentional?

Notes

1 Stephen Lawrence, a Black British teenager was murdered in 1993 in an unprovoked, racial attack while awaiting a bus. Following a judicial inquiry, the 1999 McPherson Report found the Metropolitan Police Service to be institutionally racist.

2 As Said explains, 'the Orient is not an inert fact of nature. It is not merely there, just as the Occident [the West] itself is not just there either' (Said, 2003: 4).

3 Said records that between 1800 and 1950, about 60,000 books were written about the Orient in the West, of which there is no 'remotely comparable figure for Oriental books about the West. ... beefing up the Western scholar's work, there were numerous agencies and institutions with no parallels in Oriental society' (Said, 2003: 204).

4 Snodgrass goes so far as to argue that their works are also used by many Asia-based Buddhist movements. She further elaborates the Rhys Davids' contribution: 'their unquestionable dedication, impeccable scholarship, and immense contribution to Buddhist studies and the ongoing esteem in which they are held directs one away from simplistic notions of [O]rientalism as error or colonial denigration of subject cultures. Extending the focus to the Pāli Text Society enables a consideration of Asian agency and participation in the process. It also offers an alternative lineage for modern Buddhism, one equally enmeshed in the East–West encounters of colonialism and modernity but that recognizes the complicity of academic philology and the institutional practices of scholarship in the process' (Snodgrass, 2007: 186–8).

5 Aung's contribution is found in the Compendium of the work: C. A. F. Rhys Davids, preface to *Compendium of Philosophy: Being a Translation Now Made for the First Time from the Original Pāli of the Abhidhammattha-Sangaha*, with introductory essay and notes by Shwe Zan Aung, revised and edited by C. A. F. Rhys Davids (Aung, 1910: xvii; 246).

6 Bhabha challenges Orientalist binaries of civilised/savage, enlightened/ ignorant as reinforcement of polarities (Bhabha, 1994: 218–19). He describes instead a 'third space' in which difference is negotiated as 'neither one nor the other but something else besides, in-between'. In this third space, 'hybridity [involves] strategies of subversion that turn the gaze of the discriminated back upon the eye of power' (Bhabha, 1985: 154).

7 T. W. Rhys Davids established the Pāli Text Society in 1881 which 'institutionalised the study of Buddhism' and set out to publish the entire Sutta and *Abhidhamma Pitakas* (Snodgrass, 2007: 188).

8 On the construct of knowledge, Said observes: 'No one has ever devised a method for detaching the scholar from the circumstances of life, from the fact of his [sic] involvement (conscious or unconscious) with a class, a set of beliefs, a social position, or from the mere activity of being a member of a society' (Said, 1978: 18).

9 Said's 'inaugural heroes' were 'builders of the field, creators of a tradition, progenitors of the Orientalist brotherhood; people who established a central authority, created a vocabulary, and set rules that could be used by others' (Said, 1978: 122).

10 King cleverly uses a 'border control' analogy to show the extent to which hidden forms of appropriation are underway in apparently benign acts of extraction: Western philosophies presume the superior role of homeland intellectual security who keep foreigners, immigrants, and their cultural baggage out until, their bags searched and stripped, they are considered fit for assimilation and conditional, silent inclusion (King, 2009: 44–5).

11 The term medicalisation was coined in the 1970s by sociologists such as Irving Zola.

2

Cementing whiteness: inclusion through a neoliberal, postracial lens

> The function, the very serious function of racism is distraction. It keeps you from doing your work. It keeps you explaining, over and over again, your reason for being. Somebody says you have no language and you spend twenty years proving that you do. Somebody says your head isn't shaped properly so you have scientists working on the fact that it is. Somebody says you have no art, so you dredge that up. Somebody says you have no kingdoms, so you dredge that up. None of this is necessary. There will always be one more thing.
>
> Toni Morrison (1975)

Liberal 'democracies' such as in the US and UK give the false impression that people can be who they wish to be and express themselves in any way they choose to. And yet, as Toni Morrison describes in the epigraph, people are judged, punished, disempowered, and killed based on who they are and how they identify. Describing whiteness, Morrison explains that race is constructed as a distraction that keeps people back from thriving and realising their potential. She cites the ridiculousness and many ways in which people who are racialised become tied up with anti-Black rhetoric and end up perpetually explaining and attempting to undo systemic racism and the very construct of race.

In unequal societies like the US and UK, numerous signifiers of difference such as race are used to differentiate and marginalise communities and isolate individuals. But identities are collapsed under a guise of 'equality of opportunity' and the 'freedom to choose' (Hall, 2011: 709). Equality of opportunity advocates insist that the playing field is level, granting anyone a fair chance to advance if they put their mind to it, regardless of circumstances. Their 'motherhood and apple pie' ethos ignores privileges such as access to schooling, housing, healthy food, and intergenerational wealth that advantage some at the expense of others. In racialised societies, power, resources, and opportunity are unequally distributed across race. Racial disparities in wealth, pay, education, employment, housing, justice, and health impact wellbeing. As Heather McGhee, author of *The Sum of Us* explains based on her travels across the US, 'racism is at the core of all our most vexing and public problems'. Racial divides seeded in structures and an 'us versus them' mentality, she says, cost US$16 trillion per annum (McGhee, 2021). The UK reports similar accounts of the disproportionate effects of structural racialism on poor health in People of the Global Majority (PGM) (EHRC, 2018). In contrast to 'equality of opportunity' protagonists, equality of outcome advocates acknowledge disparities and use measures like redress to ensure that those who are socio-economically and politically deprived have a fair chance at success (Caccavale, 2021).

This chapter dives into the underpinnings of the Mindfulness Industry to look at the socio-political and economic milieu in which it was forged. I probe into how neoliberalism and postracialism influence the wellness industry and, by default, White Mindfulness. Within this frame, I consider how diversity and inclusivity reinforce spiritual bypassing (Welwood, 1984)[1] and explore the implications of this for inclusion. To address the obvious question, 'inclusion into what?', I draw on Sara Ahmed's work to show how diversity claims often function as 'non-performatives'. They create an impression of a diverse sector while disguising social forces at play. This framing allows me to dip in and out of Lorde's 'master's tools' argument and to ask what is required for real transformation to occur.

Race, postracialism, and whiteness

Typically, White spaces deny, suppress, or white-wash difference, discounting people's lived realities. As the word white-washing implies, the ruse of 'equality' denies discrimination. In the interests of a dominant discourse set by White supremacy and norms, White spaces superimpose a fictitious level playing field. They belittle and nullify systemic oppression, reducing discrimination to personal, individualised acts. Such systemic aggressions portray injustices as imagined, unusual, and intermittent. The diversions Morrison names maintain dominant power structures and place the burden for attaining justice at the door of those who are discriminated against. On top of this, it makes complainants feel like they are creating a fuss when they object to unfairness. In other words, oppressive systems create the impression of 'equality of opportunity' and make it the impossible work of the dispossessed to create 'equality of outcome'.

Such weathering and wearing down as Morrison describes in the epigraph centres and recentres whiteness and creates the illusion and desirability of belonging. In other words, people can spend their lives tied up with 'gaining access' and proving their innocence and worth, while being abused. Rae Johnson, author of *Embodied Social Justice* (2017), likens this ongoing violence of exclusion to having one thousand paper cuts. Paper cuts are invisible to those who don't know they're there and might even be considered 'just paper cuts', or a small thing. But paper cuts pain and itch and irritate and burn. Just a single cut throbs.

Many systemic injustices are hidden from view even as dominant powers regenerate Othering. Postracialism, for instance, is an ideology used in advanced capitalism to camouflage the exploitation of racial difference. It conveniently sidesteps and non-essentialises race and all intersecting characteristics of difference, pretending that the exploitation of difference is an issue of the past, no longer part of contemporary societies. In this setting, the latent nature of Othering is foundational to inequality. Without it, White supremacy and patriarchy cannot thrive, since the more normative ideologies are, the fewer people notice, question, or object.

Postracialism is a significant feature of US and UK societies. Together, postracialism and patriarchy perpetuate the White gaze and provide the avenues for mental control of the oppressed. Such social controls play out in multiple ways. When coupled with Said's latent Orientalism, we see that these systematic ideologies shape and construct all minds and hearts. They reinforce white-washing and set up social and mental polarities. Commonly, those who benefit are blind to the ways power relations strip people of rights, dignity, and the opportunities to thrive.

The ubiquitous construct of race was crafted over centuries in the interests of empire and conquest. Critical race theorist David Goldberg traces its materialisation to the formation of modern

Europe. The roots of Othering reside in these histories that created race for purposes of exploitation and capital accumulation. As an expression of 'dehumanisation',

> [race] established the lines of belonging and estrangement for modern European social life ... [It] was invoked to delineate a European 'we' in defining contrast with those considered its constitutive outsiders. ... Differentiating origins, kinship, and lineage from the outset tied colour to culture, bodies to behavioural projection, incipient biology to ascribed mentalities ... From the fifteenth to the nineteenth centuries, slavery framed much if not all the thinking concerning race. Slavery was fuelled by ideas of inherent inferiority and superiority and reinforced them.
>
> (Goldberg, 2015: 7–8, 29–30)

Empire, coloniality, and Orientalism ingrained race in colonial Europe and enshrined it in the formation of US society to justify exploitation. Race infiltrates and pervades all social sectors, including secularisation processes. It is now a default technology of White supremacy. In its service, postracialism invisibilises race and encourages even more denialism than 'colour-blindness' (Armstrong and Wildman, 2007: 639).

Postracialism emerged as an ideology and instrument of power in the 2000s, replacing prior strategies of colour-blindness, in which people pretended not to see 'colour', and multiculturalism, which uses devices like cultural days or Black History Month to homogenise Black culture and then return to racism-as-usual. Postracialism conceals White supremacy and systems of marginalisation. It effectively erases race. Yet, it advances social norms, institutional arrangements, and practices that sustain racialised societies (see Armstrong and Wildman, 2007; powell, 2008). Working together with individualism and neoliberalism, systemic racism privatises race. The state no longer needs to govern the systemic exploitation of race. Postracial logic creates a material, sociocultural, and political retreat from race (Cho, 2009), so that it is no longer considered a defining feature of society. In other words, racial discrimination becomes hidden. As noted, in the 'absence of race', racist incidences are no longer regarded as systemically derived, but as episodic and individualised. In these scenarios, the racialised become the problem for even perceiving race in the first instance (Ahmed, 2018: 342).

Habits of White supremacy run deep. White prejudice which is learnt and cultivated also becomes an 'unconscious habit' or set of norms that is conditioned and socio-politically embedded in the psyche. Pre-eminent race scholar W. E. Du Bois explains:

> I ... began to realise that in the fight against race prejudice, we were not facing simply the rational, conscious determination of white folk to oppress us; we were facing age-long complexes sunk now largely to unconscious habit and irrational urge.
>
> (Du Bois, 1984: 194, 296)

Unconscious habits and norms are strategically and systematically reinforced and held in place. People's minds and beliefs become the security forces that protect and strengthen the status quo. In other words, these values and beliefs are internalised, embodied, and largely ignored by a significant portion of the population. They are sponsored cross-sectorally and reproduced socially. Yet unconscious bias training targets the individual rather than the system. By doing so, it silently retains the status quo.

Race is thus explicitly embedded structurally and facilitated through internalised social values and norms that operate as much at organisational, communal, and social levels as they do at an individual level. As a result, structural racism is fortified by latent unconscious biases and a refusal to recognise race as a signifier of White privilege. In other words, the construct of race perpetuates and permeates systemically through explicit and implicit unquestioned technologies that function as social defaults. Given these deep foundations, White supremacy perpetuates discourses of Othering, intrinsically and invisibly interwoven into social reality.

Whiteness confers invisible rights and is synonymous with normativity. It functions as 'a habit, even a bad habit' which forms a backdrop to all social activity (Ahmed, 2007a). Whiteness evades, rejects, and remains 'ignorant about the injustices that flow from [it] and its attendant privileges' (Bailey, 2014: 35; see also McIntosh, 1988). As a normative default, an institutional habit, the construct 'White' escapes racialisation. It is the norm from which Others are gauged as different and defined as 'not us'. It protects those who inhabit and benefit from its intersectional technologies ranking privilege in accordance with compliance. When challenged, 'White fragility' appeals to individualism and misunderstanding. Together with

White guilt and shame, it recentres whiteness and constitutes built-in mechanisms of systemic refurbishment.

In this world of neoliberal postraciality, the racialised now become individualised targets and the new perpetrators of racism, accused of racialising poverty, structures of power, and access to power and privilege. On top of this, all social degradation is ascribed to individual inexperience (see Goldberg, 2015: 29–30; Gordon, 2015; DiAngelo, 2010). Racist incidents are regarded as exceptions and made the responsibility of the racialised. They 'lock in' structural privilege (Roithmayr, 2014). As Angela Davis explains,

> expressions of attitudinal racism ... treated as anachronistic expressions that were once articulated with state sponsored racisms ... are now relegated to the private sphere ... they are now treated as individual and private irregularities, to be solved by punishing and re-educating the individual by teaching them colour-blindness, by teaching them not to notice the phenomenon of race.
>
> (Davis, 2012: 170)

Colour-blindness only suits dominant power which permeates from the centre and above. For those looking in from the margins, or from below, few people in positions of dominant power are incentivised to change themselves, let alone systems of White supremacy.

So how do we understand or speak about race under these conditions?

Neoliberalism

In 1988, Margaret Thatcher and Ronald Reagan were photographed happily dancing across a ballroom during a White House dinner, the last such dinner of Reagan's presidency. The image depicted the partnership and 'special relationship' the US and UK are said to share. Coming to office in 1979 and 1981 respectively, the conservative leaders shared a mutual commitment to building free market economies. Political economies in both countries advanced systems of racial capitalism to generate far greater opportunities for financial accumulation by private companies while destroying communities, trade unions, and organisations that could challenge growing inequities and exploitation. This period coincided with the advent and rise of White Mindfulness.

The term neoliberalism has become a catchphrase for multiple facets of what social activist and film maker Naomi Klein calls disaster capitalism. It refers to a global stage of capitalism, the arrangement of efficient markets and the totalising effect of valuing human life purely in economic terms. Associated with Milton Friedman, Friedrich Hayek, and Gary Becker of the Chicago School of Economics, neoliberalism emerged in opposition to Keynesian economics, which prioritised 'the common good' over profitability. Its monetary strategy emphasised instead the freedom of markets. Rooted in classic liberal economics and political theory (Hall, 2011), the new locus of power favoured privatisation, wealth accumulation, and deregulation. Socio-economic 'shocks' were exploited as economic opportunities to spread alternative ideas to existing policies until the new 'doctrine' took hold. In *Shock Doctrine*, Klein (2008) cites various countries, including Chile, China, the US, and UK, in which this method has been effective. Collective bargaining and trade unions gave way to freedoms to suppress wages, increase interest rates, introduce tax havens for the wealthy, and impose austerities for the working classes. Following different paths in different contexts, neoliberalism became entrenched in the US and UK in the late 1970s and early 1980s (Goldberg, 2009). It created what Klein calls the 'corporatist state'. For those outside the bubble of the 'dazzling rich', 'features of the corporatist state tend to include aggressive surveillance (once again, with government and large corporations trading favors and contracts), mass incarceration, shrinking civil liberties and often, though not always, torture' (Klein, 2008: 32). Although not one thing, neoliberalism always promotes individualism, encouraging competition and inequality.

Becker's deployment of 'homo economicus' – the notion that people always act in their individual self-interest – expediated individuality and individual responsibility. Noted for its discourse of individualism, neoliberalism replaces community or society with the individual as the social unit of organisation and measurement. Values of 'possessive individualism and self-interest' replaced social organisations, enabling the powerful to dominate and profit in stratified societies. Higher education, for instance, shifted from being a social right to a personal responsibility (Holmwood, 2018). Privatisation of publicly owned assets such as education, land, transport, and health paved the way to individual ownership. In the absence of social equality, individualism and consumerism rose together to widen inequalities domestically and globally.

Due to the freedom of markets and shareholder primacy, mounting socio-economic and political inequalities feature prominently in the US, the UK, and any other neoliberal state. Profit and gain are made attractive and associated with meritocracy, hard work, enterprise, and Darwinism. In this context of extremes, dispossession – a key neoliberal strategy which entails a 'loss of rights' including the right to work – restores class power to ruling elites (Harvey, 2005: 178). Because neoliberalism builds on empire, coloniality, Orientalism, and the exploitation of race, class, and gender, it perpetuates Othering of the marginalised in societies that profess democracy and freedom of expression.

Neoliberalism and wellness

The rapid spread of Westernised mindfulness occurs in conjunction with an explosive self-help industry, individualisation, and commodification. These forces promote values that act in opposition to communal and social wellness. They align with neoliberalism's discourse of individualism. In keeping with strategies of political and economic control, neoliberalism's wellbeing culture emphasises inner-being and psychological constructs of self-governance. Certain Western psychotherapy models[2] reinforce forms of separated individualism that coincide with neoliberal interests. Up-and-coming models of care promote self-reliance, self-interest, and the self-sufficient individual (see Hall, 2011; Asad, 2003). In other words, people are required to be obedient and to conform to a system that places the moral burden for wellness on them personally. Instead of feeling connected to communities, we are conditioned to think of ourselves in isolation from others. In this context, terms like 'self-regulation', 'self-compassion', and 'self-responsibility' (Bristow, 2016: 10–18), all familiar in White Mindfulness, proliferate (Lewis and Rozelle, 2016: 260). Self-governance in fact defines neoliberal culture: individuals monitor, police, and soothe themselves to relieve the state and their workplaces of such responsibility. Whether experiencing eating disorders, loneliness, or depression, all of which were exacerbated by COVID-19 isolation policies, individuals are required to self-regulate their way to wellness.

Political theorist Isabell Lorey suggests that self-regulation is an essential feature of new forms of labour that colonise the *'whole person'* (Lorey, 2015: 5, emphasis added). This neoliberal world 'exploits' corporate employees through mechanisms like an attractive salary for limitless hours or 'prestigious' internships that replace wages with status. At the other end of the spectrum, dispossession paves the way for precarity and zero-hour contracts at very little pay. Across the social spectrum, wellbeing becomes the individual's duty – an inability to withstand pressure shows weakness, laziness, and low resilience. Enduring one thousand paper cuts shows fortitude and character.

Unsurprisingly, race runs through this interpretation of 'good health' (Harvey, 2005: 65). Framed by growing privatisation of health services, health becomes a commodity rather than a human right. Doctor and professor of medicine Petr Skrabanek explains that when health became part of state ideology, it was used to justify racism, 'segregation, and eugenic control since "healthy" means patriotic, pure, while "unhealthy" equals foreign, polluted' (Skrabanek, 1994: 15). Used as a segregator, health divides the good person who toes the line and contributes to society from the bad person who burdens the health service, taxpayer, and society at large. Added to the discourse of individualism, colonising the minds of the oppressed makes them believe that they bear individual responsibility for good health regardless of adverse circumstances.

Race and ill health are of course also linked to work – dispossession leads to a malaise of ill health. Intersectional studies attest to this: Black women who are least likely to secure jobs experience extreme poor health because of this and other incessant microaggressions (see EHRC, 2016; Butt *et al.*, 2015; Bécares, 2011; Stevenson and Rao, 2014; Barnard and Turner, 2011). Despite the structural causes of this level of disease, which make race and racism public health issues, illness is met with misapprehension, racial profiling of entire ethnic groups, and, at best, symptomatic relief (Zeilig, 2014).

When societies make people ill and health becomes a sought-after, almost unattainable commodity, healthism also points to the workings of the medical industrial complex which pathologises socio-economically induced stress and then creates dependencies on big pharma. In such settings, White Mindfulness provides a much more attractive alternative to beta blockers even when it acts symptomatically rather than striking at the root of the problem. However, in the context of overwhelm and the desperation to cope, like medical blockers, it too can numb the fallout of precarity and discrimination, allowing exploitative systems to prevail.

Privatisation of health turns wellness into a rarefied, exclusive commodity accessible only to 'elite' consumers. As part of the strategy to hold individuals responsible for their unaffordable well-being, institutions use invisible actions to 'domesticate' or 'control' people. Propaganda establishes norms around weight, size, and looks for instance, that shape mindsets; activities are 'divided into approved and disapproved, healthy and unhealthy, prescribed and proscribed, responsible and irresponsible' (Skrabanek, 1994: 15). It is this same machinery that racialises belonging and being outcast. These norms extend exclusions to body shape, cis- and heteronormativity, gender binaries, ableism, age, and faith. Spun in favourable terms, the ideological sway of healthism idolises the fit, lean, White citizen who follows prescribed, 'researched' protocols. Deriding terms like hocus pocus, unscientific, unproven, and untested, downgrade traditional methods, unless these are marketable. As a result, the most deprived citizens are forced to pursue imposed systems of health care, education, and norms, often at a fee (Martinez and Garcia, 1996). The correlation of race and health recycles racism.

What of a neoliberal mindfulness?

White Mindfulness follows the protocols of healthism. It obscures the role of socio-economic and political causes in illness and amplifies personalised resilience (Cederström and Spicer, 2015; Purser and Ng, 2015). Although neoliberalism is based on a discourse of individualism, it racialises and condemns whole groups for being unwell and unhealthy. In this way healthism isolates and atomises communities. Such trends contribute to growing inequalities, as well as cultures of racialised blame and shame. They generate a numbing and sedation to the realities of inequities and an uncritical acceptance of norms.

When White Mindfulness causes us to become still and to disengage the political world, it reinforces healthism, suppresses difference, and upholds 'equality of opportunity' rhetoric. Added to this, when its primary ally, Western psychology, promotes the idea of an autonomous, responsible, free, moral self-governing citizen, it reinforces the foundations of neoliberalism (Arthington, 2016). In a critique of Western psychology, psychiatrist and academic Hussein Bulhan extends the view of a neoliberal psychology, tying it to global control: 'ascendancy and globalization of Euro-American psychology ... correlates with the ascendancy of Euro-American military, economic, and political might' (Bulhan, 1985).[3] In other words, Western psychology and its methods are tied to new forms of domination. Seen through this lens, White Mindfulness is, ironically, allied with social forces and modalities that promote personal and social distress on a global scale. Renowned psychiatrist, liberation leader, and author of *The Wretched of the Earth* (2001), Frantz Fanon, adds to this psychotherapy's inherent racism. Fanon says:

> Freud may be able to explain disorders that pertain to some individuals, but he cannot explain those that pertain to people whose lives are shaped by racism ... because he ignores the role played by social relations ... in the constitution of selfhood.
>
> (Hubis, 2015: 35)[4]

Building on Fanon, eliminating race as a factor in illness and wellness reinforces a culture of postracialism that ignores the inequalities, divisions, legislations, and lived histories that spring from racial exclusion and exploitation. This reality asks what it is that enables a system that overwhelmingly neglects difference when these are such fundamental denominators of exploitation. And how does White Mindfulness come to repeat this oversight, so uncritically? In search of answers, the following section takes a closer look at postracialism and systemic whiteness.

Postracialism, neoliberalism, and whiteness: comfortable bedfellows

Much like Said described Orientalism, ideologies function at both an explicit systemic and an intrinsic latent level. They colonise minds and create endemic habits at every level of society. When social forces like neoliberalism and postracialism come together, new concepts such as 'neoliberal postraciality' emerge to explain the coherence of strategies that exploit differences to create vulnerabilities and advance power. The way it works is

> a postracial society embeds the insistence that key conditions of social life are less and less now predicated on racial preferences, choices and resources. These include residential location, educational possibility and institutional access, employment opportunities, social networks and integration ... Postraciality amounts to the claim that we are, or are close to, or ought to be living outside of debilitating racial reference. In particular, it presumes that people (ought to) have similar life chances irrespective of their assigned race in societies ... It insists that the legacy of racial discrimination and disadvantage has been waning over time, reaching a point today where, if existing at all, such discrimination is anomalous and individually expressed. It is not structural or socially mandated ... Postraciality, it could be said, then, is the end of race as we have known it.
>
> (Goldberg, 2015: 2–5)

Goldberg's analysis highlights the 'equality of opportunity' argument. It shows the power of postracial rhetoric which grips White Mindfulness. But postracialism operates on multiple levels. It is never only about race. It is designed to hide all the mechanisms of White supremacy. Combined with neoliberalism and whiteness, individualisation of racial incidents, austerity, dispossession, and exclusion are all facets of race-making. Such neoliberal racialisation is tied to dispossession, the carceral state, joblessness, stringent immigration controls, the war on terror, Islamophobia, and the tendency to impute crime to colour (Davis, 2016: 33; Davis, 2012: 167). In other words, race is all around us, permeating society interstitially and hiding in plain sight.

The devices of transcending, privatising, and personalising race are neoliberal strategies designed to sustain power through repressing and denying identity yet using it as the basis of exploitation and power. In other words, race is suppressed to promote the ideology of the freedom of markets, equality of opportunity, individual sovereignty, and free will. It is simultaneously deeply embedded in structures of power that continue to extract capital from minoritised groups. Race is knotted with ideologies to produce racialised systems.

Whiteness represents the forging of racialised systems such as neoliberal postraciality. Indicating more than race, it includes generational wealth, legal and cultural privileging, access to schooling, finance, and housing, and is tied up with cis-normativity, ableism, income, and faith (DiAngelo, 2010). This is to say that exclusions based on difference are historic, complex, and deeply rooted in societies. Postracialism, neoliberalism, and whiteness entangle and buttress one another to generate intersectional discriminations and complex individuals and communities (Hill Collins and Bilge, 2016).

The 'discourse of individualism' runs through neoliberalism and whiteness. As a 'primary barrier' it privatises race, re-entrenches white privilege, and hides generational wealth, functioning to

> deny the significance of race and the advantages of being white; hide the accumulation of wealth over generations; deny social and historical context; prevent a macro analysis of the institutional and structural dimensions of social life; deny collective socialization and the power of dominant culture (media, education, religion, etc.) to shape our perspectives and ideology; function as neo-colorblindness and reproduce the myth of meritocracy; and make collective action difficult. Further, being viewed as an individual is a privilege only available to the dominant group.
>
> (DiAngelo, 2010)

Access to mortgages, education, justice, and health continue to be racialised. Yet these realities are now accompanied by a denial that racism has any impact. Instead, there is an insistence, an ideology in place, that 'one is fully responsible individually for one's social situation' (Goldberg, 2015: 126–7). In the current postracial, neoliberal era of free, open markets, the 'equality of opportunity' falsehood overrides systems of racialised inequalities.

Whiteness illustrates the durability and tenacity of race as a social construct. The power of whiteness resides precisely in how it plays out through patriarchy, masculinity, heteronormativity, ableism, and, often, Christianity (see hooks, 2000; DiAngelo, 2010; Lewis, 2004; McIntosh, 1988). As Kimberlé Crenshaw (1989) emphasises, these technologies mutually coalesce to create complex, intersectional discriminations. Regardless of context, White privilege retains historic, authoritative precedence, and when Black people are successfully assimilated, they too can end up protecting such privilege.

The structures and habits of White privilege function at the levels of the soma, the psyche, and the world. Whiteness racialises bodies of PGM and casts them in inferior and/or exotic ways that continue to place them beyond the borders of privilege. It demarcates the space from which 'Blackness' is excluded even when Blackness invades such spaces (see Mirza, 2015; Puwar, 2004). Drawing upon its own history, whiteness licenses and reproduces itself. Subjects are formed through and within the dynamics of its discourse and, in the absence of self-reflection and disruption, repeatedly reposition themselves in favourable relationships to power. Personal privilege becomes invested in institutions of privilege; systems become narcissistic and self-generating; habits of White privilege hide and actively impede any process of conscious reflection so that they appear 'non-existent even as they continue to function' (Sullivan, 2006: 5–6).

I have described the synergy of neoliberal postraciality and whiteness as a collection of hegemonic, self-perpetuating power structures that govern through education, health, housing, social security, legislation, and criminal justice systems. A critical race lens provides a premise from which to consider the complexities of exclusion and the possibilities for transforming White Mindfulness. As Audre Lorde reminds us: 'there is no thing as a single-issue struggle because we do not live single-issue lives' (Lorde, 2007a: 138). When race is identified as a social marker of discrimination, other markers that intersect with race become more easily visible. This allows people to organise along intersectional lines to produce queer, Black identity groups.

How does this play out?

In the world of White Mindfulness, structural racism, postracialism, neoliberalism, and latent Othering cohere to reproduce White spaces that embody exclusionary acts, avoidance, deflection, and spiritual bypassing. Downplaying race perpetuates the deafening 'postracial silences' that mark social power. Researching the experiences of GM practitioners in convert meditation circles in the US, academic Nalika Gajaweera (2021) remarks on the ways GM bodies diminish and recede in spaces in which there is no felt sense of belonging, regardless of whether they experience microaggressions. She explains how racial microaggressions are used to belittle PGM by telling them that their practice is not sufficiently evolved to transcend identity. Her *Sitting in the Fire Together* maps the now-common emergence of GM sits that allow people to experience a felt sense of safety. Whether in Seattle, California, or New York, her respondents describe the visceral release and relief from sitting together outside the 'White gaze'.

These accounts lay the basis for inquiry into how we might understand inclusion into a system built on exclusions. To address this, I draw on Sara Ahmed's body of work, especially her seminal *On Being Included*.

Can diversity help White Mindfulness?

Diversity when linked with equality, inclusion, and justice is about social change. It carries weight especially in societies that are increasingly heterogeneous, encouraging a synergy of perspectives to find solutions involving all key players to create belonging. Diverse spaces are enriching, expansive, and fundamental to growth and development. Yet, the language of diversity can be problematic. Frequent use of the term can make institutions and communities believe that they are diverse without making meaningful change (Ahmed, 2012: 51–5). But what is the purpose of diversity?

Diversity commands the potential to fundamentally transform society. Earl Lewis, previous Mellon Foundation president and diversity champion explains:

> It is one thing to define diversity, but quite another to leverage diversity and value it. Too often we find ourselves in reactive and defensive postures. We still find ourselves dealing with demographic and structural inequities. Why is economic prosperity determined by various kinds of exclusions? Can we ignore all variety of talents for the future? How can we think anew about cohesion in the 21st century?
>
> (Lewis, quoted in Mirza, 2017: 6)

Lewis links poor diversity to border controls, exclusions, and diminished economies. Compellingly, he suggests diversity can be put to work to 'leverage' difference to imagine new futures. To Lewis, diversity is imperative not only for social cohesion but for the rich advancement that benefits from difference. Futures, after all, can only be inclusive of the people who create them. But even more than this, innovative futures, new ways of thinking and approaching problems, can only arise from a coming together of different experiences, backgrounds, and contexts. When we learn from experiences, beliefs, and perspectives that are different to our own, we enrich the educational process on all levels. New lights go on, we change, the group changes, and new possibilities emerge. When learning spaces are deliberately richly diverse, new insights and innovations can emerge. Whereas racism costs societies trillions, closing the racial wealth gap is shown to benefit economies. So what is it, aside from the dominant narrative and practice of whiteness, that perpetuates business as usual? Why are systems and structures of White supremacy so intransigent? Why, when it will benefit the whole of society, do inequities and discrimination persist? Is it, as Du Bois says, that power-over is such an entrenched habit in the psyche of countries that call themselves 'democracies' that they can't imagine society-wide liberation? Or is it simply, as Trevor Noah says in conversation with Heather McGhee, that racism is a highly addictive drug (Noah and McGhee, 2021)?

Historically, diversity replaced the term social justice, regarded as too contentious a term by institutions premised on discrimination. As critical philosopher Mala Singh (2011) explains, as social justice came to challenge the status quo, it was stretched in multiple, sometimes competing, directions. Diluted, it lost its clout to shape fair and democratically enabling societies. These structures set the stage for diversity, a word that acquires meaning through its association with other concepts. When placed alongside words like equality and inclusion, diversity assumes a certain tone. Deployed by elitist institutions like Yale and Oxbridge as statements of commitment, it usually works to market the institution rather than bring about meaningful change (see Ahmed, 2012).

Through constant use, co-opted words easily become emptied of meaning and appropriated in the interests of whiteness. When a watered-down version of diversity replaces social justice, Ahmed suggests its very purpose becomes that of 'forgetting' the contexts and histories surrounding terms like race and justice. Forgetting, of course, stands in sharp contrast to mindfulness' 'remembering'. It buries unfairness and injustices deep underground in the hope that they will neither be unearthed nor interfere with the business of the day. To forget is to 'deliberately cease to think of'. It reminds us of the potentially expedient uses of diversity today to govern and control inclusion and bypass transformation.

Neither words nor policies and mission statements act or effect change on their own. They only acquire potency when people who hold or are seen to hold power adopt and breathe life into them (Ahmed *et al.*, 2006). For this reason, senior management buy-in, endorsement, and enactment of diversity strategies is foundational to transformation. Yet predominantly White institutions commonly formulate statements of commitment and dictate terms and strategies for inclusion. In such instances, diversity constitutes nonperformative, 'happy' declarations that serve to engender change without disrupting whiteness. In these all-too-common scenarios, use of the word evokes a 'feel-good politics' and uplifts organisational spirits but changes little if anything (Ahmed, 2004b; 2007b; 2012: 69, 71). Empty notions of diversity – Ahmed's nonperformatives – are then used to *not* disrupt. In other words, as with social justice, while diversity can be employed to effect change, more commonly it features in mission statements, without impact, as a technology of whiteness.

As a happy declaration, diversity is frequently used as a discourse of reparation. This purpose imagines that the word itself can heal divisions. As reparation, diversity is expected to generate collegiality, promote multiculturalism, assuage white guilt, censure objections to 'plastering the cracks', and rewrite empire as a 'melting pot' exercise and a celebration of difference (Ahmed, 2012: 166). In other words, it is paraded to do the heavy lifting of undoing systemic injustices while eclipsing those very injustices. Combined with forgetting, such non-performative applications of diversity are a far cry from leveraging diversity for systemic transformation.

Clearly, the uses of diversity are contextually determined. It can simultaneously accessorise and camouflage institutional power not always for lack of will, but poverty of understanding how to leverage difference towards justice. Intellectual Saleem Badat expands:

> A commitment to diversity does not automatically translate into genuine respect on the part of institutions, social groups, and individuals for difference. ... Nor does it imply commitment to tackling differences based on class and wealth/income inequality, which hugely constrain equity of access, opportunities, and outcomes for significant numbers of people, and impact negatively on social inclusion.
>
> (Badat, 2016: 10)

In other words, true diversity interrupts power premised on whiteness. But, as noted before, the motivation to alter such arrangements relies on commitments to innovation and justice. Those in positions to effect transformation in the interests of wider social advancement effectively disrupt their own power. Within the mindfulness sector, current uses of diversity to 'widen participation' detract from systemic change. Statements and practices of intent lean towards representational increases of minorities or raising the headcount of previously excluded constituents. Customarily, this monitors inclusion and manages 'the demands for equality while keeping racial hierarchies intact' (Saha, 2017). It is a common method used to bring GM bodies into White spaces.

Non-performative diversity strategies that incorporate minorities into existing unchanging structures are assimilationist. They bring individuals from groups that were previously outcast into the '"melting pot" of prevailing political arrangements and structures'. Outcasts are acculturated into dominant systems by 'adopting their values, habits, cultural expressions, aspirations and ways of being' (Goldberg, 2015: 19). Cast in this way, assimilation is antithetical to diversity since it entrenches social injustices and cements relations of domination. It absorbs Black people into White supremacist society without transforming that society. Ahmed calls these strategies 'the lip-service model of diversity' used to endorse the status quo (Ahmed, 2012: 58). Invariably, such strategies harden 'the set of norms and code of behaviour, the values and structures determining privilege and power already established self-servingly by Whites' (Biko, 1978: 19).

Entering the master's house, though, does not have to mean assimilation. It could be a strategy that fortifies the margins. In making this argument bell hooks suggests that

> marginality is a central location for the production of a counter hegemonic discourse – it is found in the words, habits and the way one lives ... It is a site one clings to even when moving to the centre ... it nourishes our capacity to resist ... It is an inclusive space where we recover ourselves, where we move in solidarity to erase the category coloniser/colonised.
>
> (hooks, 1991: 149–50)

In centring the margins to effect disruption from within, hooks encourages strategic border-crossing without collapsing the borders. She identifies the margins as a place of refuge for the diversity worker and as a place to which to tether and from which to nurture disruptive interventions.

Disruptive strategies and tactics are fundamental to any transformation programme. To explain the counterstrategies that keep disruptive politics at bay, Ahmed (2012) uses the analogy of a brick wall. The wall symbolises a protectionist, impenetrable construct against which the diversity worker bangs their head. It serves to guard and preserve social norms that keep whiteness in and disruptive elements out. As a technology of whiteness, the wall represents institutional norms and habits; it functions as a fortress preserving whiteness. Implicit herein is the assumption that what is guarded is at risk of diffusion, alteration, reduction, and corruption.

Cosmetic, lip-service, nip-and-tuck diversity, paraded as change, reinforces the wall. Systemic diversity strategies that challenge normativity and power encounter the wall. They expose the flexing of institutional power and privileges, the hardening of histories of exclusions, and can intimate the futility of diversity work. Yet, for their promise of seeding critical thinking and social change for the betterment of society, institutions remain sites of contestation. For this reason, the challenges for diversity work include, but are not limited to, dismantling the walls of hegemonic power built on exclusions. For White Mindfulness this raises questions of what is worth preserving, what serves the greater good, and, more importantly, what must go. For protagonists of change, whether to dismantle walls or build different inclusive spaces of belonging are important considerations.

Growing inequalities and failed diversity strategies are leading to more calls for decolonisation over diversification (Bhanot, 2015; Samudzi, 2016). Decolonisation proponents advocate institutional and systemic transformation of whiteness. The Fallist and decolonisation campaigns discussed in Chapter 10 emphasise the role of movements rather than isolated institutional struggles to transform systems and imagine new arrangements of power. The Black Lives Matter movement, for instance, emphasises collective rather than individual leadership (Davis, 2017). These 'calls to action' understand decolonisation not merely as headcounts and spatial rearrangements but demand pedagogical and systemic changes led by marginalised groups and leaders. The question begged is whether decolonisation serves as another word replacement that helps us gloss over and forget the past while looking busy. White Mindfulness' arc, as discussed here, cannot be seen in isolation from the US and UK social forces in which it proliferates. Its complexity reveals a rootedness in neo-colonial practices, norms, and narratives that thwart justice. Such histories and context require appropriate innovations to parachute or dismantle the walls that Ahmed references in order to 'reimagine postcolonial futures'.

Emergent projects that decentre whiteness defy and side-step racialised formations of mindfulness. More specifically, they advocate embodied justice as a social mindfulness cognisant of the structural forces that deplete and politically repress marginalised communities. This approach recognises the extent to which neoliberal postraciality shapes the structures, systems, relations, and language of this world, acknowledging how they engrave bodies and frame lives. The writing on the walls and signage of apartheid societies land on and inside bodies. Embodied justice celebrates the joy of many people and multiple movements who live their lives outside the parameters of White norms. It shifts the focus and calls upon all of us to do the work of decolonising ourselves, noting that this can only happen in community. It promotes agency that interrupts political arrangements of subjugation. Such agency, as noted before, is itself always complicated by questions of power and draws on lessons from different, non-competitive, and non-exploitative models of communal thriving.

Notes

1 The term 'spiritual bypassing' was coined by John Welwood in the 1980s. It refers to using 'spiritual' ideas and practices to sidestep challenging questions of discrimination, especially in contexts when the bypassing seeks to avoid guilt or shame.

2 The generalisation of psychotherapies acknowledges the multitude, contradictory, and complementary forms of therapy practiced in the West. Whether as first-, second-, or third-wave typologies, they are all noted for their uncritical alignment with the ethos of individualism and their juxtaposition to liberation psychology which correlates socio-economic conditions with mental health to treat the root of the problem rather than its manifestation (Martin-Baro, 1996; Arthington, 2016).

3 Bulhan's full quote reads: 'The ascendency and globalisation of Euro-American psychology indeed correlates with the ascendency and globalisation of Euro-American military, economic and political might. Viewed from this perspective, the organised discipline of psychology reveals itself as yet another form of alien intrusion and cultural imposition for the non-white majority of the world' (Bulhan, 1985: 64).

4 In contrast to Freud, Fanon's phenomenologically informed psychological theories and methods emphasised community. He sought to develop a human psychology determined by 'socio-historic coordinates' (Bulhan, 1985: 73).

3

Western Buddhism: a postracial precursor to White Mindfulness

There is no neutral body from which our bodies deviate. Society has written deep into each strand of tissue of every living person on earth. What it writes into the heart muscles of five-star generals is distinct from what it writes in the pancreatic tissue and intestinal tracts of Black single mothers in Detroit, of Mexicana migrants in Fresno, but no body stands outside the consequences of injustice and inequality.

Aurora Levins Morales (2013: 9)

Societies, like people, can be considered well or ill. Rather than a medical reading, these descriptors indicate how governments and states can create discomfort and illness. Racialised societies follow patterns of discrimination, oppression, and exploitation, stripping people of their human rights and dignity. Their cornerstones, roots, and values commonly generate stress and illness in individuals, structures, institutions, and societies.

As Levins Morales indicates in the epigraph, all lives are impacted by, and in turn influence, the contexts into which we are born. Those privileged are shaped by favourable social norms and values that exclude and deny others dignity and worth. But these are not homogeneous groupings. Among those privileged, some will support the status quo while others will rally against it. Similarly, marginalised groups may coalesce around certain issues, and diverge on others. Still, regardless of where we fall on the political spectrum, we all internalise aspects of society, to some extent consciously and to a large degree unconsciously. When people adhere to social norms and practices, or disrupt them, they reinforce or compromise social stability. Because some actions are subliminal and latent, certain practices like Othering persist on a more subtle level. As a result, we can find ourselves holding beliefs that we don't always believe we have. In racialised societies built on inequalities and exploitation, White is the unraced social default that simply swims unfettered in the social waters of inequities, and whiteness privileges White-bodied, cis-, heteronormative people. Here, the work of embodied justice and social justice becomes the work of everyone.

In the absence of a critical race lens our imprints manifest in what we create. The organisations we give life to are made in our image. They embody our hidden patterns as well as our interfaces with power, social structures, ideologies, and emotions that circulate in society. Embodiment is about more than individual unconscious biases; they inform beliefs, cultures, and identities and cannot be undone simply by bringing such habits into individual awareness. Unravelling the ways in which we are forged by whiteness, Othering, neoliberal postraciality, and histories of trauma takes time and requires community.

The frame of Orientalism, neoliberalism, postracialism, and whiteness allows a more critical and nuanced reflection on how Buddhism takes shape in the West. In addressing the socio-political location of the interpreters or interlocuters of Buddhism there is need for nuance. It also helps to register our influences and be open about our positions and orientations whether as critics, interpreters, or proponents of the status quo. Positionality becomes important for the reader to appreciate our stance and perspectives. This is not to say that our positions are 'black and white' or clear-cut. In fact, when we position ourselves socio-politically, we inevitably embrace texture, argument, and complexity. This same complexity applies when challenging the dominant discourse in the Westernisation of mindfulness. Leaders are, after all, also conditioned and socialised in ways that can generate tunnel vision and blind spots that shape strategies and agency.

In critiquing the arc of White Mindfulness in the West, both in relation to its antecedents in Western Buddhism and its own emergent path, its contribution to countless people's lives is evident by virtue of a steady growth. Western convert Buddhists travelled to Southeast Asia to bring the teachings they'd received from their teachers to their countries of birth. Their quests for 'a change in consciousness to curb American materialism and foster greater kindness' and their desire to 'build meditation programs as a means of personal liberation' led to a network of institutions (Kucinskas,

2019: 29). Through their teachings they granted others coping mechanisms to navigate a challenging, overwhelming world. Their contributions shaped the landscape of Western Buddhism and mindfulness. This book challenges systems rather than individuals. But even in critiquing systems, it is easy to sketch dichotomies that make individuals sound singly responsible for systemic injustices. Such reductionism denies the complexity of what Stuart Hall calls political conjunctures – the convergence of multiple influences that generate political moments. In these complex conjunctures, our politics, policies, and power play a major role in building communities, and we must be held accountable for our actions. However, it is all too easy to repeat the chasms of a polarised world by crudely categorising people and their actions as either good or bad. Such duality is enticing in a context of inequalities and unfair privilege. Mapping the complexities of how positionalities interface with systems, and reading power and nuance, is more challenging.

This chapter maps the antecedents of White Mindfulness. I consider two influences in Buddhist modernisation and the secularisation of mindfulness in the US and UK in which secularisation and modernisation are considered political processes that are flavoured by socio-economic contexts. The first influence occurs in Southeast Asia as Buddhist reform. In Myanmar and Sri Lanka, organised political resistance took form as laicisation and Buddhist revival (see Braun, 2013; McMahan, 2012). This propelled modernisation, suggesting that modern Buddhism was partly seeded by middle-class Asian Buddhists, themselves products of modernity, who sought to challenge colonialism. Their ascent depicts that of the middle classes globally.[1] The second involves the establishment of Buddhist organisations in the US by Western teachers. While these include the formation of the Buddhist Global Relief, I focus on the rise of the Insight Meditation Society (IMS) in the US as a primary influence on Western mindfulness.

Modern Buddhism: a precursor to White Mindfulness

The rise of modern Buddhism and the Westernisation of mindfulness are politically complex processes shaped by the coalescence of multiple cultures and interests. The modernisation project occurred as much in Asia as it did in the West and can be seen as a 'co-creation of Asians, Europeans and Americans [and] not just a Western construct' (Ng, 2014). It includes the migration of Asian teachers and communities to the West as well as diverse forms of socially engaged Buddhism overseen by both Asians and Westerners. As argued before, latent Orientalism extends the grip of colonialism beyond physical occupation through education and depictions of iconography. Consequently, Buddhism in the West is read through the lens of the dominant meaning maker, the Western missionary, educator, art historian, and coloniser. This goes some way to explaining a common association of Buddhist awakening with Western notions of individualisation.

To better understand the positionality of early Western interpreters, Lopez comments on the influence of the Western gaze on modern Buddhism and the transmigration of knowledges. He aligns these developments with eighteenth-century European Enlightenment thought:

> Modern Buddhism seeks to distance itself most from those forms of Buddhism that immediately precede it, that are even contemporary with it. It is ancient Buddhism, and especially the enlightenment of the Buddha 2,500 years ago, that is seen as most modern, as most compatible with the ideas of the European Enlightenment that occurred so many centuries later, ideals embodied in such concepts as reason, empiricism, science, universalism, individualism, tolerance, freedom and the rejection of religious orthodoxy. Indeed, for modern Buddhists, the Buddha knew long ago what Europe would only discover much later. Yet what we regard as Buddhism today, especially the common portrayal of the Buddhism of the Buddha, is in fact a creation of modern Buddhism.
>
> (Lopez, 2002: ix–x)

In this formulation, modern Buddhism prides itself as being most ancient and therefore most 'true'. Yet it prioritises certain Western interests and discourses and unreflexively narrates the 'Buddhism of the Buddha' with certainty and authority. In doing so, Westerners are presented as Buddhist authorities. This is not to say that convert Buddhists can't become specialists. But in the absence of naming how knowledge is extracted and that cultural appropriation by Westerners is a factor in the migration of knowledges from the East to the West, the act hints at latent Orientalism. Its obscure nature allows 'modernisers' to neglect to mention their positionalities. Aung's comment that some Western interpretations have no meaning whatsoever for Buddhists falls by the wayside.

European Enlightenment thought emboldened colonisers to commit acts of extraction, supremacy, secularisation, and universalisation of 'primitive' cultures through the 'civilising' and 'superior' lens of 'science and reason'. 'Reason and science could be applied to any and every situation ... their principles were the same in every situation. Science in particular produces general laws which govern the entire universe, without exception' (Hamilton, 1992: 21). Under these conditions, the grander mission of Westernising Buddhism appears to serve as a 'forgetting' of context, histories, lives, and power. Yet these tenets have not evaporated, and in an era of reckoning with race are resurfacing.

Southeast Asian Buddhist reform

The British colonised Myanmar in 1824 as part of the project of the British Empire of India. In response, Burmese laicisation of meditation was seen as a way of preserving Buddhism and challenging British occupation. Ledi Sayadaw (1846–1923) led this movement at the turn of the nineteenth century. His mission was to re-establish Buddhism and to challenge colonialism through regaining institutional power (McMahan, 2017). This process changed the face of Buddhism in Myanmar. Teaching meditation to large groups of lay people turned it from an elite monastic tradition to a mass-based practice. This shift sparked interest from other countries, prompting meditation's global spread. Ledi's intervention marks a significant moment for *Theravāda* Buddhism and the propagation of mindfulness as a lay practice (McMahan and Braun, 2017).[2] The main figures involved in these changes were Mahasi Sayadaw and S. N. Goenka.

Mahasi Sayadaw (1904–82) extended laicisation to foster the anticolonial agenda of Buddhist nationalism. He placed emphasis on *sati*[3] (mindfulness), for which his German-born student, Nyanaponika Thera (1901–84), coined the term 'bare attention' (Sharf, 2017: 201). Goenka (1924–2013), teaching in India, played an equally influential role in streamlining Buddhist secularisation (Hwang and Kearney,

2015: 10). Mahasi and Goenka navigated colonial landscapes of economic hegemony to reformulate their traditions. Within Myanmar
itself – a predominantly Buddhist country – Ledi and Mahasi's
laicisation could rely on culture; it escaped scientific reframe. To
distinguish their practices from what colonialists considered 'super-
stitious, idolatrous, and primitive', they both used spirituality as well
as scientific rationalism (McMahan, 2017: 117). In this way, their
projects reformed Buddhism not only for national purposes but also
for Western audiences. Both Mahasi and Goenka informed Kabat-
Zinn's reconceptualisation and Westernisation of mindfulness.

Mahasi is considered a prominent leader of the global vipassanā
movement. To make meditation accessible to lay people, he de-
emphasised ritual and prior knowledge of Buddhist literature
(McMahan, 2012). Laypeople could pursue daily life and attain
liberating insight without prior knowledge of Buddhist philosophy.
Mahasi's compact method was taught in a 10-day exportable,
standardised retreat format making it popular and accessible.
Participants learn to 'live in the now', an approach that underpins
much of the work of Western vipassanā.

In a vein similar to Mahasi Sayadaw, S. N. Goenka developed
a system of vipassanā that downplays Buddhist doctrine and
emphasises technique. Goenka reduced practice to a refined set
of instructions and described vipassanā as a universal, scientific
system suitable for anyone regardless of faith.[4] Transmigration of
Goenka's vipassanā from India to the US required cultural naviga-
tion that led to further separation from its Buddhist roots.

To globalise their teachings, Goenka and Mahasi differed in their
approaches. Whereas Mahasi mostly dispensed with ritual and
other Buddhist activities like chanting, merit-making, and devotion, Goenka's conception retains aspects of Buddhism, such as
the three marks of existence, and the four noble truths (McMahan,
2017: 117–18).[5] Alongside these practices, Goenka still expressed
vipassanā in scientific, neutral, and universal terms, saying:

> Some people take [vipassanā] as a religion, a cult, or a dogma, so nat-
> urally there is resentment and opposition. But Vipassanā should only
> be taken as pure science, the science of mind and matter, and a pure
> exercise for the mind to keep it healthy … [it] is result-oriented, because
> it starts giving results here and now. People will start accepting this.
>
> (Goenka, 2002: 28)

As Goenka forecast, vipassanā did indeed gain popularity, especially through neuroscience, allowing it to become associated with psychological wellbeing and with self-regulation. Goenka's 'mental exercise' model that likens the mind to the body, suggesting that both require fitness, ties in with healthism, individual responsibility for health, and self-governance. This is not to say that meditation and mindfulness don't support wellness. It serves to remind us how these adaptations are interpreted in the service of dominant ideologies. Now taught worldwide and translated into 30 languages,[6] Goenka-style vipassanā's influence on White Mindfulness and beyond is unquestionable. At times, Kabat-Zinn and the organisations I study repeat his words verbatim. Instances include: the Buddha taught the dhamma (Goenka, 2002: 82; Kabat-Zinn, 2005: 136); the dhamma is universal truth, not Buddhism (Goenka, 2002: 34, 104; Kabat-Zinn, 2017: 1130; 2010); and universalism is consistent with the secular and scientific (Goenka, 2002: 42, 101, 108; Kabat-Zinn, 2013: 289; 2017: 1126). These tenets echo Said's cautions against universalism – new authorities extract the 'essential ingredients' and homogenise their audiences.

Mahasi and Goenka's mutual focus on meditation and direct experience is embedded in White Mindfulness (Sharf, 1998; Lopez, 2002; King, 2004). These holy grails assumed prominence by articulating Western individualism with select Asian intellectual interpretations of Buddhism.[7] Here, modernisation in Zen traditions, and D. T. Suzuki (1870–1966) in particular, played a key role. Suzuki emphasised meditative experience to present his traditions as 'purer than the discursive faiths of the West'. Experience also provided a 'cross-cultural encounter' out of which grew an 'academic industry, complete with its own professional societies … journals … conferences and symposia, all devoted to the comparative study of 'Western' and 'Eastern' thought' (Sharf, 1998: 276).

Following these developments, the arc of White Mindfulness reifies direct experience and professionalises teacher training through academic programmes, regulation, and gold standards set through research. But contrary to critique that usually comes with the academy, these developments are largely buoyed by an uncritical scholarship and, as Kucinskas highlighted before, an elitism. What emerges here is a modernisation process that centres middle classes in both the East and the West, combining Buddhism and science in shaping the secularisation process. Alongside this, science, reason, and Western framing hide the political functions of neo-colonialism and knowledge extraction (Ng, 2016b: 72). These bold statements are not meant to cast aspersions on White Mindfulness leaders and their forbearers. It does, however, highlight the ways in which power and privilege shape our actions and positions, showing how they can create blind spots and inactions. When mindfulness, like vipassanā, is decontextualised and read as a universal dharma, it plays into the hands of power that then represents it as new, modern, upgraded, and essential for the modern citizen.

Rise of the Western vipassanā movement: consolidating whiteness

The second phase in Buddhism's Western trajectory that bore directly on Kabat-Zinn and the secularisation of mindfulness is its transmission by Western teachers in the US. Here the formation of the Insight Meditation Society (IMS), alongside Goenka's programme, contributed to the rise of the Western vipassanā movement (Fronsdal, 1995). IMS teachers who returned from Buddhist studies in Southeast Asia in the late twentieth century to establish an independent vipassanā movement were as selective in their teachings as Ledi, Mahasi, and Goenka.

In 1975 Joseph Goldstein (born 1944), Jack Kornfield (born 1945), and Sharon Salzburg (born 1952) returned from their travels and studies in Asia to establish the IMS (Fronsdal, 1998: 8; Braun, 2013: 162–3). Their teachings mostly derive from Ledi Sayadaw and Mahasi Sayadaw and are grounded in the *Theravāda* tradition. To indicate US-focused teaching, the IMS and Goenka both replaced the word *Theravāda* with vipassanā (Fronsdal, 1998).[8]

Outside a *Theravāda* culture and without direct links to traditional *Theravāda* practices, the IMS follow the Sayadaws' retreat-oriented training, dispense with Buddhist cosmology and belief, chanting, and ceremony (Wilson, 2014), and retain only meditation. Goenka's 'pure dhamma' teaching retains rebirth within his traditional cosmological worldview. In contrast to Goenka, the IMS dismiss Buddhist tenets and any serious engagement with *Theravāda* doctrine. Their intention was to leave behind 'cultural baggage' in favour of forms of practice they understood as the authentic teaching of the Buddha. This was presumably about making their teachings more accessible to an audience they assumed would be put off by Buddhist culture. Their rapid growth since the early 1980s may well accrue to their disaffiliation from *Theravāda* lineages. Indeed, Westernised teachings have seeded a 'loose-knit lay Buddhist movement, uniquely Western' (Fronsdal, 1998: 163; McMahan and Braun, 2017: 163–4). Goldstein expands:

> I'm not so concerned with any labels or the cultural forms of the tradition ... Instead, what inspires me is the connection with the original teachings of the Buddha – with what, as far as we know, he actually taught during his lifetime. Above all, meditation was presented (and still is) as the heart of those original teachings.
>
> (Quoted in Braun, 2013: 163)

Goldstein's explanation captures Mahasi and Goenka's elevation of meditation. It also reverberates with Lopez's earlier comment: Western teachers claim direct access to the Buddha's authentic teachings as if culture and doctrine are inauthentic or non-essential paraphernalia. These could be seen to comprise acts of latent Orientalism, especially where Asian Buddhists are bypassed in the process.

In the early years, Western vipassanā advocates kept their distance from Buddhist organisations such as Asian Buddhist centres and the Buddhist Churches of America. These institutions, they believed, perpetuated traditional practices from which they wished to distance themselves. As Funie Hsu explained before, their excision of traditional practices, cultural appropriation, and erasure of Asian Buddhist teachers and initiatives hurt the Asian Buddhist community. But these actions did more than strip Buddhism of Buddhism. By remaining separate from traditional Buddhists, the predominantly White convert Buddhist communities control the dominant US-Buddhist narrative. Identifying themselves as laypeople, they repackaged the vipassanā project in language and cultural terms familiar to the lay audiences they targeted; essentially, they 'Americanised' Buddhism. The extent to which this process dilutes Buddhism and meditation remains unclear.

The IMS's erasure of 'cultural baggage' and distillation of Buddhism brings to light the interests, gaze, and authority of

Western teachers as arbiters. Their elevation of meditation[9] as Buddhism's essence, now cast as a personalised practice in Western terms, privileges the individual above the community, fosters individual responsibility, and pretends at a 'spiritual egalitarianism' that ignores social context (McMahan, 2012: 161; Lopez, 2002: ix). This distinguishes the Western vipassanā movement from Ledi Sayadaw's Burmese project.

US-centric Buddhism – a form of nationalism – is familiar in Kabat-Zinn's portrayal of White Mindfulness, even though he starts from a universal premise (Hickey, 2010). This US-Eurocentric view of Buddhism is considered a 'modern hybrid tradition with roots in the European Enlightenment no less than the Buddha's enlightenment, in Romanticism and transcendentalism as much as the Pāli Canon, and', McMahan adds, 'in the clash of Asian cultures and colonial powers as much as in mindfulness and meditation' (McMahan, 2008: 5–6). In other words, US-Eurocentric Buddhism is informed and shaped as much by socio-political context as by interlocutors.

Historical accounts of Buddhism originally confine meditation to a small set of elite monks. Its reification by convert Buddhists makes Buddhism an essentialist ideology (King, 1999). Essentialism extricates religions and traditions from their local cultural contexts making them abstract, ahistorical, universal entities. This lays the basis for a universalism that decontextualises the postraciality of the US-Buddhist movement. It also overlooks the IMS disengagement from Asian Buddhists who practice and teach Buddhism in the West. The omission of these factors from the teachings of the IMS and Western mindfulness organisations reasserts invisibilised privileges and norms. Such invisibilisation works bi-directionally, obscuring those marginalised and excluded while concealing privileges of those who command power and do the obscuring.

In a further act of recontextualisation, deracination, linked to essentialism, refers to the plucking or cherry-picking aspects of Buddhist teachings from their whole. As the word implies, a plant or tree is cut off at the root, unable to grow as intended. Interpreters remove contextual and cultural tenets and choose a selection of teachings that serve the interlocuter's re-presentation of teachings. Deracination in the Western vipassanā movement constitutes appropriation performed through psychologisation and mystification.

Scholar Jeff Wilson says that these methods are 'not shared by most other religious practices in America' such as Christianity and Judaism (Wilson, 2014: 44–6). To make his point, Wilson uses the example of extracting a rosary practice from Christianity then claiming that Christianity embraces the teachings present in any and all religious tradition, that the 'early Catholic teachings are free of doctrine, that the Virgin Mary is not an object of religious devotion, that saying the rosary does not conflict with Hindu or agnostic belief' and that it enhances one's own faith as a Muslim, Hindu, or Jew. This testament cleverly turns the White gaze back on itself. It reveals the extent to which deracination disrespects and erodes whole cultures, traditions, beliefs, and values. It also demonstrates the aliveness of neo-colonialism and the subjugation of Others to Western dominion. Through this active Orientalist outlook, Buddhism, like Islam – as foreign goods alien to the 'nation' – is objectified and Othered (Asad, 2003: 7). These facets are ingrained in the fabric of Western mindfulness.

Read in conjunction with Goenka's *Meditation Now*, Buddhist teacher Gil Fronsdal's account of Western vipassanā accentuates its resonance with the arc and vocabulary of Westernised mindfulness. The two developments, Western vipassanā and White Mindfulness, may almost be seen as a continuous arc but for the latter's ambivalent relationship with Buddhism. White Mindfulness mimics Western vipassanā's relationship with *Theravāda*, depicting a steady distancing from Buddhist roots while flying the flag of universality. Acts of deracination and essentialism seem to popularise both sets of teachings.

Deracination denuded IMS teachings not only of cultural context, but also of any political associations found in, for instance, Ledi's anti-colonial mission. This depoliticisation occurred also in relation to realities in the US, with the result that teachings occurred in a political vacuum. In addition, the teachers' social realities, experiences, and interests that shaped their programmes, whether 'latently' or consciously, were concealed with implications for content as well as audiences. Our social locations and politics are precisely what nuances how we wield power or how power wields us. Our positionality becomes explicit only when we make it so. When our relations to power remain hidden even to ourselves, we responsor and enrich social norms that regurgitate unjust systems and power. Subliminally, we end up enriching systems we might think we oppose. Declaring our positionalities makes explicit our power relations, contexts, and privileges, all of which shape identities, social access, and perspectives. Commonly, when these remain obscured, they hide defaults. In postracial neoliberal societies, it is the predominance of whiteness in all its intersectional complexity that is protected and preserved.

Positionality acknowledges that the frame of the teacher reflects vested interests and interpretations. In recounting context, US-born *Theravāda* monk Bikkhu Bodhi says that when Ledi and Mahasi introduced meditation practices to laypeople, they 'opened the gates' for young Westerners to receive their teachings. This period of the late 1960s and early 1970s was marked in the West by the civil rights movement as well as student uprisings. It was also framed by a growing thirst among middle classes disillusioned with Western systems for 'the wisdom of the East'. Bodhi suggests that it was 'only natural that in their encounter with the Dhamma they would bring along the *questions and problems that reflected their cultural backgrounds and personal needs*'. But it is also the case that what they heard and learnt accorded with their own perspectives and needs. Their meaning-making corresponded to their worldviews, frameworks, and social locations. In this sense-making it seems there is a process not only of deracination and essentialising, but also one of cladding and adding. When these teachers began to teach others, it is their interpretation and understanding that they would convey in their delivery. And this is not to say that these interpretations are misguided; it is to acknowledge that the 'legacy they would transmit to their own students and down the line to future generations' would be coloured by who they are, and what they heard and perceived in answer to the questions they asked of their teachers (Bodhi, 2016: 8).

The act of deracination is coupled with that of reseeding or recontextualising the teachings and, in the process, adding new cultures to the selected teachings that are delivered. When these are called the authentic teachings of the Buddha, the impression given is that there is no history separating the audience from *the* Buddha, and that there is only one Buddha. It also suggests that the teachings are conveyed in a vacuum by an inanimate, 'apolitical', automated teacher which elides the silent politics of forgetting conveyed during delivery.

Pinpointing the chief concerns, perspectives, and positionalities of IMS teachers generates a politics of identity. Bodhi infers from his experiences of their teachings certain commonalities, such as their privilege to travel and study abroad. Within their teachings, there is a disjuncture between their psychological appraisal of individualised suffering and a socially engaged reading of Buddhism. Yet the sentiment that it is 'only natural' that we are trapped in our cultural orientation and outlook suggests that we can never step outside our frame of reference or window to the world. Positionality certainly shapes identity, but our agency, especially critical agency, can disrupt our social status. Solidarity and allyship do not undo positionality nor identity, but they deploy power differently and work to disrupt the very powers that create privileges in the first place.

Writing from an explicitly political perspective, prominent mindfulness teacher and law professor Rhonda Magee unpacks identity and political persuasions buried in secularism (Magee, 2016). She argues that social justice is distant and 'optional' to the arrangements of Westernised mindfulness and that the founders give special meaning and emphasis to personal wellbeing and individual freedoms. Their identities and White, upper-class privileges inform this arc of mindfulness that focuses on inner healing and inner freedom. It is this very spotlight that alienates marginalised communities. In its apolitical form, mindfulness seems irrelevant to those interested in changing systems that cause disharmony, division, and inequality in the first instance. The emphasis in social justice communities is that inner, outer, and interstitial healing are intertwined, or put differently, individual, communal, and social liberation are inseparable. Magee ties privilege to personalised models and practices that are distant from social transformation. The social locations, interests, and perspectives of White Mindfulness teachers and their distance from certain societal oppressions underscores their interlocutor privileges. Due to this 'chasm', the products that arise from a hyper-individualised mindfulness appear impractical or alien to marginalised communities. In this light, secularisation not only represses difference, but also camouflages the mechanisms that reproduce power.

Unless secularist processes consciously set out to circumnavigate or decolonise business-as-usual procedures, they succumb to social norms. When change makers remain oblivious to the waters in which they swim, their efforts become absorbed by institutional power. Without shining the light of mindfulness upon the teacher, what is invisible remains hidden, unseen, obscured, or avoided. This setting informs not only the structures and power arrangements of White Mindfulness; it permeates overall architectures, pedagogies, and course content. To call Westernised mindfulness secular without addressing social forces that shape movements, initiatives, and histories of oppression and pain opens opportunities for neocolonisation of the field.

Mindfulness' modernisation thus resembles the cornerstones of Buddhist modernisation. Deracination and essentialism produce a project that fits a neoliberal postracial context. Decrees of universality, delivery of 'the original teachings' of the Buddha, scientification, individualisation, and the invisibilisation of power govern the process of its secularisation. But there is a further dimension to the modernisation of mindfulness. It unfolds for specific purposes, producing particular subjects and worlds (Wallis, 2016: 496). This is addressed in Part II.

Notes

1 Influences of the printing press and easier international travel created further conditions for the modernisation of Buddhism (Lopez, 2002: xxxix).

2 *Theravāda* Buddhism, considered Buddhism's oldest school, preserves the teachings of Gautama Buddha in the Pāli Canon. It is commonly contrasted with *Mahāyāna* Buddhism, which emphasises the path to Buddhahood and tantra.

3 The Pāli term for mindfulness (*sati*) derives from Sanskrit: *smrti* meaning 'to remember'.

4 Whereas Goenka capitalises Vipassanā, Fronsdal does not. When referring to these authors, I retain their preference, but use the uncapitalised version in discussion.

5 Fronsdal expands: 'Mahasi deemphasized many common elements of *Theravāda* Buddhism. Rituals, chanting, devotional and merit-making activities, and doctrinal studies were down-played to the point of being virtually absent from the program of meditation offered at the many meditation centres he founded or inspired' (Fronsdal, 1998: 164). In contrast, Goenka emphasised the practical benefits of

meditation and retained some traditional components but refrained from linking meditation only to healing (Kabat-Zinn, 2013: 165), although Goenka himself states that it helped him cure himself of migraines (Goenka, 2002: 9).

6 Information about the Goenka's Vipassanā Centres can be found at: https://sumeru.dhamma.org.

7 Sharf asserts: 'Meditation was first and foremost a means of eliminating defilement, accumulating merit and supernatural power, invoking apotropaic deities, and so forth ... The valorization of experience in Asian thought can be traced to a handful of twentieth-century Asian religious leaders and apologists, all of whom were in sustained dialogue with their intellectual counterparts in the West' (Sharf, 1998: 272).

8 It is worth noting that the IMS founders were also influenced by Goenka's teacher U Ba Khin (1899–1971), himself a disciple of Ledi Sayadaw via his teacher, Ledi's appointed lay teacher, U Po Thet, also known as Saya Thetgyi (1873–1945), distinguished as 'one of the earliest examples of a layman empowered by a monk to teach meditation' (Braun, 2013: 156).

9 Although the IMS based their work on Mahasi's teachings, like Sharf, Caring-Lobel (2016) complicates this act by arguing that the Buddha had not considered meditation suitable for someone who had 'not renounced worldly desire' (Caring-Lobel, 2016: 195).

Part II

Wrapping mindfulness in whiteness

4

Stuck in whiteness: patterns in Western mindfulness organisations

[A]cts of appropriation are part of the process by which we make ourselves. Appropriating – taking something for one's own use – need not be synonymous with exploitation. This is especially true of cultural appropriation. The 'use' one makes of what is appropriated is the crucial factor.

bell hooks (1995: 11)

Our lives, like water, are constantly shaped as we engage and interface with our surrounding ecosystems. We in turn, like water, are forever interacting with and shaping our environments, contexts, and ourselves. Yet, despite knowing that our bodies echo their surrounding social circumstances and political realities, our lives can feel fixed, especially when our environments are oppressive and demeaning.

Renowned cultural critic Stuart Hall describes our lives as 'constructed across difference', leading us to compose the narrative of who we are: 'It may be true that the self is always, in a sense, a fiction' (Hall, 1987: 44). We are constantly making meaning and moving through society using different labels and identifiers, some of which are more temporary than others. Hall affirms that our cultural identities are never ahistorical but rooted in ways of seeing the world, with dominant histories usually dictating how and what we see. But importantly, he says these histories are always evolving and cultural identities are therefore always transforming. It is in this way that Hall describes cultural identity as much a matter of 'becoming' as of being.

This is not to say that identity is ephemeral or imagined, but that it is never fixed in ways that oppressive regimes impose and imply. Minoritised groups become free despite oppressive political architectures, and it is these expressions of freedom that flout and befuddle authorities. As trans poet-author-performer-speaker Alok Vaid-Menon (2019) explains: 'my beauty is so tremendous it has to be edited out of magazines and movements, white-washed from history, evacuated from sermons, streets and schools just to prove that it does not exist'. To neutralise difference, defiant, nonconforming acts are subsumed by dominant cultures that repeat the usual extracting patterns of cherry-picking and appropriating from them and from their socio-cultural context and meaning.

In articulating how we make sense of our lives and see ourselves, bell hooks draws on Hall's notion of 'becoming' to say that we are regularly 'appropriating', appreciating, and using what we see, hear, feel in our worlds to invent ourselves. The epigraph serves to remind us that we often step outside the confines of the White gaze as we constantly evolve our understandings of ourselves beyond the lenses imposed through coloniality. To be clear, hooks is distinguishing cultural appropriation (in which cultures and knowledges are stolen for gain, their bearers ignored and disregarded) from appreciating styles for the purposes of giving expression to one's life. Deracination, essentialism, ignoring traditional Buddhists while teaching their traditions (as discussed in Chapter 3) comprise exploitative uses of knowledge and traditions. It is markedly different to being actively engaged in overturning extraction of Buddhist knowledges, and racism towards traditional Buddhists. Often, individuals appropriate aspects of Black or minoritised cultures but maintain their privileges that are built on exploitation.

'Becoming', as in emerging, evolving, growing, and declaring positionalities so that we are not hiding our power and internalised whiteness, marks a different kind of use of what is taken or copied to disrupt power. This 'use' and 'becoming' usually disrupts rather than entrenches power. Practicing traditions that we are not born into by honouring, respecting, and naming their origins and supporting the rights of the bearers of those traditions is part of not appropriating. Acknowledging sources of inspiration, honouring the origins of ideas, whether tangible or abstract, recognising when we are stealing, and freeing ourselves from the systems that cause us to Other are all part of 'becoming'.

The previous chapters laid the ground for understanding how everyday pillars of society such as science and research, education, and self-governance are political by nature. They reside inside ecosystems of power. Such framing paves the way for understanding how mindfulness slots into Western society as if it is an independent development devoid of power dynamics. This chapter shows how the process of secularisation, informed by the social norms that hide in plain sight, makes a mindfulness that is anything but neutral or universal. I discuss the implications of presenting mindfulness as an uncomplicated concept and a universal project, without addressing its premise of Othering or its socio-political and economic backdrop. A focus on questions of power, control, and privilege reveals how mindfulness takes root in the West, especially through gateways of science and psychology, to return commodified to the East. It seems that in 'making' organisations, 'using what is seen and experienced', as well as that which is unseen, explains how whiteness becomes embedded in organisational 'becoming'. Organisations, it seems, are made in the images of their founders.

Jon Kabat-Zinn's sizeable contribution to the process of popularising mindfulness in the West is unquestionable. But his model emerges in a context of intersecting injustices from which it becomes mainstream. My attempts are not to fix Kabat-Zinn's intentions but to offer a lens through which to see how a well-intentioned intervention plays out according to historical and political contexts. There are no aspersions being cast here, but rather an effort to show how Westernised mindfulness evolves, as do we, in relation to circumstances and power.

To show the ramifications of efforts to depoliticise and universalise mindfulness, I share my 2018 findings from investigating three global organisations based in the US and Britain. A race-gender profile reveals organisations that imitate social power. White men are the primary decision-makers; racial and gender diversity at board and leadership level is poor. From this starting point of immersion in whiteness, efforts to widen participation in the Mindfulness Industry chart a course of ongoing exclusions. Talking diversity and access at an organisational level further invisibilises White privilege, hyper-individualisation, commercialisation, and skewed power, and conceals a racialised secularisation process.

'Secular' or White Mindfulness?

Jon Kabat-Zinn's definition of mindfulness is commonly understood in the West as 'paying attention, on purpose, in the present moment, and non-judgementally' (Kabat-Zinn, 1990/2013: xxxv). Its wide reach and acceptance are buoyed through extensive research and publication across multiple fields including neuroscience, psychology, and business. In short, mindfulness is scientifically and psychologically endorsed by significant voices in these fields and is shown to improve workplace productivity and the bottom line. In some quarters, this has led to its 'panacea-complex' – a mindfulness that can solve all ills.

As mindfulness crosses borders and takes root, questions of power, control, and privilege arise. The three British and American organisations I discuss all have global reach beyond their borders of origin. But they also embody the Mindfulness Industry's reproduction of whiteness. Their postracial, post-identity cultures embed White privilege and underlying conflict alongside pledges to make mindfulness accessible to all. I anonymise them as Chestnut Institute, Oak Inc., and Red Centre, to preserve their privacy. Who the actual organisations are is far less interesting than what they typically represent of the world of White Mindfulness and the nuances of their differences and sameness.

The organisations are mutually informed by the work of Kabat-Zinn. It is his thinking and early works that formulated what became the root programme of many other formulations. As a political activist who had become taken with Zen Buddhism, Kabat-Zinn had a 10-second vision while on retreat in which he conceived of the spread of mindfulness across societies.[1] The popularisation of mindfulness to heal and reduce human and social suffering was at the heart of his vision, with hospitals and public health centres as places that could roll out mindfulness trainings as an accompaniment to medical efforts. Working at a teaching hospital, Kabat-Zinn's medical orientation and his own training as a molecular biologist makes sense of his appeal to science for an evidence base. Yet neither popularisation through public health nor science are politically neutral. Even though this was meant to lay the foundations for the loftier vision of a 'second Renaissance' – a flourishing global revival that would benefit all beings 'signalling a multi-dimensional emergence of great transformative and liberative promise' – it inevitably led to its medicalisation.[2]

The mindfulness delivered through medical portals associated it with physical and mental pain devoid of structural causes. This produced a model that pathologised and individualised stress in ways that are inconsistent with pro-justice or community-led mindfulness programmes. Even though Kabat-Zinn read his intervention as patient-centred, it entangled mindfulness in the medical industrial complex, tainting it with the underpinnings of biomedicine's corporatisation and drivers. The public health pathway which should have made mindfulness accessible to anyone using it became increasingly defunded, starved of resources, and privatised. Instead, what was to become Mindfulness-Based Stress Reduction (MBSR) coincided with a burgeoning 'spiritual marketplace' that emphasised neoliberal tenets of 'personal power' and individualised wellbeing (see Carrette and King, 2005: 26–9; Eagleton, 2016). Here wellbeing trends attract attention for their resonance with the medical industrial complex (Henderson, 2010; Wiest *et al.*, 2015). Kabat-Zinn's dream of a 'second Renaissance' places the isolated individual, rather than communities and movements, at the centre of social change. Such a setting overlooks injustices and uses marketable wellbeing trends to thwart the prevention of illness or the distribution of health services to marginalised groups.

At the same time as MBSR developed a foothold, Kabat-Zinn was also instrumental in the advent of behavioural medicine, which encouraged patient-centred care and shifted focus away from pharmaceutical drugs, towards an innate human capacity for healing (Kabat-Zinn, 2014). Behavioural medicine marked a shift away from biomedicine towards an appreciation of consciousness in healing. To a lesser extent it acknowledged socio-political contexts in illness. Yet both behavioural medicine and what was being called 'secular mindfulness' emerged in contexts of overwhelming social atomisation and ruthless forms of capitalism. Noble as their intentions are to restore dignity to the patient, these movements' emphasis on the patient's healing capacity became interpreted as personal resilience and responsibility, overshadowing socio-political dimensions of illness. A mutual emphasis on 'inner resourcefulness' underplays socio-economic and political causes of and solutions to ill health and establishes mindfulness as an individualised, palliative intervention.

In the creeping frame of health privatisation, as doctors failed to attain patient recovery targets, MBSR increasingly presented an attractive, low-cost alternative (Kabat-Zinn, 2014). But the language of challenging patients to 'do something for themselves' and 'take better care of themselves', especially those 'falling through the cracks of the healthcare system', is a double-edged sword. On the one hand, it encourages patients to tap into their innate capacity to heal. On the other, it burdens the patient with becoming well on their own without addressing the cracks of public health care or other incessant discriminatory acts. This approach also denies healing cultures that are communal and collective. It was as if MBSR was propping up a failing healthcare system without disrupting it. Still, designed to encourage patients to relate to their illnesses differently, MBSR combined mind and body training to recognise the whole patient. Positioned in the overlay between Buddhism and behavioural medicine, it encouraged participants

> to do something for themselves that no one on the planet could do for them, that you can't do for them, that their spouse can't do for them, that their parents can't do for them, that their clergy can't do for them, that no one can do for them, namely that your patients have to sort of *take some degree of responsibility for their own health and wellbeing*. This was quite radical thinking in those days!
>
> (Kabat-Zinn, 2014: 14, emphasis added)

As one Chestnut Institute respondent suggests, Kabat-Zinn was offering 'an approach around developing a different relationship to physical illness that was not responding well to traditional forms of medical intervention ... to allow people to change their relationship to their illness, whatever their illness was'. As with behavioural medicine,[3] his approach departed from the mind-body split prevalent in biomedicine in which the body became an afterthought.[4] Instead, Kabat-Zinn's mindfulness emphasised individual integrity. In a neoliberal setting, this can also be read as individual sovereignty feeding individualistic rather than communal cultures. To complicate matters, Kabat-Zinn's intention to train patients in 'Buddhist meditation without the Buddhism' (Kabat-Zinn, 2014: 14) marks MBSR as extractive, taking from Buddhism only what it wanted and dismissing the rest. A case is made for hiding MBSR's Buddhist roots as a strategy to avoid alienating patients. Yet little regard was given to acts of cultural appropriation and the deep wounds created through non-engagement with Asian Buddhists. Consequently, the 'stealth' 'Buddhism without the Buddhism' strategy was questioned for the imprint of dishonesty left in its wake (Brown, 2016: 84).

In an age in which elevated stress levels, disease, and mental illness are increasingly linked to socio-economic status and political power, the burden of ill health is borne most heavily by the most marginalised. Ill health presents a far greater burden for the precariat[5] who endure multiple oppressions in contrast to wealthier classes who have better access to quality services. When mindfulness is used as a form of neoliberal governance, it can forge a complex Western subject that is somewhat narcissistic in prioritising their own inner focus, self-regulation, and obedience – sometimes at the exclusion of their community. For the precariat, this extreme interiorisation is created through the ravaging of communities and dispossession (Lorey, 2015). People are made to feel isolated and cut off from their communities and society.

One size fits all

By remaining aloof to structural conditions that construct race and identity, the Westernisation of mindfulness delivers the same programme to participants regardless of their disposition to political power. This is not to say that only some programmes ought to be politicised; I am arguing that all programmes ought to be politically contextual to avoid a one-size-fits-all approach.

Political context allows participants to see their positions in relation to others in society, to understand where the teachings they are consuming come from, and to investigate privilege and the default of Othering. It becomes possible to inquire how, when the precariat is ill, they are further racialised as weak and lazy and are morally impelled to work harder at self-improvement. Without engaging these complexities of exclusions created by White supremacy, White Mindfulness organisations pursued what they considered generic mindfulness programmes. They formed networks to strengthen their perspective and used science and research to strengthen their cause.

Scientific endorsement of Buddhist practices interacted with the rise of the psy-disciplines (including psychology, psychiatry, psychotherapy), a historical project that arose in concert with crises in capitalism, and that came to be imposed on individuals and society. Psy-specialists became authorities on 'mental health', dictating that 'the modern self is impelled to make life meaningful through the search for happiness and self-realisation in his or her individual biography' rather than as part of community (see McAvoy, 2014: 1527; Rose, 1998: 79). Further historic precursors that paved the way for mindfulness' popularisation include Suzuki's[6] 1950s popularisation of Zen among Western psychoanalysts, the 1960s psychedelic culture that fostered interest in Eastern philosophy and research into the physiological effects of transcendental meditation, and Herbert Benson's 1970s popularisation of the relaxation response framed as self-care technologies and patient empowerment. These developments, including therapeutic relaxation, were 'aimed mainly at an upper-middle class audience'; they suppressed symptoms rather than addressed cause (Nathoo, 2016: 76). In the absence of a political framing, they also seeded the psychologisation and scientification of mindfulness. As a result, authors who map the trajectory of White Mindfulness often disregard race and Orientalism and thereby buttress whiteness.

Science and diversity

In the quest to 'massify' mindfulness, science was seen as a prestigious pathway to gain traction. The premise of science is falsification: theses hold water until they are disproven. Critique, investigation, challenge, and inquiry are the bedrocks of this tradition. Progress relies on discovery of new possibilities, new ways of seeing, and innovation. Ethically, it is presumed that the community will learn from critique and dispute. But scientific investigation, we know from eugenicist studies, is political by nature. There are oftentimes conflicting and vested interests in proving or disproving certain hypotheses.

Even more glaringly, as we've seen from how science was used in the eighteenth-century Enlightenment, scientists can hypothesise and test racist and phobic ideologies that fuel racialised social trauma. Linda Smith showed in a previous chapter how science is used by Orientalists to colonise traditional and Indigenous knowledges.

This extends also to people. In nineteenth-century Europe, Sara Baartman, a South African woman, was dehumanised, exhibited, examined, and enslaved to appease Western European 'scientific curiosity'. Following her death, her remains were displayed in a French museum, perpetuating Othering, and only returned to South Africa in 2002 at Nelson Mandela's request. This narrative is not intended to dispute the scientific method but to show the impossibility of extricating it from political intent and interests.

In its methodologies, science can produce its own tensions. Randomised control trials, regarded as the gold standard of laboratory research, are intended to prove drug efficacy to be able to administer medicines safely to the public. In some instances, the method allows for sufficient testing. Yet multiple problems with this approach include vested financial, political, and social interests which can result in skewed methods and interpretations of findings. In other words, methodologies that are presented as robust may be ethically disputable. Consequently, use of the 'scientific gateway' to prove the efficacy of mindfulness comes with concerns. Despite these misgivings, the compulsion of 'scientific research' to prove mindfulness' efficacy prevailed. It may be useful then to ask: who is reliant on this form of research and science, who needs it, why, and who oversees it?

In 1982, an uncontrolled mindfulness study trained 51 chronic pain patients who were unresponsive to traditional medical care in self-regulation. Findings revealed a 'significant reduction' in stress symptoms: 65 per cent reported more than a 33 per cent reduction on the Pain Rating Index and 50 per cent reported more than a 50 per cent reduction. Kabat-Zinn read this finding as people learning to relate to their pain differently, 'to be in a wiser relationship to it' (Kabat-Zinn, 1982: 40–1; Kabat-Zinn, 2014: 19–21). But he also describes healing as 'coming to terms with things as they are', which could suggest accepting the status quo without interrupting the social causes of illness. Following this early study, further research set out to investigate MBSR's impact on chronic pain and psoriasis, as well as secondary diagnoses of anxiety and panic (see Kabat-Zinn *et al.*, 1985; 1986; Kabat-Zinn and Chapman-Waldrop 1988; Kabat-Zinn *et al.*, 1992). Research findings continued to favour mindfulness over conventional medicine: 'here were these people in MBSR [programmes] who were not doing anything medically, pharmacologically, and they were getting dramatically better, to the point where their lifestyle was improving' (Kabat-Zinn, 2014: 19). This view was buttressed by the dramatic increase in favourable research studies into Mindfulness-Based Cognitive Therapy (MBCT) (AMRA, 2018).[7]

Positive findings, a source of encouragement to the medical field and to Kabat-Zinn, further enhanced mindfulness' stature among medical staff and psy-professionals. Yet, these studies also brought into focus pathologised, psychologised perspectives of stress.[8] It seemed difficult for investigations to integrate a medical and socio-economic view of stress. As a result, mindfulness research concentrated on the bio-physiology of stress at the cost of its politicisation.

Recent investigations query the validity of mindfulness research. They comment on methodological flaws, small sample sizes, and positive reporting (see Coronado-Montoya *et al.*, 2016; Goyal *et al.*, 2014: 357; Samuel, 2014: 571; Khoury *et al.*, 2013: 763; Buchholz, 2015: 1328). For example, a 2014 meta-analysis which set out to determine mindfulness meditation efficacy 'screened 18,753 unique citations, and 1,651 full-text articles', yet only 47 of these met their inclusion criteria. The study found 'no evidence that meditation programs were better than any other active treatment (i.e. drugs, exercise, and other behavioural therapies)' (Goyal *et al.*, 2014: 358–61). These critiques pertain to MBSR and MBCT alike and highlight scientific reductionism, positivism, and inattention to critique which should be highly valued in societies and cultures that rely on science and research for validation (Lavelle, 2016; Dimidjian and Segal, 2015). Despite the flaws in mindfulness research, organisations cling to 'the gateway of science' (McMahan and Braun, 2017: 184) to popularise a universalised mindfulness that homologises difference and individualises stress, regardless of cause. And even though mindfulness does not surpass other non-pharmaceutical interventions in the treatment of stress, it bills itself as a healthier treatment choice compared to pharmaceuticals.

Quashing differential identities and inequalities, premised on uncritical research, the three organisations extended their versions of mindfulness to marginalised communities using their one-size-fits-all model. This is not to say that mindfulness cannot be put to work in marginalised contexts, but that these organisations are unsuited to spearhead such work. As extension projects show, the design and development of programmes, stripped of social context, render hegemonic models incongruous in settings for which they were not designed.

Scientific evidence also propelled corporate mindfulness programmes to improve workplace wellbeing, relations, and performance (Bristow, 2016). These popular interventions gained traction as strategies to boost corporate control and governance of the workplace. Workplace interest in worker wellbeing and growth in happiness commonly functions in the interests of business to alleviate stress costs and increase productivity. In such contexts, mindfulness regulates and assesses employees as economic resources (Davies, 2016; Cederström and Spicer, 2015). It becomes part of a strategy to control the whole workforce, which is once again homologised when viewed from the perspective of employers, and promises to enhance resilience, capacity, and performance, targeting individuals to improve profit. Healthy, happy, focused individuals competing for work take responsibility for their wellbeing and their accountability to the workplace. This style of corporatism extends beyond the workplace to include the prison complex, schooling system, and military as organs that involve and govern individuals (Davis, 2016). In school contexts, attentional regulation links to enhanced performance, and resilience links to compliance (Forbes, 2016; Hsu, 2016). The MYRIAD programme, for instance, aims precisely to 'improve resilience in young adolescents' in order to prevent the onset of depression.[9] While the programme may achieve this goal, it simultaneously subdues critical thinking and resistance to systems of inequality.

White Mindfulness programmes are, therefore, even where outcomes appear favourable, ensnared in improved control of human bodies under the guise of self-regulation. In these unseen ways it becomes complicit in a biopolitics of assimilation and co-option which pre-empts its deployment for pro-justice purposes. Regulating and blaming students rather than addressing the causes of their behaviours fulfils a biopolitical function. As an alternative, White Mindfulness could 'remove the focus on behaviour management of "problem kids" to critically examine the social conditions that create suffering for our children and youth' (Cannon, 2016: 397). This shift in accountability opens possibilities for a vastly different engagement with mindfulness.

Comfortable in its current framing, the three mindfulness organisational outreach programmes reinforce behavioural change agendas. Their premise is that as workplace decision-makers become mindful, via a cascading effect, organisations and society at large will become more 'caring'. Yet the evidence says otherwise:

> [I]t is assumed that individuals within systems, including the military, corporations, schools, and so on, who 'wake up' through contemplative practice will be effective in engendering major institutional transformations. *Not only is there no evidence for the effectiveness for this strategy*, there *is* evidence which suggests that programs that focus solely on transformation at the individual level are *not* effective in engendering systems-wide change.
>
> (Lavelle, 2016: 241, emphasis added)

This critical insight challenges the 'Buddha-nature' argument to which mindfulness appeals as a strategy for justice: the notion that the inherent goodness of our nature will be revealed with sufficient practice and that social inequalities will vanish as a result. This view in fact awaits those with power to see the light to change perspective in order for societies to change. It downplays the powerful voices from the margins and mass movements alike in forging change.

Workplace and school programmes might help individuals cope better with adversity, but they maintain the cultures that generate adversity in the first instance. From this perspective, White Mindfulness is in trouble. Regardless of noble intentions, it is embroiled in a gamut of strategies that serve the interests of advanced capitalism. Postracial neoliberalism, it seems, grips the organs of White Mindfulness.

Race-gender demographics of dominant White Mindfulness organisations

Postracial societies undo neither the false construct or exploitation of race nor intersecting characteristics of difference. On the contrary, inattention to race accords with the erasure of identity and perpetuation of power-over. In the case of White Mindfulness, this is not merely a postracial oversight. When advocates acknowledge mindfulness' Buddhist-orientation, they also use Buddhist doctrine to erase race. Notions of common humanity flatten the realities of constructed differences in the ways people experience and are valued in society. Although racial difference was acknowledged in outreach programmes, it was absent in daily operations; realities of a predominantly White, middle-class user group is largely absent in organisational literature.

White Mindfulness lexicon serves a postracial frame. Phrases such as: 'common humanity', 'we have more in common than not', 'there is more that unites us than divides us', are prevalent in Kabat-Zinn's books and interviews. They are repeated across respondent transcripts and are inherent in trainings I attended. By disregarding identity, the language fortifies postracialism. But how does this play out in organisational patterns?

Race and gender profiles of the organisations I investigated categorise organisational employees up until April 2018 when my period of active research ended. As noted, the binaries in these tables present their own trappings. My reporting also homologises groups. Both these factors require further research and disruption. These matters notwithstanding, the tables show the magnitude of the problem: a concentration of White men in decision-making positions with low numbers of People of the Global Majority (PGM).

Since the organisations are based in the US and UK, to maintain their anonymity it seems helpful to make some generic comments prior to looking at the data. In recognition of the importance of representation, the 1998 US Secretary of Education made an appeal: 'Our teachers should look like America' (Riley, 1998: 20). The US Census Bureau (2021) reports – according to their categorisation – that African Americans comprise 13.6 per cent of the population, American Indian and Alaska Native 1.3 per cent, Hispanic and Latinx 18.9 per cent, Asians 6.1 per cent, Whites excluding White Hispanics, 59.3 per cent.[10] Against these US demographics, 100 per cent White male directors, 80 per cent White board decision-makers, and 100 per cent White teacher trainers are markedly out of sync. The most recent 2011 UK Census reports an 80 per cent White population in England and Wales compared to 45 per cent White people in London (Owen, 2012). Again, the all-White directors and predominantly White boards and male decision-makers are discrepant with UK society. In his Snowy Peaks Report, Roger Kline (2014) identifies the same profile in the UK's National Health Services that Kucinskas (2019) notes in the Mindfulness Industry generally.[11] Bringing in GM consultants and improving representation of GM women at board level, even though a step in the right direction, fails to adequately address the problem of whiteness located in daily business and operations. In contrast to the three organisations, *Race on the Agenda* (ROTA), a UK social policy organisation, bases all its work on the principle that 'those with direct experience of inequality should be central to solutions to address it. Our work is actively informed by the lived experience of BME communities and their organisations' (ROTA, 2017: 7).[12]

The 2018 *BME Manifesto on Mental Health* also emphasises the need for GM participation and representation in the design and delivery of mental health services (Griffiths, 2018).[13] The remarkable absence of race and ethnicity in planning and research is not unrelated to the organisations' racial profiles. Unlike ROTA, strategies to widen participation in the three organisations are ill-informed by the lived experiences of racial, gender, sexual, and disability injustices. The *BME Manifesto on Mental Health* also sets out the devastating impact of this oversight in mental health provision on Black service users. In this light, the organisations' commitments to the eradication of suffering 'for all' and their intentions to reach marginalised communities has not yet translated into meaningful actions that inform research, policy, and strategies that change the landscape.

Chestnut Institute's race-gender profile breakdown is shown in Table 4.1.

The overall staff complement reveals poor racial diversity and a predominance of White men in leadership and decision-making positions. Two of the 18 tutors are GM women (11.1 per cent). There are no GM men because when GM men were contracted to teach 'outreach' programmes they never formed part of the staff complement. The 16 teacher trainers are all White (0 per cent GM). There are no GM administrative staff and out of 12 persons, 83 per cent are White women. Twenty per cent of 10 advisory board members are PGM, equally split between one GM woman and one GM man. In contrast to the equal split of White teacher trainers (50 per cent White women and 50 per cent men), White men (60 per cent) predominate on the board with only a 20 per cent count of White women. Up until April 2018, Chestnut Institute had only ever had White male directors (100 per cent).

Table 4.1 Chestnut Institute's profile by race and gender

	Tutors[a]	Teacher trainers[b]	Administrative staff	Board	Directors[c]	Totals
White M	2	8	2	6	3	21
White F	14	8	10	2	0	34
GM M	0	0	0	1	0	1
GM F	2	0	0	1	0	3
Totals	18	16	12	10	3	59

[a] These are teachers who deliver MBSR and MBCT programmes at or on behalf of the organisation.
[b] These teacher trainers primarily train MBSR teachers. They also teach MBSR and MBCT programmes for the Centre but are distinguished from 'teachers' or 'tutors' in the first column in that they are teacher trainers.
[c] The figure here and for the table as a whole records employees at different times in the organisation's history.

The lack of diversity across Chestnut Institute's structures suggests an institutional framework of whiteness. Decision-making powers reside in White, largely male leadership. In settings of whiteness, neglect of race and other signifiers of difference have implications for change. Strategies, programmes, and training spaces – especially where identity is erased and whiteness invisibilised – reflect the perspectives of decision-makers. Non-diversity at decision-making and pedagogical levels manifests in exclusive policies and programmes. This may explain Chestnut Institute's 'adjunctive' one-size-fits-all diversity approach, enthusiasm for universality, positive reporting, and de-escalation of diversity concerns following its 'widening participation' phase.

Chestnut Institute's history of relative racial homogeneity is further complicated by gender. Over the course of its lifespan, the organisation has consistently been led by White men employed, according to a respondent, 'on the basis of meritocracy'. Some respondents involved in Chestnut Institute's early years faulted its gendered roles and responsibilities, stating that the organisation was historically led by men yet 'carried by the work and dedication of women who were structurally subordinate to them'. They challenged paternalism and a hegemony of 'male superiority' in both the MBSR and MBCT worlds and considered gender disparities organisational failures. The academic distinction between male leaders' PhDs and female teachers' master's degrees led to, as reported by these respondents, an unfortunate gender divide within the organisation reflected in gendered pay gaps.[14]

Red Centre emulates not only Chestnut Institute's institutional White, middle/upper-class student and staff composition but that of the convert-mindfulness community (see Gleig, 2019; Kucinskas, 2019). Such concentrations of White, middle-class decision-making power reinforce political whiteness. Table 4.2 attests to Red Centre's organisational non-diversity.

Red Centre's 15 staff members include 6 teacher trainers, 0 per cent of whom are PGM. The remaining nine staff positions include administrators and research leads, one of whom is a GM woman (6.7 per cent). There are no GM men in these administrative posts. Of associates invited to their positions as supporters of Red Centre's mission, 13.3 per cent are GM women (positioned at satellite locations) with 3.3 per cent GM men. There are 0 per cent GM trustees or directors. Ten per cent of international advisors is one GM man with no GM women; 70 per cent are White men and 20 per cent are White women. When grouped together, out of 23 directors, international advisors, and trustees – Red Centre's chief decision-makers – 4.3 per cent represents a single GM man. There are no GM women. In other words, leadership of the organisation

Table 4.2 Red Centre's profile by race and gender

	Staff	Associates	Trustees	International advisors	Directors	Totals
White M	3	7	8	7	2	27
White F	11	18	3	2	0	34
GM M	0	1	0	1	0	2
GM F	1	4[a]	0	0	0	5
Totals	15	30	11	10	2	68[b]

[a] The four GM female associates are not resident in the UK or US.
[b] This figure counts people associated with the organisation from inception to 2018.

on all matters, including diversity, rests with 95.6 per cent White men and women, 73.9 per cent of whom are men.

Since its inception, Red Centre's leadership and staff have been predominantly White. In 10 years, its two directors are both White men. This profile is discordant in a sector where poor mental health is more prevalent among PGM. Notably, decision-making power and direction are held by a select group furthest removed from the GM women who experience the highest rates of mental health-related arrests in the UK (EHRC, 2016).

Oak Inc. repeats Chestnut Institute and Red Centre's racial profiles.[15] It departs from their gender norm in that it has a woman in a leadership position (Table 4.3). Since 2004, Oak Inc.'s founding members also serve as its board members. Its trainers train Oak Inc. teachers. Associate teachers are experienced and include global figures who represent Oak Inc. in different parts of the world. Staff are office administration and management team members.

Out of 18 trainers, 11.1 per cent are GM (5.6 per cent women and 5.6 per cent men). Of 28 associate teachers, 10.7 per cent are GM (3.6 per cent male and 7.1 per cent female). Of eight staff members, 0 per cent are PGM. Oak Inc. has 0 per cent GM board members/directors. Additionally, organisational data indicates that of 63 teachers trained in 2017, 7.9 per cent are GM women and 3.1 per cent are GM men.

Table 4.3 Oak Inc.'s profile by race and gender

	Trainers	Associate teachers	Staff[a]	Board members/ directors	Totals
White M	4	7	3	2	16
White F	12	18	5	1	36
GM M	1	1	0	0	2
GM F	1	2	0	0	3
Totals	18	28	8	3	57

[a] There were at the time of data gathering 12 staff members, 4 of whom overlap with previous categories; of the 4, 3 are White females and 1 is a White male. They are only counted once in the table.

Oak Inc.'s racial pattern conforms to that of Chestnut Institute and Red Centre. None of the organisation's categories correspond to social demographics, least of all its 100 per cent White decision-making directorship. Working backwards, its community-focused ethos and mission have not yet influenced the organisation's composition.

Comparisons, common denominators, and contradictions

Collectively, the organisations use the term 'secular mindfulness' to suggest a mindfulness devoid of Buddhism, even though it is not.[16] They advocate for mindfulness as an essential part of twenty-first-century life, lauding its capacities to alleviate stress and improve self-regulation for society at large. Yet the one-size-fits-all approach homologises communities and disengages difference. At the same time, racialised organisational profiles weaken accessibility to diverse audiences and hinder promises of 'mindfulness-for-all'.

Lack of critique fails to challenge White Mindfulness' complicity in advanced capitalism and its technologies of neoliberal selfhood. As a result of their uncritical stance, the organisations engage in adjunctive diversity strategies based on hyper-individualised models, designed for and by White, middle-class practitioners. By adjunctive, I literally mean that efforts to 'widen participation' – the way the organisations define their diversity and inclusion programmes – are added on to their business-as-usual without any critical appraisal of what diversification means beyond reaching 'hard-to-reach' groups. Consequently, efforts to reduce 'suffering' from a diversity perspective constitute non-performatives. In effect, the organisations collectively reproduce ideologies of postracialism that perpetuate whiteness, even while they advocate diversity. In such instances, we may ask who and what the postracial is for and what work it does: 'what racist expression is it enabling, legitimating, rationalising? Is it just … that postraciality was created to mask the effects of white privilege?' (Goldberg, 2015: 4).

These questions spotlight an implicit politics that camouflages discriminations, exclusions, and White privilege. When race or identity concerns are foregrounded within the modern Buddhist movement, they invoke responses such as: 'the genderless, colourless, non-conceptual nature of our "true self", and the private work of eliminating "the three poisons"' (Raiche, 2016).[17] Or, as Kaleem (2012) points out, there are claims from senior White convert Buddhists that 'Buddhism goes against identity. Race is a very superficial way of looking at things'.[18] These expedient responses use Buddhism's two-truth doctrine[19] to privilege ultimate over objective reality, which, as we've seen before, reduces racism to episodic encounters. Goldberg's questions become even more urgent in secularist contexts that erase race and privilege. They draw attention to White male decision-makers as the bastions of White Mindfulness, where these authorities repeat the obscuration of race, gender, sexuality, and disability, as well as the invisibility of whiteness.

To underscore the political nature of Chestnut Institute, Oak Inc., and Red Centre, Table 4.4 compresses the organisational figures to produce a snapshot of their collective race-gender demography. Here, each organisation's figures are collapsed and re-presented to demonstrate race-gender statistics across the organisations. This confirms a concentration of White decision-makers and teachers across these three key organisations, affirming the need for ongoing inquiry.

Bearing in mind that US and UK census data reports 60.4 per cent and 80 per cent Whites respectively, the figures here indicate how the organisations, and probably the industry, fall short of national averages. Although diversity cannot be reduced to representation, it is also true that diversity at decision-making level, if diverse expertise and knowledge are valued, can lead to different agendas to those currently pursued. Global figures indicate that collectively only 5.9 per cent of Chestnut Institute, Oak Inc., and Red

Table 4.4 Race-gender profile of Chestnut Institute, Oak Inc., and Red Centre

	White M	White F	GM M	GM F	Totals
Chestnut Institute	21	34	1	3	59
Red Centre	27	34	2	5	68
Oak Inc	16	36	2	3	57
TOTALS	**64**	**104**	**5**	**11**	**184**

Centre staff are GM women, while 2.7 per cent are GM men; 91.5 per cent are White: 35.3 per cent are White men and 56.2 per cent are White women.

Table 4.5 considers the race-gender alignment by organisational portfolios. Here I group Chestnut Institute, Oak Inc., and Red Centre categories to reveal more clearly the distribution of decision-making power. I bunch decision- and policy-making functions and differentiate these from directors so as not to lose sight of the race-gender breakdown of directorships. I also distinguish staff members (which includes teacher trainers and administrative staff) from associates and teachers who are not teacher trainers.

GM membership across Chestnut Institute, Oak Inc., and Red Centre comprises:

- 0 per cent directorships
- 4.3 per cent staff members (1.4 per cent are men)
- 8.8 per cent board members and international advisors (2.9 per cent are women)
- 13.15 per cent associates and faculty (boosted by Red Centre's international GM associates – 2.6 per cent of whom are men)

When figures for staff members are added to those of associates and teachers, these categories or lower pay grades show a predominance

Table 4.5 Organisational race-gender profile by portfolio

	White M	White F	PGM M	PGM F	TOTALS
Board members/ international advisors	23	8	2	1	34
Directors	7	1	0	0	8
Staff members (including teacher trainers)	20	46	1	2	69
Associates and teachers	16	50	2	8	76
Totals	66	105	5	11	187

of women. When race is not factored into these figures, they read as 72.7 per cent female as opposed to 27.3 per cent male. A focus on the upper organisational echelons, i.e. at the level of boards, advisors, and directors, inverts these figures: 67.6 per cent of boards and international advisors, and 71.4 per cent of major decision-makers (boards, international advisors, and directors) are White men. This raises questions about the gendered hierarchies in the mindfulness sector which, in my study, is overshadowed by its racialised dimension. As seen from the above figures and throughout the organisational demographics, poor diversity and the lack of GM decision-makers correlates with adjunctive diversity models, individualised mindfulness programmes, and inattention to race and gender as fundamental factors in inequality and ill health.

Tables 4.4 and 4.5 show the consistency of racialised profiles across Chestnut Institute, Oak Inc., and Red Centre.[20] When coupled with assumed authority to 'embody and universalise the dharma', this picture becomes even more contentious. It echoes Said's claims that those with dominant voices assume the authority to hold and 'speak the truth'. Their dominance derives historically from social privilege and generational wealth, allowing them to acquire academic qualifications, social capital, and to command sway far more easily. And due to the nature of power relations and social norms, such authority goes unquestioned, especially by those in power. This in effect reproduces ecosystems whereby White privilege reproduces itself, even when it does so with a smattering of colour. It also highlights how authority is constructed and reconstructed through mechanisms of 'at least some assent (or sub-servience) to power' (Stanley, 2012: 637).

When tracking the arc of White Mindfulness, the construction of 'expertise', 'authority', and 'knowledge' becomes clearer. Intersecting ideologies of Orientalism, secularism, postracial neo-liberalism, hyper-individualism, and whiteness frame this steady trajectory as instruments of power are handed like a baton from one to another. In these arrangements, the invisibility and normativity of whiteness also constitute anti-Blackness technologies that disconnect Chestnut Institute, Oak Inc., and Red Centre from communities at greatest risk of ill health. This presents a major challenge for these organisations: their positionality and chosen wellbeing frame makes their services inaccessible to those groups that are most unwell, least cared for, and further dispossessed. Put differently, the creation and roll-out of White Mindfulness which embodies current distributions of power results in its perpetuation of power-over and latent Othering.

Governed by whiteness and devoid of critical and diverse thought, the embeddedness of postracial neoliberalism in White Mindfulness goes unquestioned. A one-size-fits-all response to stress, pain, and mental health favours decision-makers and a select audience; programmes roll out systemic whiteness and reproduce notions of 'expertise' fashioned in the image of their makers. As a popular form of stress-relief, White Mindfulness continues to obscure race and difference and sustain hegemonies.

Notes

1 In Kabat-Zinn's 10-second vision in 1979, he foresaw global access to mindfulness through clinics and hospitals: 'I saw in a flash not only a model that could be put in place, but also the long-term implications of what might happen if the basic idea was sound and could be implemented in one test environment – namely that it would spark new fields of scientific and clinical investigation, and would spread to hospitals and medical centres and clinics across the country and around the world, and provide right-livelihood for thousands of practitioners' (Kabat-Zinn, 2011: 287).

2 Kabat-Zinn even perceived of his organisation, the Centre for Mindfulness, as 'the epicenter of a world-wide – sometimes people use the word 'revolution,' or a world-wide Renaissance, if you will, in mindfulness, in clinical medicine, in clinical research as well as in neuroscience' (Kabat-Zinn, 2014: 64; 1990/2013: 281; Brown, 2016: 78).

3 The first Behavioural Medicine Conference was held at Yale University, 4–6 February 1977, supported by departments of Psychology and Psychiatry, the School of Medicine, and the National Institute of Health. It defined behavioural medicine as 'the field concerned with the development of behavioural science knowledge and techniques relevant to the understanding of physical health and illness and the application of this knowledge and techniques to prevention, diagnosis, treatment, and rehabilitation. Psychosis, neurosis, and substance abuse are included only insofar as they contribute to physical disorders as an end point' (Shwartz and Weiss, 1978: 251).

4 Descartes' paradigm of 'rationality' split mind and body to create a false dichotomy between thought and affect in which the body became an 'afterthought' (Grosfoguel, 2013: 75).

5 The precariat is a social class that suffers the uncertainty of employment, job security, and emotional and psychological poor health (Standing, 2011).

6 Sharf notes suspicion cast on Suzuki's Buddhist credentials, and while not impugning his academic competence and contribution to Buddhist studies, contends that his views on 'inner experience' were derived from US-Eurocentric influences rather than Buddhist sources (Sharf, 1998: 274).

7 The Centre for Reviews and Dissemination cautions that the figure of a 500 increase in mindfulness publications in 2017 due to research into MBCT 'may be over-stated, given the poor quality and wide variation between studies' (Moloney, 2016: 276). For instance, a 2014 multitreatment trial found that MBCT is no more effective than CBT. Yet the study reports that findings 'add to the growing body of evidence that psychological interventions, delivered during remission, may have particular beneficial effects in preventing future episodes of major depression, but may be especially relevant for those at highest risk of relapse' (Williams *et al.*, 2014: 285).

8 Pathology, it is argued, remains 'the most enduring model of disease causation and progression' (Gritti, 2017: 37). Biological factors are identified as singular contributories to disease pathology; socioeconomic factors are disregarded. Meanwhile, the '"psy-disciplines", as Nikolas Rose (1999; 1998) termed them, paved the way for a therapeutic culture of the self' (Ng, 2016b: 20).

9 The *My Resilience in Adolescence* (MYRIAD) programme is funded by the Wellcome Trust. But there is little if any regard for root cause or the links drawn between disaffected students and social discrimination. The importance of this cannot be overstated: 'mindfulness is employed in a number of impoverished inner-city schools attended by many disaffected, indignant, and at times disruptive students of color. Without a critical understanding of the neoliberal education agenda, mindfulness practices geared toward stress reduction, conflict resolution, emotion regulation, anger management, and focus and concentration serve as functions of social control and reinforce emotional self-regulation that puts the onus back on the individual student' (Forbes, 2016: 360).

10 The remaining percentages comprise Pacific Islanders, and multiple or mixed ethnicities.

11 Roger Kline's Snowy White Peaks Report has contributed to redress within the NHS. It includes a Workforce Race Equality Strategy

(WRES) that monitors services and trusts in areas such as race and disability. To shift from a culture of policy formulation that fails to translate into practical meaningful change, the WRES emphasises: (i) location of strategies within governance structures; (ii) NHS boards and senior leadership good practice models; (iii) integration of WRES into mainstream business 'considered as part of the "well led" domain in the Care Quality Commission's inspection programme' (Naqvi *et al.*, 2016: 73).

12 ROTA use the term Black and Minority Ethnic in their reports.

13 The BME Manifesto on Mental Health uses the term Black and Minority Ethnic.

14 'Studies have already made it clear that women in academia generally earn less and command fewer resources such as research space on the job. They are less likely to be promoted than men to the rank of full professor, even after controlling for productivity and human capital … service work … can disadvantage women … by side-tracking their path to success' (Guarino, 2017).

15 Oak Inc. only started gathering data on race and ethnicity of teacher training participants in 2014. Because it is an optional category, in 2015 no reliable data was available.

16 Brown identifies multiple ways in which organisations include Buddhism in their training whether by stealth, code-switching, or scripting, while still calling the programmes secular (Brown, 2016). Talal Asad notes that all processes of naming the secular, secularism, and secularisation are political by nature. Secularisation carefully re-presents knowledges that have been excised of their traditions through centuries of coloniality and White supremacy (Asad, 2003). Secular mindfulness, presented as a rational, non-traditional, contemporary intervention suitable to a Western audience, serves as a good example of bypassing the politics of Orientalism, marginalisation, and whiteness.

17 Raiche says that 'an appeal to "true self," or Buddha-nature, that is blind to race and identity can all too easily redirect attention away from the very real suffering out of which a questioner may have courageously spoken. Answers that stress emptiness and personal practice also downplay our mutual responsibility to deconstruct racial fictions and to help each other heal from the deep wounds left in their wake' (Raiche, 2016).

18 Kaleem is interviewing Rodney Smith, founder of the Seattle IMS. Smith and other IMS founders also express a realisation that separate identity groups are important, but intimate that this is a GM concern that will resolve itself once GM people *advance their practice.*

This is another way in which White leaders take some distance from the issue.

19 The two-truth doctrine is present in all Buddhist traditions and differentiates conventional (Sanskrit *saṁvṛti-satya*, Pāli *sammuti sacca*) and absolute (Sanskrit *paramārtha-satya*, Pāli *paramattha sacca*) truth or reality. Conventional or relative reality pertains to the concrete world of everyday experience, while ultimate reality is said to be 'empty' of concrete phenomena that separates 'observer' and 'observed'. Its relevance for my purposes is the association of 'identity' such as race with relative reality, and the denunciation of conditional reality by those who argue for the primacy of ultimate reality in which identity is dismissed as a relative construct (Matilal, 2002: 203–8). This latter position denies the identity-based nature of inequalities: in all its forms including neoliberalism, capitalism is based on the exploitation of signifiers of difference, especially race, class, gender, sexuality, and faith.

20 In Table 4.5, the overlapping roles of Directors and Board Members are counted twice, inflating the count in this table by 3.

5

Reproducing whiteness: pedagogies of limitation

> There is no such thing as a neutral educational process. Education either functions as an instrument that is used to facilitate the integration of the younger generation into the logic of the present system and bring about conformity to it, or it becomes 'the practice of freedom,' the means by which men and women [sic] deal critically and creatively with reality and discover how to participate in the transformation of their world.
>
> Richard Shaull (1993: 16)

Every sector, new and established, takes hold and reproduces itself through some form of education and training. From theatre, engineering, plumbing, medicine, and yoga to education itself, each field involves training and apprenticing to prepare new incumbents to take up jobs. In the context of disaster capitalism, the corporatist state shapes the field of education. Increased regulation sees the rise of a quality assurance industry which comes with its own trainers and professionals. How this unfolds in the Mindfulness Industry deserves closer attention.

Educational programmes commonly reflect the interests and values of their designers. When power is racialised, so are programmes. In the case of White Mindfulness, curricula resemble homogeneity rather than a diversity of perspectives and experiences. As a result, social norms that seem sensible and logical to those in power, recirculate. As shown previously, dominant cultures in fact invisibilise power to such an extent that the arrangements of power are regarded as settled and go unquestioned. It is precisely their concealment that generates defaults and unexamined normativity (Butler, 1993). Patterns of whiteness are fortified through such norms, messages, and political silences. The repetition of these mechanisms fixes borders and divisions so that constructed worlds appear as given. When White Mindfulness overlooks or ignores social patterns of oppression and discrimination, for instance, it regenerates defaults and systems of power. Its uncritical pedagogies infused with invisible values and norms go largely unnoticed and undisputed, leading to the (re)appearance of racialised patterning within teacher training spaces.

This chapter examines the pedagogies through which White Mindfulness reproduces itself and the commercialised Mindfulness Industry. Building on the demographic profiles of my UK and US case studies, I inquire into their teacher training programmes (TTPs). This offers an opportunity to unpack the ways in which uncritical pedagogies impose norms on bodies while political claims of universalism and neutrality influence educational methodologies and experiences. In a constructed Mindfulness Industry I show how invisibilised norms that typically go unnoticed by those in power are blindingly obvious to those on the margins whose exclusions in educational spaces typically take the form of microaggressions, being overlooked, or required to 'play the game'. The discussion elaborates on earlier concerns with the expedient use of words to create illusions of diversity, accountability, and global sameness while feeding an uncritical pedagogy amenable to neoliberal postraciality. Lack of critique, I suggest, weakens social justice prospects pitting White Mindfulness education against the freedoms with which it claims to align.

A brief reminder of power within White Mindfulness

To lay the basis for this discussion it is helpful to remember the power, privilege, and antecedents of White Mindfulness as it swims comfortably in a sea of whiteness. A skewed distribution of power imprints itself on institutions and people who come to embody, reflect, and, depending on their social positioning, repel such norms. Prominent Black mindfulness trainer Rhonda Magee explains how the Mindfulness Industry inherits and perpetuates power:

> A survey of mindfulness teachers, a sampling of mindfulness training venues, and a visit to any centre of practice would reveal that social justice is often not associated as core to the practices of mindfulness.

Instead, social justice is often seen as something separate from, and optional to, mindfulness practice and mindfulness in the world. This fact is exacerbated or perhaps pre-figured by the contexts within which Western mindfulness emerged: predominantly among [W]hite, male, and upper-class students of Buddhism with a dream of taking the practices into the world. Given the relatively privileged backgrounds of many of the original teachers and practitioners of mindfulness in the West, it is easy to see why the practices have become largely if not primarily associated with personal well-being and productivity, and not social justice. For this reason, mindfulness practices are often perceived as more or less unavailable to or unhelpful for members of traditionally marginalized communities.

(Magee, 2016: 427–8)

This historical account orientates TTPs to the sector's rootedness in the systemic privileges afforded White Buddhist or mindfulness converts. By ignoring or remaining oblivious to the problem, TTPs themselves reproduce these inequalities, foster exclusionary practices, reinforce the industry's disengagement with social transformation, and embrace its affinity for adjunctive diversity strategies. Rather than bringing clarity, these blind spots epitomise poor attention to the actual outcomes of White Mindfulness.

Non-diversity everywhere

My experience of mindfulness training came through the Centre for Mindfulness (CfM) and the Oxford Mindfulness Centre via programmes offered in four different countries in the global North. I also participated in continuing professional development trainings hosted by Bangor University, retreats at Gaia House, Mindfulness Initiative UK events, and various conferences. These large-scale trainings were predominantly White and female in audience and were often led by White men. Unsurprisingly, these patterns reflect organisational demographics and social power as bi-directionally feeding off and mirroring each other. They suggest that Said's latent Othering is ever-present.

As an early starter, Mindfulness-Based Stress Reduction (MBSR) training established the foundations for the professionalisation of what was to become the Mindfulness Industry. As the field unfolded, growing emphasis on scientific evidence encouraged pedagogies shaped by research of mindfulness as well as research that predated MBSR. For example, Hans Selye's mid-nineteenth-century research on stress and the stress response are foundational to the MBSR curriculum.[1] It informs a bio-psychological interpretation of stress in isolation from socio-political determinants. This binary approach dislodges stress from social determinants and suggests that stress is either switched on or off. More recent engagement with polyvagal theory, while moving beyond the binaries of Selye's stress model, still fails to consider the imperative of context. Work by somatics specialists like Nkem Ndefo (2021) and Stacie Haines (2019), who use the 'power-over, power-with, and power-within' framing, complicate stress models by emphasising different autonomic responses that are context sensitive and that require different approaches to stress reduction. They contextualise concepts like resilience in relation to adversity, discuss the intermittent relevance of hypervigilance as a protective mechanism, and underline the imperative of community and co-regulation in lessening stress levels.

When scientism suggests that science is 'objective', like education, research obscures the norms, values, conditions, stakeholder interests, actors, and 'subjects' involved. To expose this, Harvard University published a series of articles to counter anti-Black racism in public health, space and design, science, and criminal justice. They show that despite the disavowal of pseudo-science used to bolster White supremacy, racist ideas impact not only structures and systems, but remain latent in society today, evidenced in what is regarded as unbiased research. The collection from Harvard University includes a focus on scientific racism with recommendations about how scientists may bring about change. These include becoming knowledgeable about 'science's racist history', 'increasing equity and inclusion of Black scientists', and improving Black representation in STEM subjects (see Ileka et al., 2020).[2] This is not to suggest that the mindfulness sector is knowingly complicit in scientific and educational racism. The series reveals the blind spots and mental models that chase results and outcomes regardless of flawed methods. The desire to show mindfulness' success at relieving stress, coping with 'difficulties', navigating adversity, improving productivity, and slowing down aging blindsides the multiple influences that predicate research outcomes: the paradigm in which researchers function, the select samples, and the desire for findings that prop up educational programmes and curricula.

Tied to research, education becomes a function of a particular kind of mindfulness – one aiming to achieve the outcomes promised. Put another way, education becomes the servant of certain social and market requirements such as improved productivity, obedience, and hyper-individualised self-governance isolated from a sense of community. In the world of White Mindfulness, as curricula became increasingly manualised and standardised to consistently deliver research claims, teachers were required to perform in certain ways to secure specific outcomes (McCown *et al.*, 2011).

As White Mindfulness grew beyond MBSR to include, for instance, the much-researched field of Mindfulness-Based Cognitive Therapy (MBCT), multiple TTPs embraced standardisation in efforts to 'not dilute' the teachings (Crane *et al.*, 2012). Standardisation was presented as a 'protection', but it also served as a diversion from the fact that TTPs remain divested of diversity. Moreover, standardised educational gold standards chased symptomatic relief which masked underlying causes of distress. Most importantly, they perpetuated social norms of whiteness with implications for the selection of trainers, students, and pro-justice agendas. As we see from the figures below, TTPs are mainly led by White teachers. In an industry unconcerned with critical race theory, these conditions underscore the epigraph to this chapter. In contradistinction to an insistence on neutrality, White Mindfulness reinforms whiteness.

My research suggests that correcting representation on its own won't necessarily solve the problem of making the sector more diverse in terms of expertise, knowledge, and new directions. Instead, I present these findings as a starting point from which to understand the depth and dimension of the problem of White Mindfulness generally and as it pertains to education. My data collected between 2015 and 2018 illustrates the non-diverse make-up of educational policymakers and trainers in three US-UK mindfulness institutions (Table 5.1).

Typical of the field at large, the organisational demographics indicate that 5 per cent of a total of 40 teacher trainers are People

Table 5.1 Organisational race-gender profile of teacher trainers

Teacher Trainers	White M	White F	GM M	GM F	TOTALS
Chestnut Institute	8	8	0	0	16
Red Centre	4	12	1	1	18
Oak Inc.	2	4	0	0	6
Totals	14	24	1	1	40

of the Global Majority (PGM) (1 man and 1 woman) compared to 60 per cent White women (24) and 35 per cent White men (14). As shown in previous tables, teacher trainer figures for White men and women are inverted when it comes to leadership roles, showing not only the racialised but also the gendered nature of the industry. When compared to Table 4.5 in Chapter 4, which shows director and board member decision-making roles, it is evident that many more White men than White women occupy decision-making positions. The figures reveal that the chief decision-makers and educational policy makers are 8 White directors – only 1 of whom is female – and 34 board members – only 3 of whom are PGM. In other words, there are no GM directors and only 8.8 per cent GM board members. When adding the 8 directors to the 34 board members, 30 of the 42 decision-makers (71.4 per cent) are White men, 21.4 per cent are White women, and 7.1 per cent are PGM. Inspection of these statistics tells us that the Mindfulness Industry's educational thought leaders are largely unaffected by gender- or race-based discrimination. Their positions are safeguarded by the invisibility of hegemonic whiteness. As such, they are not natural diversity and social justice protagonists, at least not in relation to race and gender, for they are affected by neither (Armstrong and Wildman, 2007). This is not to say that people's politics are determined by the colour of their skin, but it does explain, especially considering 'common humanity' and 'universalism' rhetoric, how few White Mindfulness leaders are incentivised to change the system.

Is White Mindfulness keen to change?

Critical theorist Elana Michelson says that homologous, non-reflexive, White, middle-class collectives are less capable of diversity-thought:

> [T]hose whose experience does not reflect the social norms are more likely to notice biases and problematic assumptions, so that perspectives available from those social positions are of value to epistemic communities. Similarly, knowledge communities that tend to take their own interests as the interests of the planet generally … need the engagement of those who have a specific, but different, relationship to that which is under study … *One does not have to experience the world as a woman to have insight into patriarchy or as a person of colour to investigate racism, but a fuller account is made possible if we start from the point of view of women's or Black people's experiences.*
>
> (Michelson, 2015: 69, emphasis added)

The invested nature of patriarchal power is to reproduce itself. It is disinclined to redistribute or disrupt power. In this light, if indeed there is a desire for change, the participation of those at the margins of conventional power is crucial, as are acts of solidarity. In other words, PGM and minoritised groups are pivotal to systems change. In addition, the allyship of White people, especially those in positions of power, is important to sustain intersectional justice.

Michelson's frame explains how, as the Mindfulness Industry's racial homogeneity comes into the spotlight, when asked about diversity, organisational staff find themselves incapacitated: 'we need help with the lack of diversity in mindfulness. We are unsure what to do'; 'there is a problem in that all our trainers are White, and we are only attracting people who look like us'; 'teachers are largely coming from White stock, and it's been challenging not only for us but for most meditation centres around the country to figure out how to improve diversity'. These comments point to a recognition of the problem. But of course, this lack of capacity itself needs shaking up as it is not the work of PGM to solve White Mindfulness' dilemma. The responses also highlight how poor diversity reinforces social norms and power structures that govern organisational thought and decision-making. Immobility regarding systemic racism and non-diversity shapes teacher training (TT) development and delivery and reproduces an exclusive industry and outlook. Its undoing requires radical unlearning and critical retraining.

In June 2020, Alexis Ohanian, co-founder of Reddit, resigned from its board requesting that he be replaced by a Black board member. His tweet to this effect[3] was accompanied by a pledge to invest profits from his Reddit stock in Black communities to curb racial hate. He started with a US$1million investment in Colin Kaepernick's Know your Rights Camp.[4] Ohanian's decision was spurred by the need for greater diversity at the highest levels of companies and institutions. Although improved representation at board and decision-making levels do not guarantee meaningful change, Ohanian's decision came in the wake of George Floyd's murder. With growing focus on the need to disrupt systemic racism, the call for greater diversity presumes a commitment to social transformation and justice. Through his action, Ohanian hoped to inspire other leaders to act similarly.

On *Serena Saturday* (June 2020), the show founded and hosted by Ohanian's mega-tennis star partner Serena Williams, he speaks also about the importance of stepping into uncomfortable spaces (Williams, 2020). He frames this in terms of seeing the daily forms of racism and sexism Williams deals with and realising the ease with which he occupies White spaces. Through his dialogue with Williams, Ohanian takes this further still to say that he is learning that by virtue of his social positioning and privilege he is racist and sexist and is constantly having to confront and address the undoing of these constructs in his own life. His learning, he says, is happening as part of community. Ohanian's public actions and discussion of his positionality disrupt the master's tools at multiple levels. His call for leadership in the form of action urges White Mindfulness beyond the release of pro-BLM statements.

Both Michelson and Ohanian present concrete actions that can support radical systems change work. Their frames are deliberately disruptive for the purpose of creating more equal, just societies. In the picture painted through my research, by being uncritical and unreflective of its own role in society, White Mindfulness endorses racialised social patterning and discourses of individualism. Its TTPs play a significant role in its positioning. Applying a disruptive frame to change course calls for actions that improve diverse thought leadership and engagement from key players. But this redirection assumes a desire to chart a different course in the service of social justice. White Mindfulness, after all, was not initially pro-justice, and although it issues Black Lives Matter (BLM) statements, may remain comfortable that its hyper-individualised 'inner revolution' is unrelated to social injustices.

When TTP architects design programmes in their images and when systems are designed by people who are not PGM, trans, or disabled, they misrepresent and fail marginalised groups. In the allied field of mental health, Linton and Walcott comment on the inaccessibility of services to PGM persons and communities in the UK. They outline a poor fit between therapists and patients. Speaking as two Black editors of *The Colour of Madness*, one a doctor working on a psychiatric ward and the other a 2018 PhD candidate who used the system, they write:

> Historically, the mental health system is not designed with us in mind. [It's] designed in a utilitarian way, for the masses. It serves a purpose, but it means that those who are already marginalised or disadvantaged are disproportionally harmed by it … diagnostic criteria are so culture specific … [they] come from the Western world; they weren't made by any African or South American countries, for example. The people making decisions in the room don't look like us … It shows how important it is for your clinicians to look like people they are trying to help. It seems so obvious. That's basic, you need to be able to relate to your patients and they need to be able to relate to you. When your patients are overwhelmingly [B]lack and [B]rown and your doctors are not, you're always going to have this disconnect … there is class as well. Most doctors are middle class and a lot of our patients aren't … It has been interesting to see the difference it makes when you see patients interact with someone who understands their experiences as opposed to having just read about them.
>
> (Linton and Walcott, interviewed by Kankhwende, 2018)

Linton and Walcott unpack here the consequences of diversity-poor systems. They reflect the use of selective knowledge and methodologies that perpetuate the exclusion of marginalised groups at every design stage. In a similar fashion, the Mindfulness Industry's pedagogical blueprint embeds implicit ideologies of whiteness that persistently excludes those disenfranchised by its frame. Although programme adaptation is encouraged, this extends to structural rather than pedagogical or foundational changes. For example, certain outreach programmes may adapt class times, but they faithfully follow the same 'gold standard' curriculum regardless of context and without question. There is little interrogation of the purpose of mindfulness training in a world in crisis or of what it means to 'pay attention, on purpose, in a certain way, non-judgementally' across difference. Nor is there training in political and critical engagement.

In educational settings, individualised models of stress and well-being hold little regard for collective and group narratives of politically and economically induced stress and trauma and how to end it. Trainings typically shut down narratives of collective agency that don't fit and that trouble the curriculum. This is yet another way in which TTPs reinforce a disengagement with justice-infused pedagogies that address systemic and social transformation. 'White spaces' falsely proclaim 'neutral' models and 'value-free' ethics to which Others are expected to conform (Anderson, 2015). It is into these spaces and on these terms that people are included. Nirmal Puwar (2004) calls the Black bodies in such settings 'space invaders' who commonly face the consequences of never belonging. Ironically, as noted before, these White Mindfulness spaces, formed with the intention to 'pay attention' to what arises, cause the very stress and ill health they proclaim to reduce.

A redistribution of power would require the architects of these spaces – who aren't naturally incentivised change agents – to transform, cede, or share decision-making and control. Invested in long-standing careers, powerful networks, and good intentions, their disinclination to change, or to change only on certain terms, constitutes a series of roadblocks at the heart of the sector. It keeps spaces White. Even though the business case for diversity convincingly shows that companies with diverse leadership consistently outperform those that are White and male (see Hunt *et al.*, 2020), the Mindfulness Industry remains 'snow-capped'. In the context of BLM, especially when organisations issue statements of support, notional diversity is performative and amounts to virtue signalling.

As noted, part of the resistance to change is the insistence that standardisation 'protects' the industry from dilution; that it keeps the public safe. But following the above, standardised curricula, delivery, and uniformity raise questions of what exactly is being preserved. When educationalists identify a tension between the 'gold standard' research models that govern curriculum manualisation and a TTP focus on teacher qualities, they miss the underlying politics of standardisation. Their objection is that researchers prioritise research interests over and above those of teachers and students, rather than the other way around. This, they say, downplays the ways in which teachers influence programmes. Their paradox in which mindfulness pedagogy is subservient to a dominant research agenda reveals, albeit unintentionally, a Pandora's box of how pedagogies are controlled and how they function in the service of dominant ideologies rather than change.

Starting with the realities of value-laden research as a driver for curriculum manualisation and TTP standardisation, we need to ask who governs what ideal teacher qualities are and what they look like. One set of concerns here is that 'a positivist outcome-focused research agenda' could result in teachers who are outcomes and goals driven 'rather than being deeply immersed in the practice of mindfulness on which the whole pedagogy is based' (Crane *et al.*, 2014: 1113). This valid concern still overlooks questions of who decides what constitutes the purpose and practice of mindfulness and whether there can be a one-size-fits-all curriculum that is largely set in stone. In other words, these comments supplant concerns with power. They suggest that the practice of mindfulness is a single practice that, again, is value-free.

Calling pedagogy 'the shadow side' of mindfulness (McCown *et al.*, 2011: 137, 26) implies that it is at the mercy of research agendas and unable to assert its own progressive direction. This lets mindfulness pedagogy off the hook; it is pedagogues, after all, who vet curriculum manualisation and produce a non-diverse, uncritical pedagogy. In other words, research prioritisation serves as a decoy detracting from the critical examination of White Mindfulness' pedagogy, curricula, and TTPs. To say that curricula arise through 'immersion in practice' also camouflages an uncritical pedagogy; when practice is performed within the confines of 'the logic of the present system', it preserves social norms and structural power, obstructing change.

Angela Black, founder of Mindfulness for the People, testifies that White Mindfulness is a particular practice that echoes established, racialised power:

Mindfulness curricula grounded in whiteness means that there is an overt assumption that the content presented is universally beneficial to EVERYbody. That the empirical evidence driving the curricula is 'robust and rigorous' so of course its application is relevant to EVERYbody. And all of this universality is assumed while never explaining that decades of evidence-based, well-funded, highly visible and industry standard findings that support mindfulness curricula and practices are predominantly normed on the lived experiences of White people. And quite honestly, that lack of inquiry – not having to ask which bodies receive benefit and which ones don't; which ones were included in research studies and which ones weren't, all the while garnering major dollars to further the development of this blind spot – is not only an oversight, but a demonstration of how capitalism, White privilege and White supremacy are driving the mindfulness movement.

(Black, interviewed by Alton, 2017, emphasis in the original)

Black identifies a range of issues: the claim of universality,[5] the supremacy of research which while cast in whiteness proclaims neutrality, the racialised nature of the Mindfulness Industry, and the intricate entanglement of mindfulness and whiteness. As she concurs, experiences of the curriculum and mindfulness spaces as racialised are most directly felt by those for whom these spaces are not designed. By bringing these areas together we see that curricula and research, as currently formulated, function in opposition to diversity.

But the situation, it seems, is not quite clear cut. Over two decades ago, Kabat-Zinn in a 2000 interview expressed the desire to develop mindfulness programmes for those most stressed by society. On this occasion, he drew a clear link between marginalisation and stress, acknowledging socio-economic causality. He also indicated an interest in deploying research to address questions of what kind of mindfulness would be attractive to these communities:

[I]f we created a stress reduction programme based on principles and practices, would anybody come? … Could it be offered and seen as valuable by the people who are under the most stress in our society: the poor, recent immigrants, who do not even speak English, who face economic deprivation, bad living conditions, homelessness, joblessness, very often fragmented families? These are some of the questions we wished to explore in our research and in our attempts to take a degree of responsibility for contributing to the emergent field of what has come to be called mind/body medicine.

(Kabat-Zinn, 2000: 234)

It is true that Kabat-Zinn's CfM extended their MBSR programmes to inner-city clinics and prisons and put in place child-care and transport to make the courses accessible. But even though PGM instructors were recruited to co-deliver some of these programmes, they were delivering standardised MBSR courses. What is left unquestioned here is whether the research mentioned in this quote was ever undertaken and by whom. What were the findings? Who designs programmes for the groups named? Do they represent or share the interests, concerns, knowledges of these groups? Are there even questions posed to these groups about their interests and skills, where they are as a community, and if mindfulness is of any concern and where it ranks in relation to other concerns? It would be good to hear whether mindfulness features in the traditions of these GM groups and how they have cultivated resilience without White Mindfulness. Standardisation, manualisation, and uncritical research, built on the foundations of whiteness, cannot address these concerns. They bring us back full circle to the purpose of TTPs outlined in isolation from these concerns.

To round off the picture of how TTPs shape the mindfulness project, common requirements for enrolment in TTPs include an established mindfulness practice and retreat attendance. Within the Mindfulness Industry, retreats are said to deepen appreciation of 'the dharma' and promote teacher qualities, while practice is seen as the bedrock from which these attributes spring (Kabat-Zinn, 2011; McCown et al., 2011). Those I spoke to underlined the value of retreats and practice-centred approaches to TT for their immersive features: 'retreat was a very important component right from the start – an actual seven-day proper mindfulness vipassanā-type retreat … there's something much more important than all the right techniques and that's the emphasis on personal practice and going on retreat'; 'I cannot overstate the magic of retreats, when people come on our retreats, they pick up some magic from the organisation'. These comments are from people in positions of power who aren't 'space invaders' and who benefit from the system. Their dominant voices reflect the trouble with unquestioned power.

Oppositional views state that retreats can isolate the teacher from the everyday world and foster political disengagement. Also, that they exclude those to whom this format is inaccessible financially, geographically, socially, or culturally. The model presumes an ease of domestic arrangements that allow individuals to be away from home for significant periods of time. Moreover, it presupposes that the White, heteronormative spaces that predominate in retreat settings are safe and inclusive. It is in these spaces that prized 'teacher qualities', determined by White experts, are fostered. This is not to deny that space invaders like myself, under certain circumstances, don't reap some benefits from these normative settings. Of course, they are completely transformed, as said before, by teachers like Lama Rod, but this is not the norm. With growing attention to the BLM movement, questions around power persist: who gets to attend retreats? Who designs them and for whom? Which qualities and insights are valued; which are dismissed? What, indeed, is the purpose of retreat?

Uncritical pedagogies

New public management agendas advance corporatised, metricated, skills-based education and overturn critique (see Harvey, 2005; Singh, 2011). These agendas which govern White Mindfulness pedagogy are incompatible with and diametrically oppose pedagogies of freedom. Indirectly and implicitly, they separate from social action to advance justice and discourage mindfulness teachers from engaging agendas and ideas that create inclusive futures.

The purpose of TTPs, according to some designers, is to train competent teachers to deliver mindfulness effectively (Crane *et al.*, 2012). Yet the methods and content to achieve this rest on limited research. For example, Lazarus and Folkman's transactional model of stress encourages resilience and coping strategies regardless of context (Kabat-Zinn, 2013), while Selye's 'general adaptation syndrome' and 'stress response' re-enforce an individualised, cordoned-off stress physiology. Based on these models, TTPs typically instrumentalise mindfulness as a learnable skill (Arthington, 2016) or set of coping skills (Crane *et al.*, 2010; Woods, 2009). They prepare 'competent teachers' to assimilate learners into the system and train them to endure adversity uncritically. There is little regard that minoritised groups are resilient. Aside from eclipsing this reality, it seems that curricula attune to those for whom resilience, hardship, and challenge is something new.

When TTPs claim to be neutral they hide their implicit agendas, possibly because they are unaware of these. And when they fail to spell out their pedagogical frames, they repeat their non-disclosure of positionality. As a result, they are insufficiently investigated or critiqued (Cannon, 2016; Crane and Segal, 2016). A mindfulness pedagogy that refers only to teacher qualities, ethics, and educational methods such as experiential learning does so in isolation from the politically fractious contexts in which it operates, and certainly with no reference to Angela Black's earlier challenges. For instance, the focus on contemplative dialogue within TTPs fails to examine the pedagogical principles and assumptions that shape its application. Are these dialogues honed to hyper-individualism or social justice?

Similarly, formulators of the Mindfulness-Based Interventions: Teaching Assessment Criteria (MBI:TAC),[6] a teaching assessment instrument, draw on audit and competency literature but do not discuss their neoliberal frame. They function in the normative vacuum of conventional power. Writing from a critical perspective, educational theorists such as Funie Hsu (2016) and Richard Payne (2016) critique mindfulness for its neoliberal persuasions in school curricula, although they do not fully extend this to TTPs. Candice Brown (2016) addresses code-switching and the 'stealth' nature of TTPs in hiding their Buddhist component, while Jennifer Cannon (2016) takes issue with their missionary approach, which 'brings' mindfulness to 'needful' communities. Critiques such as these help us consider TTPs in relation to social justice, remembering that their 'apolitical' stance in fact camouflages their value-laden and politicised nature.

Critical pedagogies

Especially since White Mindfulness maintains a narrow, individualised focus, it is worth considering the pedagogical implications of a social justice purpose. A critical mindfulness pedagogy embraces Angela Black's questions of 'for and by whom' and integrates anti-discrimination and building belonging training. It requires a social justice paradigm, systemic change, collective buy-in, and a shift in mindset. But beyond this, in its role as 'disruptor' of inequalities and injustices, it abandons mindfulness as a behaviour management tool (Cannon, 2016: 402).

In contrast to White Mindfulness education, critical pedagogy foregrounds communal imagination, agency, and shared vision. It comprises a practice of social rather than individual freedom and allows education itself to seed freedom:

> The classroom with all its limitations remains a location of possibility. In that field of possibility, we have the opportunity to labour for freedom, to demand of ourselves and our comrades, an openness of mind and heart that allows us to face reality even as we collectively imagine ways to move beyond boundaries, to transgress. This is education as the practice of freedom.
>
> (hooks, 1994: 207)

Educationalist bell hooks identifies liberation pedagogy as a space in which any classroom can engage, especially one invested in freedom. Critical pedagogy couples communal learning and investigation with the potential creation of fair and just societies. In these contexts, critique is prized as a means through which minoritised groups organise, challenge, and overturn dominant power structures to implement corrective justice. In fact, because critical education is foundational to vibrant democracies, the absence of such a discourse in White Mindfulness makes its transformation near impossible.

Separate from corporate interests, universities and educational spaces have long been seen as bastions of critical thinking in which students learn to 'think critically, take imaginative risks, learn how to be moral witnesses, and procure the skills that enable [them] to connect to others in ways that strengthen the democratic polity' (Giroux, 2012: 30). Put another way, politically engaged education is one of the social pillars that challenge inequalities.

Critical pedagogy is aligned with political agency. Orienting mindfulness to a social justice purpose challenges normative pedagogies. It re-exposes the tension in addressing the symptoms rather than the causes of stress and suggests that critically trained teachers can bridge its gap from social justice. Opportunities for this shift abound. Writing in a higher education context in support of the paramount role of critique, Toni Morrison explains:

> If the university does not take seriously and rigorously its role as a guardian of wider civic freedoms, as interrogator of more and more complex ethical problems, as servant and preserver of deeper democratic practices, then some other regime or ménage of regimes will do it for us, in spite of us, and without us.
>
> (Morrison, 2001: 278)

Numerous mindfulness institutions occupy higher education locales conducive to the cultivation of critical discourse. According to Morrison, it is their duty to play a disruptive role in challenging inequalities and building democracies. Many institutions and academics embrace this challenge in defiance of the corporatisation of academia. Examples include the Othering and Belonging Institute at the University of California, Berkeley, and The Centre for Humanities Research at the University of the Western Cape, South Africa. When White Mindfulness TTPs train participants to expect gradual, peaceful change without disrupting established political systems or economies, they forego this social responsibility. They prop up the status quo and abandon their claims to encourage skilful responses to adversity. Without radical change, White Mindfulness facilitates 'a mindful America [that] will still be a consumerist, capitalist nation' (Wilson, 2014: 184). In other words, mindfulness TTPs that train obedience and self-regulation rather than critique further embroil the Mindfulness Industry in accentuating patriarchal, neoliberal attempts to create docile bodies and passive minorities (Sebastiaan, 2018). They deliver political apathy and disengagement by mainstreaming and marketing self-regulation geared to not disrupt the status quo. The mechanisms of its pedagogy, including 'apolitical' curricula, retreat, and White spaces, reconstitute society and mindfulness' White, middle-class demography. In this reality, claims of neutrality mask an invisible politics that cements power structures of whiteness and non-diversity that are plainly visible to critical thinkers and marginalised groups. Uncritical pedagogies allow TTPs to remain politically disengaged while reproducing exclusions.

Following hooks' earlier insight on the potential role of education and the possibilities presented by the classroom for team learning, Jennifer Cannon proposes a 'pedagogical orientation' that uncovers power and privilege and discloses racism and other forms of discrimination. Such a training possesses the potential for social liberation. It exposes the 'White saviour trope',[7] which reinforms a mindset in which White people save 'needful' GM communities. For this to materialise, teachers require training in critical theory to engage fully with social, economic, and environmental concerns.

Critical race theory and intersectional training is threatening to right-leaning governments. By incorporating this education purposed for freedom, mindfulness can radically disrupt the form of self-regulation that ties it to neoliberalism. It can also address structural power, inequalities, and appropriate models of stress that better prepare teachers generally – and White teachers specifically – for solidarity, allyship, and actionable transformation. In Part III, I shift the needle further, arguing that mindfulness as liberation is not only forging agency for external transformation. Liberation is tied to becoming free of the very conditioning and constructs that create Othering and vulnerabilities in the first instance. Because our freedoms are bound together, this kind of training, like regulation, must be communal. It can only arise collectively.

Educational training in the Mindfulness Industry is currently devoid of the political or social justice training that turns mindfulness into a radical force. Teachers do not receive social liberation pedagogy, and in the current system, they are not meant to. Instead, any politically informed mindfulness is considered individually inspired. The suggestions from a senior White Mindfulness pedagogue that 'what people do with mindfulness is up to them. We certainly don't tell them how to think' implies that mindfulness education fosters or is at least open to critical thought. At the same time, it suggests that silence around the politics of stress and the absence of debate is inferred as 'objective' and 'neutral'. In contexts of growing inequalities and power-over, silence is more likely to mean acquiescence, especially when, despite claims of an inherent ethics, TTPs habituate individuals to political adversity (see Walsh, 2016; Stanley, 2012). The argument that mindfulness cannot change politics completely disregards the political role it plays in sustaining the status quo and systemic inequalities.

The writing on the wall: metrification, audit culture, and sameness

As the Mindfulness Industry took root and flourished, so did the demand for TT. This in turn bolstered relations between TTP providers across the Atlantic. Their mutual White Mindfulness ethos consolidated their shared pedagogical frame devoid of pro-justice aspirations. Collaboration reinforced White norms, postracial approaches to TTP development, and, subsequently, ongoing exclusions. Oblivious to their own widespread defaults and inherent politics, educators identified problems with standardisation that had little to do with race, gender, and difference. Instead, their frame spotted a tension between the demands of the 'medical, scientific paradigm' with its emphasis on 'cost-effective interventions', 'health outcomes', and an 'evidence-base', and the 'meditative contemplative paradigm' that emphasises 'non-attachment to outcome', 'non-striving', the benefits of cultivating attitudes that navigate challenges with acceptance. Highlighting the disparity between a research paradigm that emphasises measurement and outcome and one that is 'inherently unquantifiable', identified only a quant-qual tension (Crane *et al.*, 2010: 76). Detecting the square peg-round hole problem is where the tension ended. There was no opening to intersecting complexities such as richly diverse audiences, the purpose of mindfulness in the West, or questions of positionality. Nor was there any recognition that metrification, although it can have uses, is part of a neoliberal, corporatised auditing trend.

Juxtaposing quantifiable and qualitative aspects of the Mindfulness Industry without paying attention to diversity and inclusion or the socio-economic component of illness is notable. Diversity or a lack thereof is both measurable and normative, but there is a persistent reluctance to understand why it is neglected. It is simply not on the agenda and a difficulty either not worthy of attention or one that has missed the radar altogether. Instead, the quant-qual framing demonstrates how TTP designers come to bypass the politics that underpins the sector. Although they acknowledge the irreducibility of the qualities of the teacher, they take for granted the conditioned politics and social norms that teachers and teacher trainers come to embody, regarding these as unproblematic. In other words, oblivious to how their power is constructed, pedagogues believe themselves capable of 'objectivity' and 'neutrality'. Unlike Ohanian's public declaration of positionality and power as a White man and his inherent racism growing up with systemic privilege, White Mindfulness pedagogues remain silent. Their unrecognised privileges, qualities, and norms constitute TTP designs and outcomes.

By focusing on the immeasurability of teacher qualities like embodiment, designers bypass inputs and outcomes that reify whiteness. Their very power to be in positions to create these programmes in the first instance uncritically repeats itself. Attempts to reconcile the identified competing interests of metrics and the cultivation of 'qualities' yet again denies and represses questions about what mindfulness is being used to do and by whom. TTPs' diversity-poor approaches fail prospective GM teachers from the outset. In fact, it fails all new teachers who come into a fractious context that does not benefit anyone and that keeps blinkers firmly in place.

Mindfulness pedagogy continues to emphasise the individual's inner journey, projecting a level playing field on which participants are regarded as equal. In trainings, whether stress arises from microaggressions experienced within the mindfulness space or the disappointment of a cancelled holiday, participants are regarded as dealing with the same stress physiology. This insistence on 'sameness' stems from the one-size-fits-all idea: mindfulness programmes are, after all, differentiated by medical conditions not by political difference. Accordingly, among all TTPs, inner-centred learning, non-hierarchical circles, not-knowing, tacit knowledge, and co-creation are words used to describe mindfulness spaces (McCown *et al.*, 2011). But these claims are commonly made by White Mindfulness educators unattuned to power dynamics. Their insistence on collapsing difference in the classroom further obscures mindfulness' politics and hides the underlying inequalities that beset the sector. They conceal the 'control of knowledge and power' – foundations which critical pedagogy would 'unmask'.

In contrast to the Mindfulness Industry, critical pedagogies have long framed health and education in political terms (Michelson, 2015; Berila, 2016). They expose the absence of a politicised stress or health discourse in neoliberal times and the distorted interpretations of health that wholly undermine communal wellbeing. Critical interrogation of 'worldly stress' exposes a growing emphasis on personal bionic resilience as an answer to advancing global stressors. Critics challenge precarity – the requirement that employees must become more stress-resistant and resourceful to hold down their jobs. Treating symptoms rather than alleviating root causes makes White Mindfulness an accessory to new public management strategies through which a corporatised, skills-based pedagogy frames individualised coping strategies as resourcefulness. By delegating responsibility for wellness to the individual, teachers become part of the neoliberal apparatus. Their celebration of individualised 'improvements' in turn reproduces cultures of commercialised wellbeing and undermines community resourcefulness, responsiveness, and resistance to growing dispossession. Being engulfed by neoliberalism in this way limits White Mindfulness' social justice prospects.

As a medicalised therapy, White Mindfulness has undoubtedly helped many individuals cope better in an increasingly polarised world. Unfortunately, this does not contradict the ease with which the industry conforms to postracial neoliberal societies, and the role education plays to help it do so. With growing coverage of the BLM movement and pressure from the business world for industries to diversify in order to improve performance, White Mindfulness has a long way to go to unravel its sticky whiteness problem. While it does so, the world around it is changing. As the industry's pedagogy remains uncritical, growing social movements are re-posing and actioning Angela Davis's, Funie Hsu's, Angela Black's, and the Radical Dharma movement's inquiries into the relationship between mindfulness and social justice. The difference this time round is that the questioners are not awaiting the Mindfulness Industry's responses. New initiatives are being forged in different directions and away from the conventional concentrations of power.

Notes

1 The focus on Selye's work offers a good example of the value-laden nature of research which is projected as neutral and value-free. It fails to account for differences in context and in how bodies relate to adversity. More complex models are presented by experts like Nkem Ndefo, Stacie Haines, and Sarā King.

2 STEM subjects are science, technology, engineering, and mathematics.

3 Ohanian's tweet reads: 'I have resigned as a member of the Reddit board, I have urged them to fill my seat with a [B]lack candidate, + I will use future gains on my Reddit stock to serve the [B]lack community, chiefly to curb racial hate' (Ohanian, 2020).

4 Know your Rights Camp, co-founded by Colin Kaepernick, can be found at: www.knowyourrightscamp.com.

5 As Lavelle reminds us, 'universal rhetoric tends to privilege highly individualized descriptions of suffering and health, thereby eschewing social and systemic causes of suffering' (Lavelle, 2016: 233).

6 The MBI:TAC was developed through collaboration within a network of TT organisations, initially in the UK and then between the US and UK. It was first published in 2012 (Crane *et al.*, 2012; 2013).

7 Cannon draws on Freire to expand the concept of solidarity: 'Freire describes solidarity as standing with oppressed communities in their own liberation struggle, rather than extending "false generosity," acts of charity or service that perpetuate domination' (Cannon, 2016: 406).

6

Corporatising education: metrics, tools, and neoliberal skills

> Critical consciousness must deal with a multiplicity of issues – how gender is racialised in particular ways, how race is gendered, how heteronormativity takes particular forms in relation to gender, race, disability, and so on ... Critical consciousness, at its best, strives to keep asking questions across difference and does not pretend to have settled everything.
>
> Carol Moeller (2019: 194)

When groups organise and think collectively across difference, they defy the barriers that repressive societies use to divide and rule and exclude. In 1980s Thatcherite Britain, a London-based LGBT+ group campaigned for the rights of coal miners striking in Wales for better wages. They decided to come out in support of the miners, noting the commonality in their causes and how the government was denying both groups their rights. Forming Lesbians and Gays Support Miners (LGSM), they proceeded to raise funds that they delivered in person to a Welsh village.

The 2014 movie *Pride* portrays the power and creation of solidarity. It shows how solidarity poses a threat to a governmental regime set to fragment and destroy its opposition or those it wishes to marginalise and control. The historical comedy-drama tells the story of the alliance between miners and the LGBT+ London-based group. The mining community must overcome bigotry and bumps in the road. As they do, they build a cross-sectoral unity and unstoppable solidarity initiated by the LGSM. The miners and their families return the favour of solidarity when they come out in support of the LGBT+ community's Pride march. Coming under pressure from the National Union of Miners, the Labour Party incorporates LGBT+ rights in their programme.

This seemingly unlikely coupling creates a critical discourse that challenges Thatcher's 1980s right-wing government from multiple angles – both on the grounds of miners' rights and LGBT+ rights. Such rich fusions spark possibilities for change brought about through united collectives. They showcase the power of unity and expose the weaknesses in systems premised on Othering. These are, after all, regimes built on unfairness, untruths, and externalisation of their own insecurities. Much as these governments fortify themselves militarily, their very premise of Othering marks an unsustainable weakness.

Critical consciousness, says Carol Moeller in the epigraph, revolves around leveraging difference and intersectionality. It opens opportunities for disruption and removing the rigid, neat categorisations of difference that give authorities power. Such critical action as we see in *Pride* transgresses and troubles norms. It questions and defies classifications and mechanisms that reproduce dominant power. Intersectional action gradually unpicks the levers of control that create exclusions and classifications in the first instance.

White Mindfulness, with its assertions of universality, claims to defy exclusion: everyone after all is treated equally. Yet as Ramón Grosfoguel, the decolonial theorist, tells us, the academic canon in the social sciences draws primarily on a few White men in five countries who assert their knowledge as universal.[1] As Kucinskas shows in her research, the Mindfulness Industry echoes this elitism. Its edicts hide its cultural appropriation, authoritarianism, and whiteness. Education and training play an important role in the pretence of sameness and the performance of equality. In fact, White Mindfulness' pedagogical mechanisms further bind it to the instruments of postracial neoliberalism.

One form of control educational authorities use is to regulate an uncritical pedagogy that props up the status quo. Another is to adopt instruments that professionalise discriminatory practices. This chapter addresses the specifics of how audit culture and competency-based education shape Teacher Training Programmes (TTPs). They frame the production, measurement, and domestication of mindfulness teachers who reproduce normative values. I look especially at one such instrument, the Mindfulness-Based Interventions: Teaching Assessment Criteria (MBI:TAC or TAC), a primary measure of teacher competency which provides an example of squeezing mindfulness into a corporatised education and training system. Through this discussion I show that the omission of difference in White Mindfulness leads, in effect, to an embodiment of whiteness which becomes embedded in educational programming, thus re-informing elitism. This embodiment is overlooked, unseen, hidden, and silently reproduced through mechanisms like the TAC that appear to equalise and standardise the educational experience for aspirant mindfulness teachers.

Audit society, skills-based training, and social justice tensions

In neoliberal pedagogy, by which I mean a pedagogy in the service of neoliberal governance and values, shrinking states privatise services and values and replace a sense of the public good and community with individuals taking responsibility for themselves. This ideology promotes an 'utterly privatised ideal of freedom' (Apple, 2001: 55). As the free market increases corporatisation, new public management strategies shift the purpose of education from its public values designed to safeguard the common good, to market interests (Singh, 2011; Olssen and Peters, 2005). In this setting, contrary to Toni Morrison's forewarning, the role of universities morphs from critical engagement to the production of neoliberal subjects; teaching is no longer naturally aligned with social transformation but fosters elitism, individualism, and 'technologies of the self' (see Gonzalez-Calvo and Arias-Carballal, 2018: 413; Ng, 2016a: 139; Reveley, 2016: 498). These developments coincide with the diminishing yet increasingly urgent role of critical discourses and transformative education; it increasingly measures right performance and outcomes using tools and metrics. To embed its agenda, corporatised education adopts audit culture as a primary strategy of control.

Corporatised education instrumentalises being human, reducing it to a set of criteria and performance outcomes that deny the very histories that bring us to the point of grossly unequal societies. It flattens difference and makes 'clients' act in uniform fashion in the service of some 'greater good'. Compliant with these trends, White Mindfulness pedagogy comes to serve the skill requirements of knowledge societies in which knowledge extraction and control persist. Dressed up as 'apolitical', TTPs conform to values and trends that individualise and privatise freedom. Rather than support vibrant democracies and movements for social equality, TTPs which claim to subtly subvert corporate interests in effect serve these through skills-based education (Singh, 2011; Eaton, 2014; Davies, 2016). On closer examination, an inspection of what is being measured reveals a series of domains divorced from the values of social equality, access, and justice.

Given the extensive investment in deciding how to standardise TTPs, it could be said that critique is not altogether absent from the mindfulness sector; that it has played an important role in thinking through how best to help teachers attain minimum standards to build their proficiency. Critique, however, can be utilised in ways that do not disrupt social norms. It can function within what Ronald Barnett calls 'a horizon of utility; that is to say, critique is tolerated provided it points towards changes with a use-value ... located within ... relevant boundary conditions' (Barnett, 1994: 165). In other words, such inquiry is neither disruptive nor overly critical. It poses questions and provides answers 'within the boundary conditions' of White Mindfulness, making it acceptable and unthreatening.

Non-disruptive change validates rather than transforms the sector. Adjunctive diversity models that perpetuate normative White Mindfulness programmes serve as an example. Views that challenge the sector, on the other hand, are generally discouraged. The argument made in favour of adjunctive programmes is that centres can only offer what has been tested and scientifically endorsed. Central to this thinking is the belief in an uncompromised, objective scientific method. Further approaches such as co-creation through collaboration take time. They require flexibility, responsiveness, communal decision-making, and slowing down on the part of the provider to be guided by participants. Values-driven, aligned, vision-building programmes centre participant engagement in shaping the process. Audit culture, or audit, serves to preserve neoliberal arrangements of power, shifting societies increasingly towards 'metricated' futures (Singh, 2010: 193). Everything that can be measured and shown to entrench dominant power is assimilated; anything subversive is cordoned off, downplayed, overshadowed, or ignored.

Sketched in its political context, audit culture is typically associated with management, and functions to preserve power and control. It emerged in education as part of quality assurance to measure teaching performance, judge research quality, and assess institutional effectiveness. In other words, audit seeks to control and produce teachers who conform to systems of governance that domesticate them for the marketplace. Promoting quality rather than equality, audit and its purpose is largely unquestioned. And yet, instead of improving quality, 'a peculiarly coercive and disabling model of accountability has emerged' in which innovation, transformation, and radical change which defies the boundary conditions, if it can't be assimilated, is shut down (Shore and Wright, 1999: 557).

It is important to note that performance measurement is itself not new. Prior to outcomes-based education, as we've seen, rational, 'scientific' approaches were valued over traditions that could not be understood in Western terms. In other words, dominant systems have always found ways of measuring and assigning value and worthiness to knowledges that are extracted or essentialised. This process, after all, governs Orientalism, White supremacy, and heteropatriarchy. The only difference today is the degree to which audit is embraced by society at large and normalised as 'benign solutions to the problems of performance, management, and governance' (Singh, 2010: 192; Shore and Wright, 2015: 423). New specialisations, academic departments, structures, and consultants have sprung up. New quality assurance specialists with new 'expert knowledge' now classify how knowledges are structured and consumed. They consult and design institutional procedures and preside over 'new regulatory mechanisms and systems' judging those who conform or diverge from these. They administer their expertise to individuals keen to improve, self-regulate, and comply with the new norms. Called 'staff development trainers' and 'teaching quality assessors', they are bearers of a new education culture (Shore and Wright, 1999: 560). In its normalisation of 'new' knowledge, expertise, and authority, the rise of White Mindfulness conforms to audit's trajectory and norms. It too has audit experts, knowledge curators, programme designers, monitors, and consultants who oversee the regulation of TTPs.

White Mindfulness' teacher training (TT) architects, pedagogues, trainers, and supervisors are normalised as audit experts and guardians of mindfulness. Themselves leaders and decision-makers, they mostly preserve privileges, norms, and claims. In this way, the naturalisation of audit serves as another strategy that conceals power, reinforces dominant ideologies, and further entrenches hegemonies of control. Quality assurance, possibly unbeknownst to its designers, operates as a technology of exclusion, not of charlatans from whom the public are being kept safe, but of mindfulness teachers who subscribe to a social justice and community agenda, many of whom are PGM. One of the primary mechanisms through which White Mindfulness audits prospective trainers is the TAC.

The MBI:TAC

As demands for TT grew, the MBI:TAC set out to standardise TT assessment to ensure consistency of delivery (Crane *et al.*, 2010). As a respondent explained: 'it's a bit of a wild west out there in terms of teacher training with people setting up trainings without very much experience of their own. The university sector, working with the network, is building clarity around this'.[2] The clarity they sought came in the form of the TAC. In a further motivation, formulators expressed concern that 'second-generation' educators – those originally trained by first-generation mindfulness teachers – were less qualified than their predecessors. By implication, the TAC preserves TT in the image of its founders.

In efforts to measure teacher performance, 'highly experienced MBI teacher trainers' from a UK cross-institutional alliance designed the MBI:TAC (Crane *et al.*, 2013: 682–5). First published in 2012 to assess teacher adherence and competence in the delivery of Mindfulness-based Interventions (MBIs) (Crane *et al.*, 2016),[3] the instrument identifies six learning domains across which the trainee is assessed for competence. These domains assess the teacher's:

(i) coverage, pacing, and organisation of material and curricula; it considers faithfulness to the curriculum as well as flexibility and responsiveness, the teacher's level of organisation and the flow and pace of the session.
(ii) relational skills or the ability to convey course themes through interactive inquiry and didactic teaching; it also assesses authenticity and compassion, curiosity and mutuality, recognising the difficulty in measuring these.

(iii) embodiment of mindfulness and attitudinal foundations even though these are less easily measurable; this domain covers presence, focus, responsiveness, calm, and disposition.

(iv) guidance of mindfulness practices and use of clear, precise language to convey key learnings such as where to place attention, how to work with the wandering mind, and how to cultivate the attitudinal foundations.

(v) ability to convey course themes fluently through interactive inquiry and didactic teaching including ability to train learners in noticing the facets and inter-relation of direct experience, convey learning and teaching skills.

(vi) group facilitation of the learning environment demonstrated through creating and sustaining a learning container of safety and confidentiality with clear boundaries that enables risk-taking and exploration; leadership capacity that shows authority, the ability to convey common humanity moving from personal to universal learning and opening the learning process towards universality.

Auditees' abilities in these domains are categorised according to six levels of competency. The idea is that trainees will progress from incompetent, through beginner, advanced beginner, competent, and proficient to advanced (Crane *et al.*, 2012; 2016). The instrument and its methods are presented as logical, rational, and comprehensive, providing an equal measure that does not discriminate between one teacher and another. It assumes an 'apolitical' power relation between the auditor and auditee and perpetuates the myths of an 'apolitical', ahistorical, and decontextualised mindfulness. Politics are ignored both in the formulation of the TAC and its application. Consequently, a myopic focus on standardising delivery ends up recycling the problems of mindfulness pedagogy.

Understanding how the TAC functions affords the opportunity to consider how things could be done differently. Given the reality of an audit culture that now grips education, such a discussion helps us inquire into the possible relation between quality assurance and social justice. It's worth asking if it might be possible to integrate race, gender, and social justice pedagogy within White Mindfulness' audit frame. But this requires understanding of the use of competencies in the development of the TAC.

Assessing competencies to measure people

The MBI:TAC uses competency-based education and training (CBET) as a way of standardising outcomes, achievements, and competencies for the mindfulness teacher. As more teachers trained, CBET was seen as an opportunity to replicate the styles and proficiencies of first-generation teachers. However, when this happens in racialised contexts replete with blind spots and biases, these become baked into the very instruments that are designed.

CBET governs performance- and outcomes-based teacher education; it claims to improve 'public accountability and control' (Hyland, 1994: 1). Yet historically, there was little research to support CBET's implementation in the early 1970s. Its supremacy over other teacher training approaches was unproven (Tuxworth, 1989). Still, the methodology grew prominent in the US and UK through advocacy of 'social efficiency', which, based in skills-training, sprang from expanding markets and a quest for increased worker efficiency. CBET draws on a German model of conservative social philosophy, stress-response psychology, industry needs, and supreme efficiency (Wirth, 1991). These principles reinforce education's link to industry, quality assurance, and market interests. In other words, CBET is a function of audit and corporatised education. It drives competency approaches that are usually expressed as simplistic behavioural outcomes. A critique of the 'so-called competency-based movement' notes that it has 'spawned mounds of curriculum formats ... devoid of any significant inputs from adult learners and teachers. They are characterised largely by ... simplistic behavioural objectives' (Collins, 1991: 90). A lack of co-creation reinforces authoritarianism while a behavioural change agenda conforms to hyper-individualisation.

Protagonists like Barnett concede that while competence is important for training doctors, accountants, engineers, and any discipline that requires precision, it can become problematic under certain circumstances. These include situations when 'competence becomes a dominant aim ... diminishing other worthwhile aims; or ... when competence is construed over-narrowly' (Barnett, 1994: 159). These two conditions provide a helpful frame for an MBI:TAC review.

As an audit instrument, the TAC conceals its own political orientation and does not engage social justice. It prioritises competence in chosen domains over transformation, fulfilling Barnett's first condition. Assessment is decontextualised both in relation to what is being assessed and by whom, and competence is treated as an end in itself. Of course, this poses the question: if there were a domain/s assessing socio-political competence, would this make the instrument more palatable? In other words, can the CBET framework be used to assess political understanding?

In succumbing to the drive to measure and quantify, MBI:TAC formulators state that efforts to standardise training result in manualising less quantifiable qualities of the teacher (Crane *et al.*, 2010). As a result, embodiment and authenticity – terms associated with the mindfulness teacher – are included in the instrument as objectifiable measures, satisfying Barnett's second condition. But these qualities, as shown before, are themselves conditioned, contextual, and contingent (see Mitra and Greenberg, 2016; Payne, 2016; Wilson, 2016).

Embodiment is intimately interwoven with alterity in that bodies are differently inscribed by social forces and conditions. The body is described as 'a discursive category, a site of struggle ... Pedagogies which are embodied ... involve a more complex understanding of how the body is culturally and socially constructed and experienced' (Butterwick and Selman, 2012: 66). Following this thought, residents in the US and UK already embody whiteness and related ideologies, albeit differently, through repeated exposure to norms of whiteness such as White spaces. Bearing in mind that borders are porous, the influences of whiteness of course spread beyond the constructed borders of these countries through all forms of media, foreign policies, proxy wars, and global pacts. Whiteness is expressed through inequalities, violence, injustices, vulnerabilities, privileges, entitlements, biases, blind spots, and Othering. Privilege, however, is protected or invisibilised through underpinning social norms that protect certain bodies by damning others (see Darder *et al.*, 2003; Sullivan, 2006). Black joy is not simply an antidote to White privilege but is rooted in long-standing traditions remembered in the body and invoked in community. In contexts of whiteness, White Mindfulness becomes part of its camouflage.

Uncritical mindfulness teachers, regardless of their ethnicity, embody an unfettered whiteness which is reinforced through a postracial TTP. They are trained to proclaim neutrality and promote ideologies that obscure difference. The embodiment being judged according to the TAC is a performance of an ahistorical, universalised, 'apolitical' mindfulness that fits the commercialised Mindfulness Industry. This mindfulness does not remember community, political context, and teachings of justice. In its role, it assesses the teacher in isolation from their contexts and histories as if they are discrete entities, unconditioned, objective, and unaffected by society. The MBI:TAC, in other words, anonymises and neutralises the mindfulness teacher. It evades questions around power generally, including the power dynamics of assessment.

White Mindfulness' political metrification and TINA

The MBI:TAC aims to preserve and standardise existing systems, methods, and practices. Like audit culture it is faithful to uncritical pedagogies, norms of whiteness, and a normative neoliberal education framework. Read in this way, the instrument pre-empts transformation because the purpose of preservation appears irreconcilable with social justice aspirations that address systemic change. Audit instruments embed teachers in a culture of regulation and compliance. Good practice guidelines and teachers' registers function as disciplinary gatekeepers for both teachers and training institutions. A lack of compliance prohibits membership of teaching networks.[4]

As an instrument that pretends to operate in a vacuum, the TAC has little sense of its own politics. Because it regards itself as 'apolitical', it assumes that teachers are objective, neutral bodies untainted by society. There is little awareness of the instrument's whitewashing role. In mental health settings, Linton and Walcott (2018) explain that patients or students resonate with health practitioners or teachers who share their racial/ethnic identity. Poet, playwright, and academic Yolanda Nieves shows the same 'recognition' and sense of 'knowing' in her work with other Puerto Rican women to tell the stories stored in their bodies (Nieves, 2012: 35). Yet in keeping with a culture of silence around identity, audit has not been applied to questions of diversity. Nor has it investigated teachers' cultural competence in relation to diverse audiences or social justice issues. By obscuring difference, formulators and hence teachers either fail to see or deny the impact of whiteness and will likely interpret prejudice in behavioural rather than structural terms.

Grosfoguel's statement that most of the academic canon is constructed by a few White men correlates with the figures Edward Said called Orientalism's 'inaugural heroes'. These figures are furthest removed from most people's everyday lives. In making the case for how distant the White Mindfulness curriculum is from the lived realities of PGM, Cannon notes that it neglects any critical inquiry into learners' 'socio-political conditions … poverty, institutional racism, the school-to-prison pipeline, or the multitude of reasons teenagers' may disrupt their learning. Nor is there any consideration of contemplative practices young people may already use at home or in their communities (Cannon, 2016: 403–4). Not only is the TAC devoid of such content or thought, the dominant culture constructs students also as 'defective and lacking' and excludes large 'groups of people from the political process where they might have a say in democratically determining what education should look like in their communities' (Ladson-Billings, 2007: 321). As with the critique levelled against CBET, there is no co-creation. Poor connection to broader thinking about changing the world stems from and reinforces an 'ivory tower' Mindfulness Industry delivered mostly by remote 'White saviours' and celebrated in much the same way as the elitist academic canon.

Audits claim to generate improved accountability to the public and the profession. All White Mindfulness teachers in the UK and US undergo assessments based either on the MBI:TAC or other models. Even though audit presents, at least to White Mindfulness, rational, academicised responses to standardisation, there is more to the story:

> [A]ccountability and transparency have been conceptualized in market-like terms, with the negative impacts of neoliberalism and audit regimes (e.g., work intensification, growing inequalities, anti-democratic practices) treated as externalities outside accounting's scope … Neoliberal reforms have been portrayed by their advocates as not only beneficial but as though there were no alternatives … People also understandably hesitate to look as though they are

against accountability, efficiency, and good governance, albeit that the real issue is arguably the need to contest the meanings ascribed to these concepts under neoliberalism and the related marginalization of other values (e.g., social justice, democratic participation, ecological sustainability).

(Shore and Wright, 2015: 432)

Shore and Wright capture Margaret Thatcher's famous TINA – 'there is no alternative' – making audit sound normal, worthwhile, and rational. It appears interested in the public good, even as the public good is eroded. But in addition, the quote reveals a tightening of the neoliberal grip through the use and appropriation of language as we saw with diversity. It puts critics on the back foot when they challenge terms like accountability, making them sound anti-accountability, anti-standardisation, and anti-competency. When audit appropriates terms like 'accountability', 'efficiency', and 'good governance', people become won over and seduced by what sounds not only reasonable but sensible. There is no recognition here of the grasp of whiteness.

Is the MBI:TAC simply a measure of performance?

The first MBI:TAC domain covers course content and delivery. It judges the trainee's skill in their interpretation of Buddhism and transmission of 'secular' material. Aside from the political nature of secularisation and appropriation, the ambivalent relationship with Buddhism complicates this domain. As one of my respondents says, the integration of Buddhism into mindfulness teaching generates its own difficulties:

> You are trying to turn [mindfulness teachers] into secular dharma teachers. If you look at people from my generation … we have gone through a huge amount of training. I didn't start teaching until the 80s and started practicing in 1970 and so I have this huge training and accumulated material, hearing it over and over again, and yet we're asking someone after – I don't know how many hours it works out at – to suddenly start being upfront in a fairly short period of time, to start conveying some of those meditative approaches in a traditional context that is usually only expected after a significant period of time, a long time.

This leads us back to the Buddhist critique of convert mindfulness: aside from questions of its cloaked nature and what exactly participants are being taught, there is a misalignment in the time required to cultivate understanding of Buddhism, and the speed with which mindfulness teachers become qualified. The MBI:TAC assumes that trainees can become proficient in Buddhism and mindfulness in relatively short periods of time. It considers it fair to assess their Buddhist comprehension even though the assessor may themselves not be Buddhist. The teacher is also expected to secularise Buddhist material, without attention to the politics and implications of secularisation, and almost more importantly, without regard for the interpretations of Buddhism they are taught.

The tension described above pertains to a TTP which initially favoured teachers with Buddhist training, even where this was uncritical of cultural appropriation. Over time, as the Mindfulness Industry exploded, trainees without foundations in Buddhism joined mindfulness organisations. A teacher trainer recollects:

> As time went on and mindfulness became more popular, people were coming in through professional doorways so it was all the different healing arts you might say but not necessarily with an understanding of the dharma and the roots that this whole programme rests on.

The problem with an uncritical, ahistorical lens is, in other words, compounded by a 'cramming of skills and understanding'. To support Buddhist training on TTPs, various documents such as Bob Stahl's *The Heart of the Dhamma* were used. In it, Stahl pinpoints expressions of the Four Noble Truths, the Three Marks of Existence, and the Four Foundations of Mindfulness in the eight-week curriculum (Stahl, n.d.; Brown, 2016: 81). This constituted sufficient evidence of MBSR's commitment to the programme's Buddhist underpinnings. Code-switching and camouflaging are thus embedded in the training process in multiple ways. Teachers themselves need to find ways to secularise their understanding of Buddhism as well as universalise and 'neutralise' the teachings, adding to multiple layers of complexity underpinning the stealth nature of White Mindfulness. When teacher trainers remain uncritical, they become complicit by default in instrumentalism, camouflage, and dishonesty about the messiness of White Mindfulness' history and its present-day uses.

Auditing the TAC itself

MBI:TAC functionality has been tested in two studies. The first, conducted in 2013, aimed to measure its reliability. The instrument was used by 16 assessors who evaluated 43 teachers (Crane *et al.*, 2013). In 2017, a further study deployed MBI:TAC to assess the effect of MBCT TT on participant outcome (Huijbers *et al.*, 2017). The 2013 study, undertaken by its formulators, found MBI:TAC to be a reliable tool for use in the assessment of MBSR and MBCT teachers. The 2017 study noted no significant correlation between competence and participant performance. Its authors explain that they found the tool to be less reliable than its founders did. They account for this discrepancy by saying that whereas the formulators of the TAC collaborated for a significant period – several years – they themselves had no prior experience 'with the instrument, were trained in MBCT at different institutes, were less acquainted with each other, and evaluated teachers of whose teaching they had no or little prior knowledge' (Huijbers *et al.*, 2017: 968).

This suggests that the MBI:TAC may not be a reliable measure when used outside the setting in which it was developed or when used by assessors who are not immersed in the culture in which it was developed. The 2017 authors also argue that MBCT's standardisation and manualisation, coupled with an emphasis on participant self-reliance, may diminish the role of the teacher: 'It is possible that the role of the teacher relative to the curriculum, the group, the mindfulness home practice, and the participants themselves is overestimated' (Huijbers *et al.*, 2017: 971). This opens new queries around the digitisation of mindfulness. Safiya Noble's *Algorithms of Oppression* (2018) suggests that the same pedagogues who embody whiteness, and who in this case generate White Mindfulness, will embed whiteness in digitised versions. White Mindfulness more than likely spreads whiteness through digital platforms.

Reservations of the TAC notwithstanding, to customise it for their own purposes, some organisations adapted the instrument giving priority to the 'soft qualities' of the teacher such as compassion, embodiment, and kindness. Again, the lack of inquiry into what is embodied and embedded is worrying in a context of uncritical pedagogy and the absence of positionality and reflection. This pertains even when the MBI:TAC plays a role alongside other methods. Outlining a multimodal approach to audit, a respondent says:

> [T]here are *ways to assess objectively* as well as subjectively the strength of a teacher ... who knows if it's good enough but it's good enough to begin. I think the fact that we can have some kind of standardisation, that we can look at MBSR teachers in Denmark and Sweden and Worcester and San Diego and Kalamazoo and South Africa would be of value. We'd learn something from employing it in some way. So, we are employing it here; we are employing it within our teacher training. But we are not relying on it as the central measure. We are saying it's one way [alongside] supervision by senior teachers, peer supervision, observation, reflection – these all play a part in this thing called the ongoing assessment and evaluation of an MBSR teacher without the MBI:TAC.

These reservations still assume assessor objectivity, although the respondent acknowledges positionality by naming subjectivity as part of the assessor–student engagement. Still, the overarching power structures governing context, processes, and curricula remain intact.

In another context, MBI:TAC remains integral to training: 'With escalating training demands, we use the MBI:TAC to make sure our assessment is standardised.' However, concerns include design flaws and the irreducibility of certain qualities:

> At the moment they are giving equal weighting to the various components. I was very much arguing a few years ago that embodied mindfulness is a huge part and should have a heavier weighting in it than some of the other elements. The ability to explain didactically is less important than the ability to explain what is going on in the mirroring when someone is actually giving a mindfulness approach in their being.

This highlights the extent of uniformity applied across qualities of the teacher which results when the rhetoric of universality is so well established that it frames uniformity and standardisation. Equalising the weighting of domains in the instrument mirrors also the rhetoric of sameness. Domains are given equal regard, differences among teachers flattened, and assessors regarded as 'apolitical' and unbiased experts.

Indicating the complexity of trying to measure what may be immeasurable, others express similar reservations: 'We are in discussion with ... colleagues about measuring embodiment ... we're not sure that's an easy undertaking'; 'We appreciate efforts to standardise assessment. It's difficult to evaluate teacher qualities and be fair when we are training people across different continents. However, we lose something when we put qualities into a grid'. All organisations expressed concern at the instrumentalisation of mindfulness. Yet in the same way that research supersedes teaching, audit takes precedence over the politics of mindfulness and teaching qualities. There is an assumption that qualities like empathy and compassion are independent of social norms. Healthy critique within the boundary conditions may open the door for more rigorous inquiry. When White Mindfulness entrenches itself ever more firmly in neoliberal education, Lorde's master's tools guideline weighs heavily in the absence of any inquiry into justice.

Despite reservations about its shortcomings and the opening for debate, the sector continues to use MBI:TAC and audit uncritically. In fact, a respondent indicates ongoing subscription to an audit culture:

> I think there are also more formalised potential accreditation processes that are being discussed. In the longer term, the MBI:TAC will have a role in that as well ... there might be different tiers of registration and teachers will have needed to be assessed by MBI:TAC to appear on the most prominent lists. In a sense, hopefully this will help to put pressure on those training organisations that are not in line with the Good Practice Guidelines of TT organisations to come into line with them.

Confirmed recourse to MBI:TAC reinforces a narrow view of assessment focused on norms and tighter controls. The framing of quality assurance prioritises the teacher's self-improvement in accordance with a narrow set of concerns. Domains that assess the teacher's cultural competence, anti-racism, critical thinking, and social values are glaringly absent. At the same time, claims of neutrality and an absence of social justice aspirations demonstrate the multiple ways in which White Mindfulness reproduces itself. Audit's disengagement from social justice polarises individual and collective care. In this way White Mindfulness seems to create a binary rather than a synergy between individual and collective action. This satisfies Barnett's second condition, in which competence reinforces a diminished, reduced version of mindfulness. Satisfaction of both Barnett's conditions suggests the need to reconsider quality assurance and to interrogate its purpose more fully and broadly.

Can quality assurance better serve White Mindfulness?

In defence of audit, some suggest that quality evaluations, rather than 'policing', promote self-reflection and the improvement of educationalists (Barnett, 1994). This view postulates an audit ideology of enhancement, betterment, and self-governance that resonates with the White Mindfulness sector. In contrast, a more critical perspective warns of audit bureaucratisation in academia and the instrumentalisation of learning itself. Here, audit does not necessarily lead to improvements, especially when designed by the architects of the systems they measure. Instead, they presume a naive positivistic link between the auditing agency and those being measured, producing hierarchical and paternalistic relationships of power between scrutiniser and observed (Harvey, 2006). This uneven relation is not dissimilar to that between teacher and learner in the classroom.

Student–teacher relationality is a contentious area. First, TTPs claim that skilled teacher trainers are guided by the innate wisdom of the learner. To quote Saki Santorelli, former director of the Centre for Mindfulness: 'The essence of mindfulness [is] to draw forth that which already is, rather than imagining that we must fill others or be filled from some outside source to be complete' (Santorelli, 1999: 82). In other words, there is an assumption that White Mindfulness education is liberatory rather than conformist. But as we see below, this presumes solidarity with a shared purpose of social liberation. There is little recognition that what is being 'drawn forth' is filtered through the teacher's lens.

Second, some challenge the assertion that mindfulness constitutes an equal, dialogical relationship between teacher and student. Based on research of an MBSR course, researchers Stanley and Longden (2016) believe that teachers are directive and subtly authoritative.[5] Their findings reflect the complexity of mutual learning and the absence of critical inquiry into the educational process itself. They highlight a disparity between the characterisation in TT manuals, conduct within TTPs, and mindfulness programmes.

Third, in White Mindfulness' hyper-individualised culture, mindfulness teachers constitute social units of measurement. As such they are constantly audited and encouraged to self-audit to enhance their performance and output. Set within an asymmetrical power relation, as opposed to Santorelli's flattened structure, the auditee aims to fulfil requirements set by an 'expert' who then scrutinises and grades them (Shore and Wright, 1999). This approach conforms to Paulo Freire's 'banking education model': invested with superior knowledge and expertise, the mindfulness trainer deposits their knowledge in 'deficit' trainees (Freire, 1993: 53; Cannon, 2016: 402). In contrast to mindfulness' 'impartial' politics, Freire's *Pedagogy of the Oppressed* (1993) foregrounds liberation, the role of solidarity in the cultivation of education as the practice of freedom, and education's purpose to eradicate social inequalities and cultivate vibrant democracies. Despite the stark distinction between its hyper-individualism and Freire's collective liberation, White Mindfulness pedagogy seeks to align itself with an education of liberation and believes that its curricula are co-created and that social change will come about through a ripple effect of compassion (Santorelli, 1999). These assertions make for uncomfortable discussion of what White Mindfulness thinks it does as opposed to what it actually does.

Can audit serve a social justice agenda?

Considering White Mindfulness' entrenched audit culture, a pedagogy of freedom requires calibration of new public management strategies with equity. Is it possible for metrics, transparency, and accountability on the one hand to coalesce with a politicised mindfulness geared to fulfil a social justice purpose on the other? Their directions appear diametrically opposed: audit aims at personal self-improvement of the neoliberal subject; social justice is a political project that aims to redistribute power.

Few examples exist of collaboration between quality assurance and social justice wherein audits remedy intersectional exclusions. South Africa's post-apartheid educational reforms provide evidence of integrating social justice and transformation goals into quality assurance systems. The example reinterprets quality assurance and educational effectiveness in the interests of social transformation.[6] It highlights tremendous challenges because of trying to merge a progressive, emancipatory agenda with neoliberal intent and values. Nonetheless, I apply the South African experience to White Mindfulness.

The South African education system found that articulating 'quality' with social purpose demands a policy framework that centres ethics and calls for equity and societal transformation. Such a shift requires the production of new curricula and pedagogies that prioritise systems change. It also needs to interrogate the ways unjust institutional systems that inform educational experiences and outcomes become prominent in the first instance. In other words, radical change would have to consider the stickiness of social norms. Such a framework would need to value and leverage diversity in all its forms. It would also embrace changes in institutional cultures, curricula reforms, innovative scholarship, and academic freedom, and establish education as a public good (Lange and Singh, 2010). To learn from this example, TTPs would need to prepare teachers through pedagogies geared towards social transformation. Teacher trainees would require competencies to live, work, make choices, and act in diverse educational settings. This requires an education that dismantles underlying ideologies of Othering.

Social mindfulness would centre the traditions, cultures, strengths, and interests of communities, highlight how mindfulness features in these, and integrate any additional practices appropriately. Research ambitions would serve social rather than individual output measures. These requirements, in turn, call for critical philosophies and pedagogies. To bring about reform of this nature, any intervention would constantly be reviewed for its 'fitness of purpose' in social justice terms. It would entail systemic changes that uproot convert mindfulness' whiteness, challenge foundational claims of neutrality, universality, authority, and expertise, and foreground community. It would also have to interrogate the roots of mindfulness and ensure that it is correcting injustices and not generating further harm. Such dramatic changes pose legitimate questions of power. Who develops curricula and how? Who reviews and changes them? Can these shifts themselves foster inclusion and reduce fractures and chasms?

Aspirational justice

Instrumentalist strategies that adjust for representation without changing underpinning ideologies do not address diversity deficits. Affirmative action programmes, for instance, commonly constitute non-performatives. These programmes fail to engage the diverse expertise and knowledge that increased representation may bring. The eradication of systemically embedded cultures of Othering is essential to achieve a sector able to grow from difference and innovation. By the same token, inclusion does not necessarily enhance equality. In fact, they share an ambivalent relationship, and we must ask what systems and values people are being subsumed into. Is inclusion a form of assimilation on the terms of dominant power or does it signal a systemic shift that hints at the potential to create spaces of belonging for all? In other words, cosmetic reforms can use 'inclusion' to maintain unequal power and bypass systemic transformation. The inclusion of minorities into current power configurations will fail to induce significant changes if they reinforce dominant ways of thinking. It is only systemic transformation that can challenge the tacit ideologies of whiteness that sabotage social justice.

Within the frame of White Mindfulness, without a critical approach to transformation, adjunctive diversity strategies comprise non-performatives. Improving the intake of GM teacher trainers and trainees under current conditions puts a new face to the same problem. It is performative in that it constitutes window-dressing and suggests that social justice innovation compels policy, pedagogy, and curricula disruption of the order of decolonisation rather than diversification (see Arday and Mirza, 2018; Bhambra *et al.*, 2018). Such radical change requires quality assurance modalities designed to achieve social justice in the long term. This necessarily challenges the confines of bounded critique.

In much the same way that White Mindfulness assumes the ideologies of neoliberalism and postracialism, audit culture, focused on the individual as a social unit of measurement, depoliticises and decontextualises assessment, perpetuating social norms and defaults. There is scope to broaden the instrumentalist view since the CBET field recognises the need for a 'more holistic model which identifies the role played by knowledge, understanding and context in the assessment of competence' (Hyland, 1994: 23). A shift would place social justice centre stage.

Many questions remain including whether it is possible to re-imagine methods of training and assessment that draw on the knowledge and skills of prospective teachers, and what comprises a decolonised TTP that is inclusive and driven by fairness and justice.

Notes

1 It is considered normal to have Western men from only five countries produce the canons of thought in all the academic disciplines of the Westernised university. Grosfoguel suggests that there is no scandal in this because it reflects the normalised racist/sexist epistemic structures of knowledge of the modern/colonial world (Grosfoguel, 2013: 74).

2 In the UK, standardisation was tied to the Mindfulness Initiative's attempts to train enough teachers to respond to anticipated demands for programmes to be delivered through the NHS and schools and in prisons (Loughton and Morden 2015). In the US, quality assurance training was emphasised to secure insurance for teachers.

3 The Dreyfus and Dreyfus (1986) competency scale, further developed by Sharpless and Barber (2009) in the evaluation of psychologists, underpins the tool's production (Crane *et al.*, 2013: 2).

4 In 2019, the British Association of Mindfulness-Based Approaches replaced the UK Network for Mindfulness-Based Teacher Training Organisations. It oversees good practice guidelines which teachers uphold to be listed on the teachers' register. In the US teachers are credentialled by their training centres to teach.

5 Stanley and Longden explain: 'Three-turn sequences are one of the most familiar organisations of pedagogical discourse (Lee, 2007). Often referred to as Initiation–Response–Evaluation (IRE) sequences, they take place when the teacher poses a question, listens to a response from a member of the group and feeds back with what may be viewed, on a superficial level, as a summary or confirmation of what they have heard ... formulations have been defined as a method of con-tinuously and actively listening to, evaluating and interpreting talk,

while simultaneously creating an opportunity for the speaker to omit certain parts of an account and to emphasise other parts, to advance their own institutional interests'. They explain that teachers learn to repeat certain words back to learners and omit others to convey their chosen teaching points: 'Formulations are the means by which mindfulness teachers transform the accounts given by participants in order that they fit the pedagogic and institutional aims of the course' (Stanley and Longden, 2016: 312–13).

6 The interests of new public management and social justice are commonly antagonistic. As Singh explains: 'The challenge [in South Africa] was to develop a workable fit between the neo-liberal lineages and functions of quality assurance and a local emancipatory agenda which stressed social justice and social transformation. There were potential gains from using a social transformation agenda to mediate and re-orientate what is usually regarded as a new public management strategy but the broader, more progressive intent linked to the transformation agenda was, in turn, likely to be vulnerable to and in danger of being eclipsed by the origins, lineages, values and effects of traditional quality assurance' (Singh, 2011: 490).

Part III

Embodying justice, changing worlds

7

White Mindfulness, Black Lives Matter, and social transformation

What if the way we respond to the crisis is part of the crisis ...
resistance not only feels inadequate to the task of decoloniality but
programmatically linked to the continuity of the status quo.

Báyò Akómoláfé (2021)

Social change is not always planned. In March 2015, students at the
University of Cape Town, South Africa, birthed the Rhodes Must
Fall campaign after a student threw faeces at the bronze statue of
White supremacist and imperialist, Cecil Rhodes. Within a month,
the statue was taken down, but the protests galvanised global
action, awakening similar acts against institutional racism. Birthing
the Fees Must Fall movement in October that year, students called
for the removal of colonial symbols, opening of universities to
students from historically disadvantaged communities, and institutional and curricula changes. What is now known as the Fallist
movement – a term coined by female activists – spread through the
global South and North, seeding multiple studies and actions that
are expanding the decolonial focus.

Global decolonial movements reverberated in the US and UK, the
birthplace of White Mindfulness. More specifically, they birthed, for
example, Oxford University's Rhodes Must Fall campaign linking
education to empire, Georgetown University's plans to redress its ties
with slavery (Swarns, 2016), the UK National Union of Students'
campaigns Why is My Curriculum White? (El Magd, 2016)
and LiberateMyDegree. Edited works include *Decolonising the
University* (Bhambra *et al.*, 2018) and *Dismantling Race in Higher
Education* (Arday and Mirza, 2018). These historic developments,
in tandem with the Black Lives Matter (BLM) movement, demonstrate a keenness to dismantle de facto apartheid as it continues to

present itself as a colonial hangover. Adding tremendous value in pushing forward debate, action, and agendas on what decolonisation constitutes reveals the inadequacy of using an equity, diversity, and inclusion (EDI) or diversity, equity, and inclusion (DEI) frame to promote transformation.[1] DEI/EDI's euphemistic attempts at change tend to produce nip-and-tuck cosmetic changes that sustain underlying philosophies and politics even when these are unknown to their perpetrators.

In the build-up to the Cop26 gathering, activist Greta Thunberg (2021), although unconcerned with coloniality, challenged world leaders for their talk of 'build back better, green economies, and net zero by 25', reducing their words to nothing more than words, or in her critique, 'blah, blah, blah'. Her challenge to act to stop the human destruction of the earth and to bring about the changes needed to sustain life on earth echoes talk of diversification within the world of White Mindfulness and repeated failures to make progress beyond paying lip service or making cosmetic changes. The earlier parts of this book have shown how such intransigence comes about. So ingrained is White Mindfulness in the systems in which it swims, it makes disentanglement from the tides appear impossible. In fact, so successful is the social saturation of White Mindfulness that the term is used today without reference to Buddhism. Mindfulness is referred to as if there is only one type – the now fully modernised Western version. It is Buddhist forms of mindfulness that must now distinguish themselves from commercialised models and the Westernisation of its knowledges.

Lorde's master's tools challenge echoes loudly in Part II, which reveals pedagogies entwined in audit cultures in service of an education that lacks critique. In the quest to escalate the spread of mindfulness, dissociation from widening systemic cracks has helped mainstream White Mindfulness. As a result, even though we can outline the possibility of merging audit and social justice agendas, incentive to do so may well be lacking. More importantly, it is unclear how a decolonised White Mindfulness might serve processes of transformative justice.

This part of the book attempts to break free of bifurcations, binaries, and polarities to appreciate a both/and perspective. Communities can be both politically underserved and marginalised and culturally rich in tradition, social, and network capital. By the same token, communities that are socio-economically and/or politically privileged can be culturally impoverished and stripped of their humanity which pivots on the deprivation of marginalised groups and communities. This is not to suggest a flattening of different experiences of power. On the contrary, it serves as a reminder that the greed behind cultural appropriation and the rapacious looting of lands and people over centuries has hidden deep within it fragility, divisiveness, and the absence of integrity. Such revelations do not centre whiteness but recognise its complete incapacity to transform itself, let alone act in the service of People of the Global Majority (PGM). The building of inclusive futures entails the dismantling of dominant ways of seeing and being from the vantage point of freedom. Decolonisation is only one part of liberation.

This chapter looks at why decolonisation is gaining traction. It asks questions of White Mindfulness to understand its incentives and prospects for change. To address these questions, it looks more carefully at its conceptual basis through Kabat-Zinn's 'second Renaissance' thesis. This inquiry reveals a troubled, contested concept. While the previous parts of this book have carefully mapped the rise and fortification of White Mindfulness via Othering, whiteness, uncritical pedagogies, and neoliberal curricula, I have spent little time on the concept of mindfulness itself. Much has been written on this, especially with regard to deracination and consumerism. I consider it more closely to understand its construction in whiteness and its conceptual distance from PGM and minoritised groups.

Kabat-Zinn's 'second Renaissance' thought underpins his reconceptualisation of mindfulness, which becomes more politicised over time. My intention is to determine whether the shifting sands of White Mindfulness open possible doorways to advance a social justice agenda. I believe that this deeper dive gives some insight into what decolonisation in this context must address and entail, even though it is unclear what a decolonised practice of mindfulness is, or what it might look like.

A closer look at decolonisation

Decolonisation is both theory and praxis that is critical and creative. It guides processes of transformation that involve legislative change as power shifts either from one dispensation to another or as new policies and practices emerge through unchanged power structures.[2] But in the quest for freedom, decoloniality inevitably comes up against the strong imprint colonialism leaves in its wake. It builds on multiple forms of resistance to colonial rule while acknowledging the ways in which colonialism remains imprinted in ideologies and systems that seep into society and blend into normative ways of thinking, seeing, and being. White supremacy, whiteness, advancing forms of capitalism, neoliberalism, and postracialism are all forms built on and benefiting from the colonial project. These isolate individuals, generate insecurities, anxieties, precarity, and isolation, and, in relation to mindfulness, induce a sense of wellness as 'me-first' and 'time-out'.

The practice of decolonisation takes on the disruption and dismantling of such ideologies deeply ingrained in social structures, economies, legislation, policies, policing, the media, and systems of education and health. It exposes ways in which constructs such as race serve particular interests and helps us question how our own constructs, realities, and worlds take shape. When tackling the education sector, for instance, the practice includes disrupting entrenched whiteness in structural power, research and scientific paradigms, and curricula often steeped in Eurocentric eighteenth-century Enlightenment thought. It also challenges our acceptance of these constructs and philosophies.

At a personal and collective level, decoloniality invites other, often Indigenous or innate, ways of seeing that bring completely different perspectives to the solution space. It questions the Western notion of the individual as a 'distinct entity', offering instead a view of entanglement and constantly becoming (see Akómoláfé, 2021; Hall, 1987). Decolonial praxis presents alternative ways of being in the world and embraces cosmologies, relationships to the land, Indigenous paradigms, methodologies, and psyches. Drawing on Patrice Maidona Somé's writings on the Dayara people of West Africa, anthropologist and abolitionist Karine Bell (2021) explains: 'Indigenous psychologies often reflect an entangled and relational universe of which we are but one element. Not supreme within it, but in relationship' to it. Such a frame provides a much wider perspective from which to consider White Mindfulness' disentanglement.

One of the ways postcolonialism shifts systems, ideas, and thought is by 'writing back' to persistent colonial narratives and ideas about histories, people, and cultures. This practice constitutes Hall's endless 'becoming' referred to in Chapter 4. It takes form as generative thought, ideas, and enterprises that offer different perspectives and new ways of narrating and being. For our purposes, this form of disruption illuminates the contested spaces in which White Mindfulness emerges and evolves. Writing back does more than register vocal discontent with historic accounts and systemic inequities. It opens possibilities that embrace the convergence of mindfulness with other initiatives and justice agendas. Following hooks' description of 'appreciation', it points the uses of mindfulness and other contemplative traditions towards social transformation and redress of systemic imbalances.

New, evolving ideas of wellness based in communal and collective thought and Indigenous rather than consumerist cultures are reviving notions of care. Importantly, the bearers of these traditions are also today's innovators, centring and honouring their traditions in the ways they write back. In the epigraph, author, speaker, and trans-public intellectual Báyò Akómoláfé encourages an opening to possibilities that don't centre colonialism. He talks about turning to the cracks, understanding the individual and their experiences as communal rather than isolated, and paying attention to the living universe. His cosmological view awakens reconnection and recalibration of the person as an integral part of a vital, vibrant, unbounded cosmic system. It disrupts hyper-individualism.

White Mindfulness and decolonisation

The first free democratic elections in South Africa followed a long-fought battle for freedom in which many people, young and old, sacrificed and lost their lives for collective liberation. These heroes challenged the 'put your own oxygen mask on first' culture of White Mindfulness. Despite their sacrifice, lives continue to be thwarted by systemic exploitation and the oppression of most South Africans. Sisonke Msimang (2021) describes the desperate lives of many people living on the brink of an untenable lack of services, increasing violence, poverty, and gross neglect, their voices ignored. They are asked to be a bit more understanding and to await change for a little longer, as the gulf between rich and poor widens. Patience is familiar to the lexicon of White Mindfulness. But this story is not unique to South Africa. It is as alive in the US and UK, with growing underserved communities slipping further into poverty. And it is in such circumstances that there is uncertainty about how White Mindfulness can support a social justice agenda and avoid a repeat of the Heygate residents' experience discussed in the Introduction. Can mindfulness as a practice of freedom support decolonising society and ourselves to change the world, or will decolonial processes side-step White Mindfulness entirely?

At a time of rising inequalities, bar a few pro-Black Lives Matter (BLM) statements posted on websites, White Mindfulness institutions remain silent on the conditions, norms, and constructs that feed and perpetuate White supremacy. Their silence continues to erase minoritised experiences and White privilege. Performative acts help them continue to bypass coloniality.

The work of decolonising White Mindfulness, if such a thing is possible, confronts the problem of bifurcation and binaries. The concepts that allow us to deliberate this world of colonisation-decolonisation makes positions and experiences sound fixed and exact. For example, the terms privilege and marginalisation start from the socio-political and economic vantage point of hegemonic power. It measures privilege in relation to the centre of that power which in our context is the source of whiteness and White supremacy. While this lens is helpful in clarifying dominance, authoritarianism, positionality, and control, it becomes unhelpful when casting the margins only in these terms. We saw this with the need to subvert the colonial and the White gaze and with Black joy. The notion of 'becoming' allows for constant meaning-making as we navigate the world. It helps avoid the pitfalls of a 'them-and-us' polarisation and opens us to ask whether those who find White Mindfulness helpful can become more interested in broader social change.

A postcolonial perspective on the realities of colonialism reminds us of the enduring nature of its imprints. The construct of race imprints on the psyche, becomes normative, and is reinforced daily by structural power and the circulation of racist ideology. Writing back claims the space to tell these histories from the perspective of those who stand in a different power. The presence of such a mindfulness in organisations such as the East Bay Meditation Centre (EBMC), the Buddhist Peace Fellowship, the Buddhist Global Relief (BGR) programme, and the Radical Dharma movement suggests that writing back is well underway. These organisations centre justice at collective, communal, social, institutional, systemic, and planetary levels rather than a one-size-fits-all strategy. They leverage difference for purposes of transforming all bodies, ecosystems, and the planet.

The prevalence of such initiatives points to a liberatory mindfulness that is embedded in a larger vision of freedom, not as an end goal but as a process of ongoing emergence. It also suggests that such mindfulness may not be commodifiable, that it may be found in multiple traditions, that it bends to freedom taking form according to context. In case this is beginning to sound like the commercialised version of mindfulness that could mean anything to anyone, the examples cited are clear on their purpose in service of political and socio-economic transformation. They are not imagining justice in the image of coloniality but in new terms unfettered by the constraints of dominant power.

The White Mindfulness brand

To consider whether a commitment to social transformation is likely to spread, it is worth remembering that White Mindfulness mimics the 'Americanisation' of Buddhism, constituting a consumable embedded in the Western middle- and upper-class psyche. Its popularisation follows a marketing strategy:

> [F]irst Buddhism is made palatable via mindfulness in order to sell Buddhism, then mindfulness is made palatable via eliminating Buddhism in order to sell mindfulness, then mindfulness is so appealing and denatured that it can be used to sell other products, such as financial services, vacations, clothing, computer software, etc. ... it promises everything: it can allegedly improve any conceivable activity and provide unlimited practical benefits. Perhaps it can even save the world.
>
> (Wilson, 2014: 73)

This process normalises a commercialised mindfulness and legitimises its appropriation. It is now, says independent scholar

Wakoh Shannon Hickey, 'trans-religious, trans-cultural and trans-historic' in the ways it erases past injustices and simultaneously authorises interlocutors with expertise and power to present their socio-cultural, historical viewpoints as universal (Hickey, 2010: 172–3).[3] As a consumer-based product it normalises a brand, while it appropriates, exoticises, and marginalises. In a two-for-one deal, the consumer imbibes both the new brand of White Mindfulness that brings happiness as well as its invisible ideological undergirding of whiteness, individualisation, patriarchy, and postracialism.

The White Mindfulness brand departs from Buddhist doctrine but conveniently dips in and out of it. Commenting on his own experiences of Western vipassanā teachings, the Western-born Buddhist monk Bikkhu Bodhi, founder of BGR, describes the Westernised linkages between mindfulness, happiness, and this-worldliness in contrast to his original training:

> [P]ractices prescribed for attaining the supreme good, liberation from the round of birth and death, were presented as a means for attaining well-being and happiness here and now. Mindfulness, concentration, and wisdom became not the means for breaking the fetters that bind us to [cycles of worldly life], but qualities that 'free the heart' so that we can live meaningfully, happily, peacefully in the present, acting on the basis of our perception of the interconnectedness of all life. The aim of the practice was still said to be freedom, but it was an immanent freedom, really more a kind of inner healing than liberation … in the classical sense of the word. This reconceptualization of the training may have made the practice of mindfulness much more palatable than would have been the case if it were taught in its original context. But the omission may have set in motion a process that, for all its advantages, is actually eviscerating mindfulness from within.
>
> (Bodhi, 2016: 13–14)[4]

Conflating mindfulness with happiness or immanent goals facilitates a self-absorbed 'selfing' and blends into an instant gratification culture. Although Mindfulness-Based Stress Reduction (MBSR) emphasises non-striving, there is an implicit promise of living with greater ease – an outcome measured through baseline and post-intervention self-reported tools. Mindfulness-Based Cognitive Therapy's (MBCT) emphasis on coping skills that are also audited trains a familiarity with mind and body patterns to encourage greater responsive choice rather than reactivity. These worldly concerns are helpful in certain contexts in which they help arrest rumination or reduce stress. But the models also fortify the already individualised self through self-regulation to constitute an 'improved' hyper-individualised entity. Still, they have proved significantly helpful to many participants, so the question here is not the value of the interventions but the cultures they are perpetuating. In US and UK settings, White Mindfulness forgoes aspirations of justice. It implicitly trains an obedience to and equanimous acceptance of a racialised neoliberal status quo beset with growing inequities and crises. But it is unclear whether a pro-justice mindfulness that emphasises collective liberation rather than individualised gratification corrects Bodhi's observations. Would this qualify as being for the 'supreme good' and for 'liberation from reincarnation'? Is our project to return mindfulness to Buddhism and/or to find a version that supports social transformation in the West? In a partial answer, based on his experience of an engaged Buddhism conference, Bodhi distinguishes those seeking to live peacefully within the confines of society from those seeking social change:

> [A] majority camp ... accepted the present structures of society and sought to use Buddhist teachings to enable people to function more effectively and peacefully within its contours; a minority camp ... sought to draw from the Dharma a radical critique of the dominant social ethos and its institutions.
>
> (Bodhi, 2013)

Extracting and decontextualising mindfulness from its cultural and 'religious' origins serves dominant discourses and functions. According to Bodhi, this completely distorts the purpose of mindfulness, reducing it to something it is not. As a respondent says:

> [W]e know the dangers of just taking one bit and calling it mindfulness. In fact, if you're just taking one bit and teaching people how to be more focused while they're shooting other people then that's not really mindfulness, that's something else. That's concentration training – that's fine, go do that but don't call it mindfulness, call it something else.

Without relocating mindfulness in its rich Buddhist literature and multiple traditions that display a sophisticated exposition of mind, I want to pose the question of whether putting mindfulness to work to support social justice incurs the same appropriation and extraction charges that I've levelled at White Mindfulness.

Bodhi suggests that Buddhist doctrine lends itself to radical critique, suggesting it is possible, if one is not using mindfulness for commercial gain but towards a just cause such as levelling up societies for social liberation, to use it respectfully. This suggests that teacher positionalities and contextualisation of the histories of White Mindfulness can provide a more legitimate frame from which to train teachers. This allows the question of whether we might consider mindfulness not only in relation to its Buddhist origins but also in relation to the many Indigenous cosmologies in which versions of being together in circle, in ritual, in contact with community and the cosmos offer spaces for communing, processing, digesting, being, and becoming. When we call forth these cosmologies, we seem to be departing from the master's house to change society.

To consider these matters, I discuss Kabat-Zinn's accounts of mindfulness to pose a counter narrative. In this overview I revisit some prior discussions but do so now in the conviction that White Mindfulness is the bedrock of the Mindfulness Industry.

Kabat-Zinn's 'second Renaissance': universal social leveller or divider?

Kabat-Zinn, as said before, has made a lasting impression in formulating a programme that offers sanctuary to many. His mission has seeded large-scale operations and investigations purposed to relieve stress. Although his audience is limited by race and class in the US and UK, Kabat-Zinn boldly moves beyond therapisation to relieve suffering with an emphasis on human and universal inter-connectedness.[5]

As shown in the previous sections, his work unfolded in a larger context of social forces bent on consumerism and steeped in postracialism, neoliberalism, and White supremacy. These are now inextricably entwined in White Mindfulness. In considering Kabat-Zinn's early reconceptualisations, I select certain excerpts to show how these lent themselves to dominant ideologies discussed at some length in the earlier parts of this book. The version of mindfulness we are left with fails minoritised groups.

Kabat-Zinn is well known as a scholar, scientist, meditator, and anti-war activist. However, because the construct of race invisibilises whiteness, reflections fail to locate him as a White, cis-gendered, middle-class man, as a privileged subject within a society defined by inequality – or what bell hooks (2000) has called the imperialist White-supremacist capitalist heteropatriarchy. And yet these dynamics, and Kabat-Zinn's relation to them, are foundational to his early conception of mindfulness. Although sincerely devoted to changing the world, his vision fails to take account of fracturing societies and the evisceration of communities and mass organisations.

Entering a divisive period, Kabat-Zinn clarified his intention behind developing MBSR as never wishing 'to exploit, fragment, or decontextualise the dharma, but rather to recontextualise it within the frameworks of science, medicine and healthcare' (Kabat-Zinn, 2011: 288). And yet, although he explained his own understanding of 'the word Dharma' as pointing to something that really is universal (Kabat-Zinn, 2011), he sought to use language to 'Americanise' it. And while his reluctance to call his work 'secular' honours a desire to merge it with the sacred, his own conception of the sacred does not accommodate 'the cultural aspects of the tradition out of which the dharma emerged, however beautiful they might be' (Kabat-Zinn, 2011: 287, 301).

We might understand Kabat-Zinn's desire to honour the sacred as aiming to counteract the disenchantment of modernity and as a desire to re-enchant 'the modern epoch' (Asad, 2003: 13). Yet, this process involves, for him, selecting what constitutes acceptable teachings for a US audience. The lens through which he makes his selection is oblivious that use of the word 'dharma' can be a trigger because it represents the extraction of knowledges typical of the violence of colonialism. It also assumes a homogeneity, suggesting that the US is an 'integrated totality'. This lens that generates models for specific groups becomes invisible and these particularised models are then universalised.

The word 'dharma' is claimed as a universal concept that describes the quality of human attention in relation to suffering and

166   *Embodying justice, changing worlds*

happiness (Kabat-Zinn, 2005: 137). Assumed authority of this kind conceals mechanisms of exclusion and displaced ownership. While this strategy may improve access to a certain kind of mindfulness, it

> erases two or three millennia of Hindu and Buddhist history – and the monks, nuns, monarchs, nobles, and ordinary laypeople who preserved and developed it. Kabat-Zinn himself learned mindfulness from Buddhist teachers, in Buddhist communities. I do not actually think there is anything inherently wrong with practicing medita-tion or yoga or lovingkindness for better wellbeing. It is recognized as a legitimate goal within these traditions, albeit a lesser one than enlightenment or union with Brahman. What I am critiquing here is a rhetorical erasure of the past, and the assumption that one's own social, cultural, and historical perspective applies universally.
>
> (Hickey, 2010: 173)

Orientalist practices such as cultural erasure are acts of predatory modernity. White Mindfulness embeds these practices of appropri-ation and dominion in models and courses marketed for therapeutic gain. By casting itself as a 'universal dharma' and 'skilful means', it conceals dynamics of privilege, and the immorality of appropri-ation and erasure. At the same time, it exacerbates the inequalities which typify the operations of privilege and access in the US and UK contexts in which White Mindfulness flourishes among certain groups. Edicts of neutrality and universality imply a compatibility with all social settings, regardless of circumstances. Packaged as an 'apolitical', ahistorical, 'social leveller', White Mindfulness is said to be available to anyone. As a wellbeing technology, it is projected as neutral and available to those who take responsibility for them-selves and who wish to be well. At this point, 'apolitical' branding erases socio-political differences and the causes of suffering.

Following the early rise of White Mindfulness, although Kabat-Zinn's early definition of mindfulness did not address social ethics, it did proclaim a desire for an egalitarian society – at least for the global North. Presenting to The Contemplative Mind in Society Working Group, 29 September–2 October 1994, he explained:

> As I see it, a profound social/cultural revolution, or what I prefer to think of as a second Renaissance, is possible, at least in first and second world countries, if not globally. It is driven by strong currents of desire for greater meaning and fulfilment, health and well-being,

leisure and comfort and the expectation of relative longevity that the past several centuries of technological progress in first-world countries has generated. The power of this strong inward longing in our society for well-being, meaning, and connectedness should not be underestimated ... One might argue that conditions are ripe, at least in the US, for the beginning of a new and more enlightened and broad-based Renaissance.

(Kabat-Zinn, 1994a: 3)[6]

This positioning reveals a US-Eurocentric frame that privileges the interests of certain social classes, 'at least' in the global North. Such binary framing has implications not only for the global South but also for marginalised communities within the US and UK. Uncritical of the balance of world power that constitutes and privileges the global North and protects elite pockets of society therein, the 'second Renaissance' thesis proposes revolution in the social and cultural spheres, without addressing structural inequalities nor the problematic origins of these teachings. The idea either disregards – or is unaware of – invisibilised social norms, implying that mindfulness is equally accessible to all, that there is a level playing field, and, moreover, that mindfulness can transform the structural causes of stress. Such claims of universality reposition the hetero-, cis-normative White man as 'the invisible subject at the centre of discourse' (Walsh, 2016: 156). Individualised mindfulness, it suggests, will generate a personal desire for social justice. This optimistic view that a particular brand of mindfulness will generate a pro-justice critical mass misses many beats along the way, not least its deep roots in whiteness and its depoliticisation.

In sharp contrast to this positivity, White Mindfulness' hyper-individualism suggests that 'second Renaissance' thought is antagonistic to community and cultivates qualities and values antithetical to 'commoning' – a term used increasingly in emergent, pro-justice mindfulness ventures to denote the reclaiming of mindfulness for the betterment of society (see Hickey, 2010: 174; Doran, 2017; 2018). Dalia Gebrial locates hyper-individualisation among broader neoliberal strategies that substitute political, collective, resource-based demands with 'self-help models of change' (Gebrial, 2018: 30). She substantiates her reasoning with Paul Gilroy's explanation of the displacement of mass mobilisation with 'the individual' as the essential, indivisible social unit of change.

The discourse of individualism foregrounds 'self-reliance and economic betterment through thrift, hard work and individual discipline', as social atomisation accompanies privatisation and elevates health and happiness as attributes of the model citizen (Gilroy, 1990: 71). As noted, medicalised 'labels "healthy" and "ill" relevant to an ever-increasing part of human existence [promote] a belief in the omnipresence of disorder ... [and an imperative] to feel, look or function better' (Zola, 1972: 475–6). This critique of a perennial quest for perfection opposes Kabat-Zinn's project of mindfulness as a pathway to become 'whole', transcendent, and more human (Kabat-Zinn, 1990/2013: 177). It suggests that White Mindfulness' claim to 'the sacred' obscures its complicity in healthism. Throughout its emphasis on 'wholeness and interconnectedness' (Kabat-Zinn, 1994b: 266), it legitimises individual discipline.

'Second Renaissance' thought indirectly sanctions neoliberalism's disruption of community and effaces the genesis of ill health. Universality and individualism symbiotically produce an 'apolitical' subject 'as a unique entity – one that appears to have emerged from the ether, untouched by socio-historic conditioning' (DiAngelo, 2010). By a sleight of words and framing, 'second Renaissance' thought places this universalised individual at the centre of their own healing process for which they are singularly responsible. This strategy elevates homogeny, entrenches postracialism, and denies identity as a mechanism that organises experience and mobilises communities. As such, blindness to the richness and complexity of difference enchants White Mindfulness only for elite audiences and individuals.

Following on from this early period, Kabat-Zinn's own conceptualisation of mindfulness became increasingly politicised over the decades. In 2005, in *Coming to Our Senses*, he anticipates that individualised mindfulness will awaken an interest in community: 'we cannot be completely healthy or at peace in our own private lives, inhabiting a world that itself is diseased and so much not at peace, in which so much of the suffering is inflicted by human beings upon one another' (Kabat-Zinn, 2005: 507). Here he links personal wellbeing to the wellbeing of all. Yet this view still treats White Mindfulness as a private strategy, or individual tool, to achieve social peace. Neglect of structural power continues to reinforce the privatisation of politics and ethical action.

Half a decade later, in 2011, Kabat-Zinn again suggested that the individualised mindfulness model would serve prosocial advancement: 'as a public health intervention, a vehicle for both individual and societal transformation ... as common-sensical, evidence-based, and ordinary, and ultimately a legitimate element of mainstream medical care' (Kabat-Zinn, 2011: 282). Yet this society-wide health services strategy unfolds in the context of the increasing privatisation of health services in both the US and UK (see Riggins, 2018; Davies, 2016), a trend which undermines public health services as viable channels through which to widen participation in mindfulness. As NHS experience shows in the UK, roll-out of MBCT is erratic (Cook, 2016) and services are racialised (Griffiths, 2018), thereby exacerbating existing social inequalities. This is not to say that some people do not benefit from these interventions, but it does note the models' dislocation from changing the lived conditions for participants which harks back to mindfulness as a balm rather than a disrupter.

In the same year, Kabat-Zinn restates his thesis as a 'flourishing on this planet akin to a second, and this time global Renaissance, for the benefit of all sentient beings and our world' (Kabat-Zinn, 2011: 281). Although this seems to correct part of the elitist problem, it adheres to a hyper-individualism that relies on a ripple-effect model of social change. His thesis presumes that programmes will make a growing number of individuals more compassionate, ethical, concerned about others, and community-oriented, and that the institutions in which they practice will 'naturally' transform to become forces of good attuned to social human flourishing (see Payne, 2015).

In 2015, when the activist-philosopher-scholar Angela Davis, herself a meditator, challenged mindfulness' contribution to social justice, questioning its application to rising trends of dispossession and inequalities, Kabat-Zinn offered his 'second Renaissance' model of societal change. He added that mindfulness offers 'transformative practices that are capable of moving the bell curve of the entire society toward a new way of understanding what it means to be human' (Davis and Kabat-Zinn, 2015). Their debate captures the 'apolitical' stance of White Mindfulness, which defaults to the 'second Renaissance' idea to explain its contribution to racial and social justice. But when racial and social justice are not mentioned in the training, it is unclear how this is meant to happen. It is also unclear how we decide what being human means and who is asking. Still, their dialogue helps us think about what purpose White Mindfulness serves in an unjust world.

'Second Renaissance' thinking was reinforced in Kabat-Zinn's 2015 foreword to the (UK) Mindful Nation Report in which mindfulness is seen as a pathway to personal insight, clarity, discernment, ethical understanding, and awareness (The Mindfulness Initiative, 2015). As social justice gained traction in the public domain, the model illustrates the sector's failure to recalibrate its operational definition in response to widening social divides and inequalities. The guideline of a mindfulness 'for our time' increasingly exposed choices, interests, privileges, and political biases within the sector. Political neutrality continued to threaten a meaningful link to social justice, working to demarcate White Mindfulness audiences from those whose political oppression the model could not accommodate.

Speaking the following year at the World Economic Forum Annual Meeting 2016, Kabat-Zinn's description of mindfulness remained 'apolitical'. While he again referenced his concept of a 'Renaissance', he dropped the outdated descriptor 'second', instead locating it in the context of rapidly developing confluences in physical, digital, and biological technologies called the fourth industrial revolution. Kabat-Zinn here packaged mindfulness in the rhetoric of the era, saying for example:

> There is now scientific evidence for the effects of mindfulness on the brain, on the genome, on biological aging; when the mind does know itself then you get the potential for a new Renaissance that restructures itself in terms of our relationship to life, our relationship to the planet, our relationship to work.
>
> (Kabat-Zinn, 2016)

Yet as the United Nations cautions through their adoption of the Sustainable Development Goals in 2015, in contexts of growing inequalities, unless economic systems address the needs of every human on the planet, skewed provision of services exacerbates the problem.[7] Strategies of social transformation become meaningless without taking structural and systemic inequalities into account.

By neglecting to address such inequalities as causes of communal oppression, White Mindfulness models fall into the trap of deepening divides.

The following year, seemingly for the first time and perhaps in response to the urgency of rising inequalities and resultant challenges outlined above, Kabat-Zinn began to interlace politics with his 'Renaissance' idea:

> This is probably one of those 'key moments,' if not the most critical key moment ever on the planet, auguring a potential Renaissance in all senses of the word, if we can come to grips with our own endemic enmity, fear, and self-centeredness as a species, as nations, and as individuals. Never have we needed the wisdom and freedom of the dharma and our inborn potential to realise it as we do now, for the sake of all beings and for the sake of the planet itself.
>
> (Kabat-Zinn, 2017: 1134)

In this instance, although Kabat-Zinn roots inequality in individual emotions rather than social structures, again appealing primarily to individual sovereignty, he recognises the additional need to act also at national and global levels, invoking a collective sense of responsibility. It is unclear, however, who exactly he hails with this communal 'we'. In effect, a sense of universality accompanies an ongoing silence around inequalities hinging on race, socio-economic class, sexual orientation, gender, faith, age, and ability. Consequently, while still rooting systemic change in individual behavioural change, the demands for actions on a national scale leave little room for understanding nations as heterogeneous, fractured entities that impose injustices upon their own citizens (see Asad, 2003). Ultimately, this positioning of mindfulness reinforces individualised models and highlights the absence of social ethics. It also assumes that a single model and its variants will save the world.

As if in response to this critique, later in 2017 Kabat-Zinn reframed the role of mindfulness in fractured societies:

> For me, this trajectory has always been one of generating an ever-growing number of hopefully skilful approaches for effectively addressing widespread suffering and its root causes in the human mind. These classically take the form of (1) greed; (2) fear and

aversion, and the disdain, enmity, and vilifying that frequently
accompany them, including the racial/ethnic dehumanising phenom-
enon of 'othering'; (3) delusion, namely, mistaking appearance for
reality; and (4) the toxicity, ignorance, and blindness that arise from
ignoring intrinsic human values such as kindness and compassion,
and the humanity in others.

(Kabat-Zinn, 2017: 1126)

Here Kabat-Zinn paraphrases the 'three unwholesome roots'[8]
in his description of US and UK contexts. He concurs, to some
extent, with Loy's argument regarding the institutionalisation of
'greed, anger and delusion' (Loy, 2016: 20). However, whereas Loy
interprets mindfulness from an engaged Buddhist perspective that
acknowledges the role of community, Kabat-Zinn emphasises that
the route to change is personal. He follows 'second Renaissance'
ideology that locates the 'root causes' of change 'in the human
mind'. This stance once again individualises Othering and appeals
to innate ethics as part of the ideology of postracialism in which
'second Renaissance' thought functions, and in which racism is
episodic. Perpetrators of racism are encouraged to change their
behaviours, while targets of racial injustices are encouraged to
increase their coping strategies and resilience. White Mindfulness
after all, contrary to Kabat-Zinn's vision and sentiment, was never
intended to direct social transformation.

While change is evident in Kabat-Zinn's thinking over the
decades, universality and individualism underpin his 'second
Renaissance' belief, meaning that White Mindfulness globalises the
causes and solutions of stress.

Troubling neo-colonial racism, individualism, and universality

Through its discourse of hyper-individualism, White Mindfulness
positions behavioural change as the route to systemic change.
Merging with psychology, it ignores systemic inequity and
obscures and individualises race. Historian Leah Gordon's theory
of racialised individualism upends the notion that individuals can
on their own overcome systemic racial bias by adopting common

solutions to vastly different experiences of the world. This, after all, is what the current mindfulness model asks of its participants. Like Gilroy, she highlights US discourses of racial analysis that targets individuals as units of analysis in change: 'Racial individualism brought together three of our most powerful post-war American discourses: psychological individualism, rights-based individualism and assumptions about the socially transformative power of education' (Gordon, 2015: 2–3, 27, 80). These deep-rooted histories of individualised, racialised psychologies show how twentieth-century psy-disciplines ignored the systemic roots of racism. Using studies that favoured 'racial individualism [they] created obstacles for advocates of systemic and relational approaches to the race issue'. The psy-world, in other words, a significant channel through which White Mindfulness has gained social traction, detracts from systemic accounts of racism, and personalises racialisation. Seen in this light, it seems inconceivable for the current models to perform a politically transformative function.

When structural causes are disregarded, stress is psychopathologised, and personal resourcefulness to withstand or transcend such causes becomes a primary focus, the White Mindfulness model can even be considered antithetical to stress reduction for marginalised groups. Through training, the individual is made either partly or wholly responsible for coping with their experience of structural oppression and discrimination. In addition, racial and now postracial individualisation impose the responsibility to overcome systemic racism upon individuals rather than power structures.

The underpinning ideologies of universality and individualism are cast in European and, increasingly, in US-Eurocentric terms. Central to this thought is the bifurcation of the 'White man' as the universal model of humanity, and the created subaltern or precariat – a lower ranking class, race, or group – which is excluded from the hierarchy of humanness, Othered and paternalistically assimilated and/or controlled (Bhambra, 2014: 125). To exemplify this point, White Mindfulness frames stress and its solutions not only in individualised terms, but from a White, male, heteronormative perspective. At the same time, it universalises the biopsychological model and homologises suffering.

When respondents use White Mindfulness rhetoric to bypass structural inequities, they demonstrate the success of its ideologies. A lexicon of 'common humanity' promotes a notion of interconnectedness and sameness that denies power, as shown by this respondent:

> [C]ommon humanity is one of the great foundations in MBSR ... a person might come in with a diagnosis but is not defined by their diagnosis. We all suffer and to me what that does is erode and loosen the illusion of a separate self ... we're unifying experiences of human beings accessed both in pain and the potential for freedom.

Breaking the illusion of a separate self sounds appealing until it becomes clear that it hides both White Mindfulness' hyper-individualism and the unequal contexts in which lives, stresses, illness, and wellness are forged. The lexicon of 'common humanity' functions to collapse difference and perpetuate universality.

The decolonial response

Trainers do not sit outside political contexts. Yet their conditioned beliefs, biases, and cultures are presumed to be erased and replaced by an implicitly transmitted ethics that replaces their embodiment of privilege, whiteness, and postracialism. This echoes Kerr's counterpoint to Said that educationalists are objective thinkers untrained by context. Because White Mindfulness avoids an inquiry into relational power, the individual who conforms to its dominant culture and helps it recycle itself is presented as universalised. By the same token, it excludes those with divergent views, who are often people with minoritised identities, through the whiteness of its spaces.

Decolonising these tenets of White Mindfulness requires foundational shifts in conceptualisation. For a start, White Mindfulness needs to acknowledge sources, histories, and positionality more readily. It must challenge and undo its hyper-individualised discourse, claims of universality, and social norms such as Othering. Reckoning with the impact of coloniality and racialised neoliberalism in shaping the sector is a challenging but necessary requirement if there is incentive to serve social transformation aspirations. Undoing ourselves in the broader frame of decolonisation is but one facet of this work that is fundamental for changes in direction, ethos, and purpose. As long as we expect justice to only happen on the outside, our liberation is incomplete.

Stepping outside the frame of White Mindfulness as a decolonial strategy allows its tenets such as 'second Renaissance' thought to become crystal clear. But decolonisation is not only about unravelling and undoing dominant discourses. It includes forging new initiatives, approaches, and narratives. When we locate ourselves culturally and historically within the power of our communities, we disrupt the White gaze. Defying and refusing the position of the Other is part of the process of decolonisation. Such challenges to universality and modernity underpin works informed by embodied justice.

Notes

1 While the US uses the term diversity, equity, and inclusion (DEI), the UK uses equity, diversity, and inclusion (EDI). I capture both acronyms by using DEI/EDI.
2 Macrostructural changes do not in and of themselves guarantee political changes. In some instances, despite colonial force withdrawal, policies, systems, and structures remain intact and upheld by surrogate local administrators. At other times, decolonisation efforts are slow in the wake of rapacious colonial regimes that leave countries economically devastated. This book acknowledges but does not engage with the decolonial–postcolonial debate. I use the terms interchangeably with respect for the serious debates that engage scholars like Gayatri Spivak and Homi Bhabha.
3 Stanley and Longden say this framing constitutes the premise of universality: 'In most professional, scientific and Buddhist literatures, "the mind" tends to be understood as "universal": trans-social, trans-cultural and trans-historical. The growth in popularity of MBSR can be partly attributed to the recent historical re-interpretation of Buddhism as a universal "scientific religion" compatible with the principles of rationalism, evolutionary biology, materialism and psychotherapy' (Stanley and Longden, 2016: 306).
4 White Mindfulness' immanent goals are measured, rated, and used to contrast and polarise 'the strong and the weak showing the weak how much stronger they might be, and confirming to the strong that they are winning, at least for the time being' (Davies, 2016: 179).

5 Kabat-Zinn used a quote from Albert Einstein in his public lectures to underline his emphasis on interconnectivity, which he saw in cosmological terms: 'A human being is a part of the whole, called by us "universe", a part limited in time and space. He experiences himself, his thoughts and feelings as something separated from the rest – a kind of optical delusion of his consciousness. This delusion is a kind of prison for us, restricting us to our personal desires and to affection for a few persons nearest to us. Our task must be to free ourselves from this prison by widening our circle of compassion to embrace all living creatures and the whole nature in its beauty. Nobody is able to achieve this completely, but the striving for such attainment is in itself a part of the liberation, and a foundation for inner security' (Einstein, quoted in Kabat-Zinn, 2005: 338).

6 Although there is no consensus among postcolonial scholars, 'first-world' and 'third-world' terminology is critiqued for its colonial overtones. I deploy the concepts of global North and South to indicate histories of economic, political, and cultural dispossession that generate the bifurcation in the first instance. However, the global North and South terminology is itself critiqued for the elision of the complexities of societies such as the rise of a global precariat – undefined by national borders and equally present in countries in the global North (Thérien, 1999: 723).

7 The United Nations Development Programme explains that 'The 17 SDGs are integrated – they recognize that action in one area will affect outcomes in others, and that development must balance social, economic and environmental sustainability' (https://bit.ly/3xKs 2Gp). This serves as a reminder of the need for a holistic approach to wellbeing – that mindfulness cannot be extricated from socioeconomic and political conditions.

8 Kabat-Zinn is referencing the three unwholesome roots of greed, hatred, and delusion, named as such in the *Theravāda* tradition (Sanskrit *akuśala-mūla*; Pāli *akusala-mūla*) and referred to as the 'three poisons' in *Mahāyāna* (Sanskrit *triviṣa*; Tibetan *dug gsum*) (Buswell and Lopez, 2013: 546). We are seeing here the choiceful referencing to Buddhist traditions to select aspects that help position or re-position White Mindfulness in relation to Buddhism which at this point had become socially acceptable. But this still happens without reference to Orientalism.

8

Taking back the future: beyond Eurocentric temporality

love and justice are not two. without inner change, there can be no
outer change; without collective change, no change matters
angel Kyodo williams, Lama Rod Owens,
Jasmine Syedullah (2016: 89)

When Safiya Noble was urged by her friend to google 'Black girls',
she was shocked to be directed mainly to porn sites or results that
·commodified young Black women. Noble tells us that Othering is
found not only in the structures and cracks of systems of discrimination but that it circulates widely in social media. In *Algorithms
of Oppression* (2018) she explains how discrimination is presented
and perpetrated through search engines that contribute to inequality
especially for women in the Global Majority (GM). That they privilege whiteness, racism, and sexism is no surprise given their normative contexts and producers. Algorithms are, after all, created by
people and show that systemic Othering runs deep in society and
psyches in ways that make discriminations appear incidental even
while they are amplified. Othering and racism reproduce themselves through ideologies, philosophies, daily exclusions, and the
back door. The scale of their societal permeation requires decolonial
agendas that address underpinning norms that come to reside in the
very warp and weft of all social and personal bodies.

The waters of White Mindfulness are synonymous with Noble's
algorithms. They recycle underpinning social values – not the ones
publicly listed, but those that are lived. But these are increasingly
being challenged and disrupted. The growing Black Lives Matter
(BLM) movement and the emergent pro-justice movement give new
meaning to wellness rooted in systemic change, and community.

They challenge the hyper-individualised notions that underpin the Mindfulness Industry. This community orientation is affirmed by recent stress research that points to co-regulation as a prerequisite for self-regulation (see Ndefo, 2021). Indigenous knowledges, as noted before, also offer alternative perspectives to the dominant Western frame of individuality and universality. Cosmologies that revolve around interbeing, to cite the Zen monk Thich Nhat Hanh, require little need for terms like interconnectedness and interdependence.

From within White Mindfulness, it is evident that decolonisation entails far more than an upgrade of curricula or DEI/EDI trainings. It calls for stepping outside the given frame to chart a new course of inquiry. As numerous decolonial models show as they dismantle systems, structures, and patterns of marginalisation found in board rooms, education systems, and numerous sectors, undoing the embodiment of whiteness requires more than improved representation, antiracism, and social justice training. To gain traction, such work necessarily requires a different, non-extractive worldview that draws on global South methodologies and knowledges that centre communities and transformation. The undoing of White Mindfulness requires the kind of thinking that leverages difference and diversity in the service of building just and fair worlds. The disruption of social norms and dominant narratives requires both a renegotiation of institutional power as well as an acknowledgement of initiatives positioned outside the formal White Mindfulness sector. In preparation, it is helpful to become clear on what exactly White Mindfulness is selling.

This chapter considers a foundational pillar of White Mindfulness – present-moment awareness – to establish whether its conception of time holds sway among People of the Global Majority (PGM) and minoritised communities. Drawing on queer perspectives, I discuss this US-Eurocentric keystone of White Mindfulness and bring new light to the notion of nowness. I look more closely at temporality to reveal the normativity of a Eurocentric perspective that unquestioningly reasserts its worldview. White Mindfulness' premise of 'the present moment' presents a singular, separable, isolated, 'apolitical' moment sandwiched neatly between a linear past and future. Disrupting this notion invites complexity and an engagement with difference to enrich a conceptualisation that troubles the boundaries of authority and dominant perspectives. I am less interested in a reconceptualisation than in embracing different ways of seeing and being in the world to undo the neatness of definitions carried forth in dominant worldviews.

Present-moment awareness, temporality, and futurity

The White Mindfulness model uses Kabat-Zinn's operational definition of 'the awareness that arises through paying attention, on purpose, in the present moment, non-judgementally'. The concept follows a Western notion of time that presents a past–present–future linearity. It is usually conveyed as 'present-moment awareness' to impart a sense of 'nowness', constantly guiding awareness to the 'here-and-now'. Using it also to emphasise the quality of presence allows practitioners to gauge how distracted the mind is, and rather than allow it to wander, to bring it back to the notion of the 'present-moment'. Ideas of convergence and divergence are built into the concept to accommodate focused and wide-open awareness. The former encourages undivided, absorbed attention and the latter, spacious awareness. There is deep respect here that in Buddhist and other cosmologies, concepts like presence, awareness, and consciousness signify far more than the Western construct of time. While this is not necessarily missing from White Mindfulness, 'moment-by-moment awareness' as a popular discourse and as taught through White Mindfulness is predominantly related to a linear notion of time and self-regulation.

The challenge to present-moment awareness is posed on several fronts. These include the need, at times, to distract the mind from certain events to protect it from danger that can take form as incessant experiences of micro- or macroaggressions, familiar to minoritised groups. Proponents of the concept might answer that the distraction, as a place of sanctuary, becomes the new focus of the mind. But mostly, the concept is used to encourage a mental training of individual presence and of the self to better regulate, improve, self-censure, or 'show up' with a particular disposition. The latter could be a genuine level of compassion or, as business professor Jeremy Hunter (2021) suggests, a passive-aggressive smile.

Generally, White Mindfulness teachers deliver trainings based on Kabat-Zinn's definition believed to apply to everybody. A respondent explains:

> Mindfulness is developing a conscious awareness that has a particular orientation which is about living in the present moment as best we can and what that means simply is a way to practice, to attend to internal triggers and to be situated in our external environment.

The present moment becomes a gateway to individual sovereignty. Through self-discipline and regulation, White Mindfulness suggests that we can change the world by changing ourselves. This view is upheld as universal. Yet, as Bodhi reminds us, the construct encourages a 'particular style of meditation' linked to innate goals such as 'peace of mind and a more stable grounding in immediate experience' and instant gratification (Bodhi, 2016: 6). The fixation with outcome, Bodhi says, aside from being anti-Buddhist, reaffirms an obsession with individualised 'selfing'. Kabat-Zinn pushes back against this association with outcome, although in doing so, he emphasises acceptance:

> The emphasis was always on awareness of the present moment and acceptance of things as they are, however they are in actuality, rather than a preoccupation with attaining a particular desired outcome at some future time, no matter how desirable it might be.
>
> (Kabat-Zinn, 1990/2013: 290)

Kabat-Zinn's emphasis encourages practitioners to turn towards and accept, making White Mindfulness 'as much about acceptance of experience as it is about remaining in the present moment' (Lewis and Rozelle, 2016: 257). In true liberatory fashion, Angela Davis challenges this notion, saying: 'I'm no longer accepting the things I cannot change. I'm changing the things I can no longer accept.' In Kabat-Zinn's statement, the acceptance of things 'as they are' encourages pain sufferers to avoid second-arrow reactivity. Recalling Buddhist scripture, a respondent says it also encourages an appraisal of thoughts, sensations, and emotions as 'not me, not mine', or a remembering that these are 'impermanent events in the mind'. A focus on transience, constantly shifting awareness from moment to moment, is intended to train a 'letting go' and an acceptance of new moments (Stanley and Longden, 2016: 320). However, pain is treated as homologous. When social inequities are imprinted on our bodies, tissues, and cells, the guidance is to call forth that part of us that can hold the event in awareness and endure even as we are experiencing devastation. For generations of marginalised people this is like teaching one's grandmother to suck eggs. It disregards histories of trauma and fortitude, or restraint and resilience, in movements that 'still are rising'. There is also unawareness that White teachers are homologising pain and instructing PGM and marginalised groups to accept gross inequalities as they are. In addition, the agency to change that which is untenable, as Davis says, is absent.

Pain can occur in nature or through illness. But it also includes the pain that nations inflict on some of their own citizens, on refugees and migrants, and on other nations through war and globalisation. When contextualised and acknowledged, our relationship to pain can change to reduce the stress it causes us if there is clarity that injustices must end, so that White Mindfulness is not asking people to be long-suffering. Without this distinction, politically induced pain meted out to minoritised communities over centuries and generations becomes equated with that caused by a single accident that causes temporary harm. Flattening pain equates discrimination experienced by a cis-White, racist, gay man with that experienced by a Black, queer, trans-woman. This gay man may well experience political homophobia but remains protected by systemic whiteness which privileges him at work, socially, financially, economically, educationally, politically, and otherwise. This is not about oppression Olympics; it calls for understandings of how intersectionality functions systemically and structurally and how some minoritised groups marginalise other groups. Without this complexity, EVERYbody, as Angela Black says, is treated as experiencing the world in the same way.

In Buddhist terms, the framework of acceptance involves 'taking refuge': '[w]hen difficulties come along, we have something in which to take refuge, something that will sustain us through the time of darkness' (Brazier, 2016: 73). In taking refuge, turning toward difficulty is accompanied by recollection and non-forgetfulness of the three jewels – both of which can be read to disrupt 'present-moment' notions (Tomassini, 2016: 222). It depicts an active engagement with the present moment to bring clarity and wisdom rather than only noticing what arises. Spiritual and communal refuge are of course common to many traditions. In White Mindfulness settings, these sites of refuge are replaced by the body and breath. But, as the brutal murders of Eric Garner and George Floyd illustrate, these refuges are not always dependable: they can be made inaccessible and/or unsafe. Some are denied their right to breathe or safety in the body, based on race, socio-economic positioning, and difference. Again, we see that the present moment is neither a level playing field, nor universal.

From a decolonial perspective, the 'present moment' is meaningless in numerous cultures in which past and future are non-linear. Speaking at the Planetary Utopias 2018 opening plenary, Nikita Dhawan (2018) tells us that '[t]he terms for past and future in many non-European languages like Aymara, Mandarin, Urdu and Hindi [are] the same'. Within these cultures, pasts and futures are commonly understood as intertwined and indistinguishable rather than as linear progressions. 'Temporality', she says, is tied to 'hope, desire, and imagination for non-dominant futures'. It is also linked to the construction of a more nuanced 'self'.[1] In certain African, American, Māori, and Indigenous traditions, elders and ancestors are generally present in communal spiritual spaces (see Smith, 1999; Ige, 2006; McCabe, 2008; Mitchell, 2021). In these traditions, the 'self' may include relationships with the community and the land. These perspectives tell us that time is inextricable from context; that some cultures and traditions do not separate the 'self' from the collective, at least not historically; that 'self' is a collective, cosmological concept.

When White Mindfulness follows a Eurocentric view of the present moment and when it extricates the present moment from history and context, it assumes that individualised participants arrive in a 'present moment' equally and that 'nowness' has the same tone for every body. By critiquing the notion of the present moment, my effort is to show that the construct of time is marred by a deepset dominance of certain cultures and outlooks that fail alternative perspectives. Linear temporality excludes traditions with rich cosmologies and cultures of non-linearity that have been colonised and violently stamped out. There are many ways in which we reinforce Eurocentric linear time. White Mindfulness language, for instance, depicts history and tradition as past and done and uses the present participle to reinforce an idea of life happening in the present moment. Notions of pausing, reflecting, visioning, strategising are all seen through a present-moment lens, with little regard for how much this lens imposes forgetting and a selective remembering. Troubling it at least allows us to accommodate other ways of seeing and to embrace dimensions that are yet unknown. Queer theorists help us introduce some further complexity. Alongside global South perspectives, they write back by disrupting the assumptions and building blocks of structural power.

Queer theorist Heather Love (2009) presents a different yet related challenge to White Mindfulness' temporal framework to those mentioned above. Love's work builds upon the anti-relational turn in queer studies which steps outside heteronormativity to establish ground that is less hostile and conducive to queer belonging. Theorists like Love say that heteronormative society tramples queer desire. From this vantage point she emphasises 'turning backwards' to struggles that have informed queerness – not to liberate them from the darkness of shame, but to recollect depression, pain, and regret, to understand the present. For Love, the present necessarily involves the past not as rumination, but as 'remembering' – as refuge. Her work stands in opposition to Linehan's 'detachment' in MBCT, in which participants dissociate from pain. For Love, 'feeling backwards' into a painful past defines being alive in a way that differs from meeting pain only ever in the present moment with no recollection of the past. She amplifies the power of the past and engages remembering as reflexion and not-forgetting to create a space for queerness. Gajaweera's respondents similarly describe a 'reaching back' to return to an intersubjective, collective sense of intergenerational trauma and to remember together a 'shared past – recognising the historical effects of … socio-political contexts on the present' (Gajaweera, 2021: 13–15).

We might understand José Muñoz's work (2009) on queer utopianism, on the other hand, as part of what Drew Daniel (2010) has referred to as the anti-anti-relational turn. Queer theorists of the GM like Muñoz suggest that anti-relational theorists like Love assume individual sovereignty that those who live intersectional lives neither have nor subscribe to. Muñoz and others emphasise the 'imagination of a utopic future' as a refuge that offers hope (Cheang, 2020: 158). For him the present moment is premised upon and constituted of inequalities, while also infused with 'queer potentiality', or the possibility of queerness which is 'yet to come', necessarily in the future 'not yet here'.[2] Instead of White Mindfulness' 'here-and-nowness', Muñoz advocates for a politics of transformation that emphasises a 'then-and-thereness' (Muñoz 2009: 29). In this line of thought, the past is essential to the present in that the present is 'history still', and queerness, as an ideality, is what 'tells us that something is missing, or something is not yet here' (Muñoz, 2009: 86). It is 'a temporal arrangement, one that is a being and a doing for the future' (Warner, 2011: 256). This understanding of temporality counters White Mindfulness' 'present-moment beingness', revealing it to be devoid of *remembering* or *imagination* to create a different world. Muñoz's temporality embraces striving and agency. As madison moore (2018) puts it: 'the present moment is awful for most of us. Why would we want to live in it? We have to create a different moment.'

Muñoz's 'futurity' emphasises the imperative for marginalised groups to *actively* occupy the present moment, to do rather than be, to alter inequalities by creating an inclusive world. There is purpose and judgement here. His political sense of agency infuses temporality with understandings of power. While this may be read as happening nonetheless in a present moment, temporality is marked by agency rather than time. Neither Love nor Muñoz are interested in occupying the present moment with compassion for the purposes of attaining calm and happiness. For both, queer life is defined by its defiance of the normative trend to accept the present moment as a blank canvas without striving for it to be any different to what it is.

From a perspective of Indigenous wisdom, Sherri Mitchell Weh'na Ha'mu Kwasset, a Native American attorney, activist, and teacher from the Penobscot Nation, recovers the Indigenous way of life. For Mitchell (2021), space is timeless and honours the reverence for the earth and elements. Her insight into traditional cosmologies embraces asynchronous worlds that require much richer understandings of a decolonisation process, one that opens doorways to spiritual realms for healing. For her, temporal linearity is misplaced in a cosmology alive with entanglements trans-generationally and trans-species. Neither the present moment nor individuals are discrete entities in the ways presumed in White Mindfulness. Life and vitality are multi-dimensional and never only 'here'.

Theorists such as Muñoz and Mitchell defy normative, 'apolitical' notions of 'time' or 'self', while others show that the present moment is inseparable from the past as it expresses the ways in which bodies and lives are continuously reconstituted in relation to power.[3] Contrary to the reification of the present-moment and the 'letting go' of the past, these scholars contend that narratives that unearth invisible 'pasts, presents, and futures', transform temporality (see Ahmed, 2014: 34; Smith, 1999: 149). From this queer perspective, time, like other norms, is a construct:

> [T]he past and present are not ... discrete categories, but are, rather, complex human constructs. The present is not a quarantined, autonomous thing. What was begun does not end but instead intensifies so that the past and present become indistinguishable.
>
> (Dillon, 2013: 42)

The constructedness of temporality sheds light on White Mindfulness' discourse as part of US-European modernity, amplifying the political nature of the present moment and what could easily become a lost sense of agency.

In a further challenge, philosopher David Scott critiques the present moment for a 'presentness' (Scott, 2017: 56) that belies it as a 'conjuncture'. In his commemoration of Stuart Hall's work, Scott echoes what queer theorists and critical feminists argue: that the present moment cannot conveniently be reduced to a temporality that occurs between the past and future. He asks: when does it begin and end and who decides? Hall's 'conjuncture' encapsulates the political, economic, and ideological materiality of conditions that lead to action and subversion. The idea is not merely to denote the present as a political culmination of the past, but to acknowledge the interplay of multiple events and responses that constitute many different 'presents' and realities. Beginnings and endings, demarcations of time so neatly packaged in linearity, deny complexity and multidimensionality. Hall adds to conjuncture the notion of contingency, through which he argues that futures are not yet known or determined by temporal 'pasts' or 'presents'. His appreciation of possibility, which ties agency to contingency, takes account of the political crises that dominate power and the imperative of political action. For Hall then, the present cannot be differentiated from power. Contingency and conjuncture are complementary aspects that alert us to the entanglement of worlds beyond linear temporality.

This critique marks yet another challenge to White Mindfulness' apolitical claims. Its presumptions about the linear progression of indivisible units of time and enchantment of the present moment reveal hegemonic discourses and perspectives that bury rich, diverse worldviews. These multiple perspectives test notions of universality and complicate the construct of time as being separate from an agent with positionality. Authors from different perspectives caution against a colonisation of time that embeds a political messaging of universality, acceptance, non-judgement, and non-striving.

Discussion of temporality shows its intricate link to the historic roots of pain and emotion. The language of conjuncture, agency, indigeneity, and futurity offers multiple perspectives that break with US-Eurocentric notions of linearity and universality. Yet this framework continues to govern the ways White Mindfulness programmes target pain in their aim to reduce stress and depressive relapse and build resourcefulness and coping strategies. Queer, Indigenous, and global South perspectives offer different, non-homogeneous lenses through which to relate to the realities of life. Leaning into these richly diverse worldviews could allow White Mindfulness to expand its understandings of context. Currently, these multiple perspectives illuminate further ways in which White Mindfulness excludes communities, suffocates rich worldviews, and misses out on embracing difference.

Notes

1 Nikita Dhawan's opening address on Resignation, Disenchantment and Reenchantment presented at the third symposium to the Colonial Repercussions Planetary Utopias – Hope, Desire, Imaginaries in a Post-Colonial World, 23 June 2018, can be found at https://youtu. be/OlzDe2rgfzs. The full programme of the conference can be found at www.youtube.com/playlist?list=PLfJugoeO9YFervitRNBaD8GJes 9tiZhIa.

2 Muñoz employs a critical idealism to emphasise the importance of concrete utopias which involve collectives and groups. He states: 'The

here and now is a prison house. We must strive, in the face of the here and now's totalizing rendering of reality, to think and feel a *then and there*' (Muñoz, 2009: 1).

3 Dillon explains that the present 'is possessed by the logics and protocols of racial capitalism's past – by a perfectly routine massacre that was and is repeated endlessly across space and time in the (post) colony, prison, frontier, torture room, plantation, reservation, riot zone, and on and on. Racial terror returns from a past that is not an end to take hold (of bodies, institutions, infrastructure, discourse, and libidinal life) and does not let go' (Dillon, 2013: 42).

9

Disrupting space: the politics of pain and emotion

Black ... people are expected to educate white people as to our humanity. Women are expected to educate men. Lesbians and gay men are expected to educate the heterosexual world. The oppressors maintain their position and evade their responsibility for their own actions. There is a constant drain of energy which might be better used in redefining ourselves and devising realistic scenarios for altering the present and constructing the future.

Audre Lorde (2007c: 115)

Nationalism is as much part of neoliberal regimes as individualism. In *Peace Love Yoga*, academic Andrea Jain explains how these seemingly oppositional terms coincide through conservative controls that encourage individuals to bear allegiance to the state. She highlights the uses of what she calls neoliberal spirituality to foster nationalisms in ways that generate borders and divisions within societies. Jain cites India's declaration of International Yoga Day as an 'instrument of domination through which [Prime Minister Narendra] Modi mainstreamed Hindutva', building a sense of national pride based on a single religion. She suggests that such acts foster social divisions and disunity; those religions and practices that are not Hindu become foreign in their own lands (Jain, 2020: 15). Conservatism, neoliberalism, and embedded forms of divide and rule are entangled and give rise to increased coercion, policing, incarceration, and pain meted out within the nation. Jain uses this argument to show the intimacy between India's commercialisation of yoga and its nationalisation agenda, which together entrench intersectional privileges and heteropatriarchy. Her thesis complicates appropriation as not simply happening across constructed national borders but as a means of monopolisation geared to build global elites engaged in the hyper-individualised self-help industry. This multi-faceted spin captures the complexity of Hall's conjuncture in which divisive nationalism and control arise in what appears to be a single, almost rightful, proud act of re-appropriation.

Lorde's epigraph points us to the intricate inner workings of societies premised on the exploitation of difference, and the creation of divisions and pain. In the context of Jain's work, it underlines the role spiritual practices can play in social marginalisation. But Lorde's words, like Toni Morrison's before, also underscore the burdens commonly inherited by the minoritised in correcting injustices. They underpin Jain's conceptualisation of neoliberal spirituality as a mechanism of domination and recall the marginalisation for Asian Buddhists and other People of the Global Majority (PGM) in contexts of the 'Americanisation' of Buddhism and White Mindfulness. To further explore emotionality and exclusions, in contrast to the normative, clinical definition of pain in the secular literature,[1] this chapter compares mindfulness' interpretation of pain – an interpretation derived from Buddhist doctrine – with Sara Ahmed's 'sociality of emotion'. Following on from the discussion of temporality, 'apolitical' models conceal multiplicities of pain that go unacknowledged in the universalisation of suffering. In a vein similar to the imposition of the linearity of time, the 'apolitical' flattening of human suffering functions as a denial of the inequivalences of adversity, and the administering of such affliction by some humans upon others. In building this case, I reject the depoliticisation of pain and compassion and emphasise their role in power structures that proclaim some emotions more significant than others.

Pain or stress – White Mindfulness' proxy for the Buddhist concept of suffering – draws together multiple threads of White Mindfulness: temporality, the body-mind, and the therapeutic. In Buddhist discourses, suffering is understood to comprise three levels (Purser, 2015: 680). First, the suffering of suffering comprises chronic pain, stress, and depression. Mindfulness programmes address this kind of 'unsatisfactoriness' through the 'two arrows' doctrine, which attempts to avoid the recycling and worsening of pain.[2] The aim is to unlearn mental reactivity to unpleasantness since the 'second arrow' – which we shoot ourselves – is believed to exacerbate suffering, and by training the mind away from it, practitioners learn to respond more openly and wisely. In this interpretation, reactivity is assumed to be negative, while responsiveness has a measured, positive tone.

Second, the suffering of change is associated with 'clinging' to the pain/pleasure and denying its impermanence. Mindfulness cultivates recognition of what are regarded as unwholesome attachments, using the teaching of impermanence to encourage 'letting go'. Third, suffering of conditioned existence or all-pervasive suffering includes the prior forms and relates to a fixed view of the 'self'. Third-level suffering is considered inaccessible to ordinary experience, comprehensible only through deep meditative insight. White Mindfulness is not designed to address this final form of hidden suffering. It aims only to stabilise attention and cultivate an ability to hold stress in awareness without judgement (Dorjee, 2014). Designed for therapeutic purposes to address 'this-worldly' suffering and stress reduction, White Mindfulness lacks soteriological aspirations found in Buddhist teachings. Comprising self-regulation and coping strategies, we can ask whether indeed these constitute any form of enchantment.

Ahmed's investigations of diversity and social justice work within UK and Australian higher education systems and among Indigenous Australians challenge homologous categorisations of pain and emotion. For her, thoughts, sensations, and emotions are not objectifiable; emotions drive effect and generate power. Even perception, regarded in White Mindfulness as pre-subjective, is for Ahmed (2014) preconditioned. In a similar vein to Ahmed, Asad (2003) says: 'A crucial point about pain is that it enables the secular idea that "history-making" and "self-empowerment" can progressively replace pain by pleasure – or at any rate, by the search for what pleases one'.[3] He implies that pleasure or coping does not undo pain and that agency and sovereignty are not equally available to all people. In talking about the body, the assumption is that all individuals can act unfettered even though agency is a constantly wielded power, always under threat.

In the Buddhist literatures, pain is associated with unpleasantness and is instinctively avoided. Perception follows a point of 'contact' which generates what is regarded as a pre-subjective 'feeling tone'. Mindfulness trains the ability to intervene before the feeling tone evolves into emotions and thoughts, presenting this liminal field as a decisive point at which autonomic reactivity can be interrupted and replaced with 'wise response'. In other words, mindfulness cultivates an awareness of 'feeling tone' or sensation as part of a strategy to arrest secondary suffering and alleviate further trauma that arises from unconscious reactivity (Piyadassi, 1959/2008). It also trains a non-reactive response to pain, regardless of its causes. As a respondent explains:

> Mindfulness is there to engage with the process of perception. It's not a stand-alone thing – I'm not developing mindfulness in isolation from other categories. What empowers one is if I can begin to see more clearly into a situation and that situation might have ethical consequences; it might have other issues such as seeing this turmoil as just part of life – this is what happens – so you get clarity … In our confusion, perception is skewed by all sorts of things such as the drive to have or not to have. What mindfulness is geared to, is cleaning up that process of perception so that perception becomes more: *what can be changed, what can't be changed.*

Considered pre-subjective and autonomic, perception is a gateway through which to learn to respond rather than react to pain. More importantly, it is a pathway to cultivating discernment. Within this frame, the notion of pre-subjectivity and personal agency to discern – seemingly objectively – what can be changed and to affect the desired outcome are taken as given.

Ahmed's work challenges the premise that the sensation that arises through contact is pre-subjective and unconditioned. She says:

> [W]hether something feels good or bad already involves a process of reading, in the very attribution of significance. Contact involves the subject, as well as histories that come before the subject. If emotions are shaped by contact with objects, rather than being caused by objects, then emotions are not simply 'in' the subject or the object. This does not mean that emotions are not read as being 'resident' in subjects or objects … I want to suggest that the distinction between sensation and emotion can only be analytic, and as such, is premised on the reification of a concept.
>
> (Ahmed, 2014: 6)

In her fluent fashion, Ahmed questions the depoliticised assumptions that 'pleasant' and 'unpleasant' perceptions are momentary and pre-subjective. While it is taught in mindfulness to discern pleasant from unpleasant and neutral, Ahmed suggests that this type of cognition is inextricably bound up with subjectivity. It privileges certain subjects, histories, and perceptions such that constructions of pain depoliticise bodies and impose normative understandings of suffering and healing.

To illustrate how power constitutes 'selves', 'relationships', and 'structures', and makes only certain pain and emotion intelligible, I draw on an example from the writings of Frantz Fanon. I use Fanon's theorisation to disrupt White Mindfulness' claim to pre-subjectivity, indicating instead an understanding of pain and emotion as politically constituted.

Fanon narrates the medical examination of a man in France who had migrated from North Africa. He describes clinical interpretations of politically induced pain. In conventional terms, the pain produced through violent dispossession is unclassifiable and non-clinical. It is interpreted only as a 'vagueness':

> What's wrong my friend?
> I'm dying, *monsieur le docteur*.
> His [the patient's] voice breaks imperceptibly.
> Where do you have pain?
> Everywhere, *monsieur le docteur*.
> When does it hurt?
> All the time.
>
> ... the North African, spontaneously, by the very fact of appearing on the scene, enters into a pre-existing framework.
>
> (Zeilig, 2014: 203–5)

Because such pain does not fit the medic's classification scheme, the patient either articulates pain in terms the doctor understands or relents and remains plagued. In both instances, the patient is neither understood nor attended to. The political roots of the patient's condition are diagnostically ignored. Here language reduces affect – as in the noun, emotional affect – to what is expressed and what can be heard, and leaves behind that which remains unsaid (Clough and Halley, 2007: 8). For Fanon, such disservice is due not necessarily to the ill will of the doctor, but rather a system that is not designed to accommodate the needs of the patient, and which conditions and trains the doctor in its service. The patient, already beleaguered by incessant pain, is hardly 'seen' in this scenario of misrecognition by the doctor.

Fanon's work highlights, to borrow Ahmed's terms, the insufficiency of both a psychological 'inside-out' view of pain which individualises experience, and a sociological 'outside-in' perspective in which emotion becomes a social article that overrides individual affect. Ahmed explains:

> Both assume the objectivity of the very distinction between inside and outside, the individual and social, and the 'me' and the 'we' … emotions create the very effect of surfaces and boundaries that allow us to distinguish an inside and an outside in the first place. So, emotions are not simply something 'I' or 'we' have. Rather, it is through emotions, or how we respond to objects and others, that surfaces or boundaries are made: the 'I' and the 'we' are shaped by and even take the shape of, contact with others.
>
> (Ahmed, 2014: 8–10)

In this light, sociological perspectives cognisant of the structural causes of suffering are important but ultimately insufficient to account for the complexity of emotion. Equally, psychological perspectives that deal with isolated individuals and their emotions fall short. Developing her idea, Ahmed rejects unchecked assumptions that individual and social bodies are defined by distinct borders in the first instance. Such borders, she argues, are constantly construed relationally across all contexts. They are created through the circulation of emotion. This applies, of course, in the context of mindfulness programmes as well. It fosters deeper appreciation of cosmologies in which the 'self' is not discrete, isolated, or singular.

In Fanon's example, the patient is diagnosed by the doctor as vaguely ill, with no reference to their structurally or systemically induced illness. As much as the root of what we might understand as the patient's wound goes unacknowledged, the patient too goes unseen or is perceived and objectified in social interactions only through their woundedness. They are essentially seen as 'wretched' and burdensome to social services. This is due not to a refusal of the patient's wholeness as a multidimensional being, but rather to White Mindfulness' refusal to attend to the patient's identity as politically constructed. Although Kabat-Zinn emphasises the whole patient in his conception, pain is the doorway through which they enter mindfulness, and it is through their wound that the patient is encouraged to find their wholeness. But the patient is only classified as a wounded body by a system of oppression that then applies a normative lens through which they are perceived. There is little sense here of their contribution to society, of their talents, skills, desires, and knowledges.

To explain how bodies are defined, Ahmed posits an almost indiscernible distinction between bodily sensation and emotion. Emotions, she says, create borders that are irreducible either to the psychic or social:

> In suggesting that emotions create the very effect of an inside and an outside, I am not then simply claiming that emotions are psychological *and* social, individual *and* collective. My model refuses the abbreviation of the 'and'. Rather, I suggest that *emotions are crucial to the very constitution of the psychic and the social as objects, a process which suggests that the 'objectivity' of the psychic and social is an effect rather than a cause.* In other words, emotions are not 'in' either the individual or the social but produce the very surfaces and boundaries that allow the individual and the social to be delineated as if they are objects ... even when we feel we have the same feeling, *we don't necessarily have the same relationship to it.* Given that shared feelings are not about feeling the same feeling, or feeling-in-common, I suggest that *it is the objects of emotion that circulate, rather than emotion as such.*
>
> (Ahmed, 2014: 10–11, emphasis added)

Ahmed highlights normative tendencies to understand borders as fixed and to assume that feelings/emotions are fleeting and common across these borders. She uses an example of nationalist fervour enticed by British National Front rhetoric in which inflammatory language is used to describe a 'swarm of illegal immigrants'. The 2021 storming of the US Capitol is a further example of such nationalist fervour that does not dissolve but continues to circulate, (re)produce, and draw lines and structures of power. In these examples the objects of emotions – nationalist fervour – generated and embodied by dominant groups, remain in circulation. Those of the marginalised commonly dissolve or are interpreted through a dominant lens, reflecting relational power.

When White Mindfulness defines emotions as mood states, these appear as discrete states that occur in already bounded bodies and nations. Yet the emotions are not simply in an individual as a mood or state. They are social practices that follow power and their circulation as objects will favour and reinforce certain perspectives and not others. When privilege is challenged, and the world becomes uncomfortable for those in power, we see the emotional objects of White guilt, shame, and fear in circulation. These objects come to overshadow any injustices that preceded them.

Because they are not equal, dominant emotions circulate to create impressions of individual or national sameness without recognising that they create and reproduce White supremacy, heteropatriarchy, and other dominant ideologies. Circulating emotional objects create the illusion of sameness around fear, sorrow, and anger, when in fact they are different experiences, constructed through differential operations of power. In the examples cited, nationalism is used to generate a sameness and to camouflage difference and denigration when it suits. The sameness and rhetoric of interconnectedness is discarded as soon as difference departs from heteronormative, patriarchal White supremacy. But it also creates situations in which PGM and minoritised groups are assimilated into discourses that revolve around dominant emotional objects.

Misrecognition of the role of emotion in generating psychic and social difference supports an understanding of emotions as 'apolitical'. The pain felt, for example, by Fanon's patient, is discerned as an object to be negotiated independently of its effects. We might, following Ahmed, understand the pain felt in Fanon's patient as a historic map of causes and effects. The doctor's and patient's experiences of and relationships to pain are different. Mindfulness teaches that this pain is momentary and impermanent: feelings of pain are objectified; they come, and they go, some teachers even suggest, 'like clouds passing across the sky'. Such practices are inimical to recognising that pain is socio-politically constituted, generative of 'surfaces and boundaries' and difference. Some emotional objects and bodies are more welcomed than others. In the storming of the Capitol for instance, despite its categorisation as domestic terrorism, police were seen to take a markedly lenient approach to the sizeable contingent of angry White men.

This is especially significant when compared to their heavy-handed ruthlessness towards Black Lives Matter (BLM) protests.

When pain is flattened and homogenised, there is no space for the oppressed, precariat, or subaltern. In mindfulness, alleviation of secondary suffering is expected to alter the primary pain or our relationship to it. However, as Ahmed argues, pain always represents histories and power. It could be argued, therefore, that a focus on alleviating secondary suffering overlooks primary suffering, thereby leaving no room for the recognition of difference in suffering. By denying the effects of pain, mindfulness works to erase sociopolitical injustice and exclusions. We can see in Fanon's example that the patient is treated by the doctor according to the doctor's script. In the same way, we can see that although all injuries are not equal, they are treated so by White Mindfulness.

Because the present contains the past, memories and histories inform experiences. As Scott (2018) explains, the present cannot but express experiences of slavery, coloniality, and related legacies inscribed on bodies. When liberal concepts such as 'common humanity' express the principle of equal treatment of all individuals, White Mindfulness refuses to recognise inequalities represented by differences in pain and its effects. This is borne out also in its circles by downplaying narratives that are regarded as peripheral to the here-and-now, but which contextualise pain. In this way, difference and context are muzzled. Instead, common White Mindfulness discourse homologises human experience and, in doing so, epitomises the ideals of postracial neoliberalism.

White Mindfulness' homogenising function is concealed in its rhetoric: 'contemplative practices that are spiritual and/or religious centre us, bring us away from mental dispersal, and connect us with our immediate experience' (Monteiro *et al.*, 2015). Yet as theorised by Muñoz, Ahmed, and Scott, for example, the present moment and experience are politically and historically contingent. The guidance to return to the body and breath implies that they are discrete, ahistorical objects rather than effects of the circulation of power. And yet Fanon's patient has an experience that is different and inequivalent to his doctor's, based on unequal access to power. Their spiritual-religious worlds inevitably differ. White Mindfulness' efforts to connect these differing experiences would, as noted before, privilege the doctor.

In settings in which teachers homologise unequal experiences, empathy and compassion are complex emotions. Relationality commonly centres those with more privileged identities and decentres experiences and narratives outside the normative frame, thereby further marginalising already marginalised voices. To compound matters, wounds can become fetishised as ahistorical entities so that the histories surrounding pain are erased and pain itself becomes objectified with no regard to its role in producing inequalities.

To demonstrate the inequivalence or inverse relationships of pain and political power, Ahmed reports on the Australian government's dispossession of Indigenous Australians. Her study of the Bringing Them Home Report on the Stolen Generation in Australia shows that initiatives geared at 'healing' are themselves infused with power; that permission to heal and to empower, and to decide when hurts are resolved, is not granted universally. She argues that when narratives of pain are heard, they are not necessarily heard justly, explaining how historical oppressions can become 'hijacked' in contexts that seek 'resolution':

> [S]ome forms of suffering more than others will be repeated, as they can more easily be appropriated as 'our loss'. The differentiation between forms of pain and suffering in stories that are told, and between those that are told and those that are not, is a crucial mechanism for the distribution of power.
>
> (Ahmed, 2014: 32)

In this example, 'reconciliation' is used as a means of assimilating Indigenous Australians into the White nation which cleanses itself through expressions of shame at past actions. It demonstrates that those who cause the pain and benefit from its effect also get to decide when and how it will be 'resolved', thereby relinquishing further responsibility and maintaining power. The Australian government appropriates the pain as 'our national identity' without re-arranging perpetuating structures, thereby consolidating their own power, while casting the process as 'compassionate and caring'.

Ahmed's testament illuminates the precarity of White Mindfulness' claims to social transformation. Through concepts such as universality, it invisibilises inequality and fails to interrogate the social norms that perpetuate it, thus continuing to recycle exclusions and

Othering. It claims support for the BLM movement without altering any of its power arrangements or questioning its curriculum and pedagogy. Fanon's medical model typifies the teacher–student relationship, and White Mindfulness' relation to marginalised communities. This is not to suggest that marginalised groups are at the behest of hegemonic power, for subversion and disruption are inevitably and constantly underway. Yet White Mindfulness, framed by postracial, neoliberal discourses, appears to acclimatise participants to their pain. When it does issue pro-BLM statements, it admonishes the pain caused by systemic White supremacy as an opportunity to register 'compassion' without transformation.

The following contribution from a respondent illustrates White Mindfulness' orientation to emotion as residing solely in the participant. They present a charitable intervention that helps participants overcome depression and rumination to transform their lives:

> Mindfulness is really about 'clear seeing' – you know that's obviously very congruent with the Buddhist understanding of mindfulness, that it's about clear seeing – and improving peoples' agency – I think that's a lovely word to use for it – really improving peoples' capacity to make decisions about their own circumstances. For instance, it seems that around mindfulness and unemployment, mental health and depression that so often beset people who are long-term unemployed is a barrier to agency, and a preoccupation with rumination impairs people's capacity to make good decisions ... so one can make a good psychological as well as a social case for mindfulness being extended to populations of much greater deprivation, and personally I'm really passionate about that ... really wanting to see mindfulness developing in these sorts of ways and it's very much an issue [my organisation] wants to put centre stage in terms of its developing role in its vision and mission.

Within the frame of the therapeutic model, the pitiful patient is given an injection of coping strategies to liberate their agency to transform power. The ripple effect is at play: the more people can be reached in this way, the greater the social shift will be. This spin that individualised models transform society reiterates the inability of Fanon's doctor to comprehend the problem. Because they hold the view that depression resides in the patient, there is something wrong with the patient rather than with society and the interstitial tissue – the social norms – that generates 'society' in the first instance. Such inside-out thinking lies at the heart of White Mindfulness' decolonising problem.

The doctor in Fanon's example is trained to perform 'apolitical', ahistorical work because of decontextualised models. This does not preclude the doctor's compassion, but it limits it to bringing symptomatic relief. In this sense, the model may appease the doctor more than the patient, for the doctor sends the patient away feeling they have done something helpful. Similarly, White Mindfulness' dislocation from political transformation and community-based programmes reinforces models that are disengaged from political inequalities. As with Fanon's doctor, the mindfulness teacher may feel empathy but may be more affected by their compassion than their participants are.

In its emphasis on healing, an underlying unequal power relation that sees the participant as pitiful persists. A respondent who works therapeutically with trauma clients shows how the notion of healing and empowerment can become tied to a 'White saviour trope' complex:

> I worked as a trauma therapist and asked: *how do I meet this suffering skilfully?* Then I heard about this programme which is something I knew myself has tremendous value and capacity to bring about healing. So, for me, mindfulness was an extension of my own meditation practice and professional training.

Here again, 'suffering' is seen as the effect of structural causes that resides exclusively in the patient rather than defining the borders between the patient and teacher. If seen in this light, the patient becomes a vessel to be saved and filled with power and wholeness. White Mindfulness becomes a generic healing modality that 'empowers' trauma survivors even while it disengages the politics of transgenerational trauma. The desire to heal detracts from interrogating unequal distributions of power and circulating economies of emotion. There is little proximity to participants, nor any desire to negotiate or co-create curricula that draw upon the knowledge and skills of participants to transform systemic injustices. Like Fanon's doctor, outcomes of mindfulness programmes may appease teachers more than participants.

The decolonial project

Ahmed's work recognises how deeply people are affected by state, governmental, and cultural violences that land deeply in bodies. She highlights how the constant generation and recycling of emotional objects interstitially and trans-generationally reproduces systemic injustices, inequalities, and norms. Equally importantly, Black joy and Muñoz's futurity are explicit about lives that are lived outside the confines of dominant structures and cultures. When White Mindfulness focuses on sensations, emotions, and thoughts in isolation from power and the construction of lives, and treats inequities as things to be resolved through behavioural change without any attention to the politics of emotion, it adds to the problem.

The work of structural and systemic transformation must necessarily involve a dismantling of approaches that are non-collaborative and exclusive such as normative, elitist, US-Eurocentric worldviews that reproduce dominant power. New perspectives on temporality and emotionality, discussed above, suggest that White Mindfulness is constrained in its role and its audience. In the context of growing critiques of how we read and make meaning of the world, and social movements that question how agency too is constricted, its US-Eurocentric orientation locks it into a linear time continuum and a limited psycho-social frame. A lack of engagement with multiple cosmologies, communities, and worldviews makes White Mindfulness provincial. Audiences able to adopt its coping strategies gain, but invariably do so through making projects of their lives. Overall, White Mindfulness' underpinning architecture dislocates it from PGM and groups it is so keen to enlist. Changing course requires sincere dismantling of White Mindfulness' building blocks at every level. As the epigraph says, change must be profound and multidimensional.

Notes

1 In Chapman's definition, pain is nuanced and subjectified: '(a) pain is subjective; (b) pain is more complex than an elementary sensory event; (c) the experience of pain involves associations between elements of sensory experience and an aversive feeling state; and (d) the

attribution of meaning to the unpleasant sensory events is an intrinsic part of the experience of pain' (Chapman, 1986: 153).

2 The *Sallatha Sutta* found in the *Samyutta Nikaya* as SN 36, which addresses 'feeling', contains the two arrows doctrine (Thānissaro Bhikkhu, 1997). The descriptor reads: 'When shot by the arrow of physical pain, an unwise person makes matters worse by piling mental anguish on top of it, just as if he [sic] had been shot by two arrows. A wise person feels the sting of one arrow alone.'

3 'Empowerment', says Asad, is 'a legal term referring both to the act of giving power to someone *and* to someone's power to act' (Asad, 2003: 68, 79).

10

Politicised twenty-first-century mindfulness: creating futures of belonging

The kind of change we are after is cellular as well as institutional, is personal and intimate, is collective as well as cultural. We are making love synonymous with justice.[1]

Prentis Hemphill (2022)

Prentis Hemphill reminds us in the epigraph that our bodies and lives do not end at the boundaries of our skins; we are as much our personal lives, influenced by and influencing the world around us, as we are the structures and cultures that govern our societies. In Indigenous traditions, we are also cosmological beings, inseparable from a living macrocosm and our communities. Since societies mark our bodies and shape our lives, it is the full gamut of circulating affects that imprint themselves on us. This includes communal joy and support, victories won through collective action, celebration of cultures, and the capacities of the heart to connect with one another. But, of course, it also includes dominant cultures and norms that continue to marginalise, diminish, dismiss, exclude, and erode.

In efforts to address the imprints of colony and empire, movements for justice are turning the camera 180 degrees to apply intersectional methods to how they function. There is growing concern with how we reflect and reinforce on a social level the waters that we resist on a political and economic level. As we advocate for liberation, insidious structures, values, and norms – like heteropatriarchy, colourism, and other injustices – continue to confound us. To impact meaningful change, the liberation agenda applies equally at the level of our very being as it does to external structures.

This final chapter looks more carefully at what is to be done at this juncture of crisis and opportunity to create futures that naturally decentre and dismantle whiteness. It considers mindfulness in relation to a liberated society and shines a light on decolonising actions outside the White Mindfulness space. While imagining together can create worlds of belonging, I reflect on the lessons learnt from established and emergent projects grounded in contemplative traditions that are building inclusive futures. Without recentring whiteness, these projects reframe mindfulness as a politicised contemplative practice. They help us discuss meaningful transformation and questions that take us beyond what is known. These burgeoning examples confirm that decoloniality requires radical social transformation rather than cosmetic reforms enacted through improved representation on boards and committees. They highlight collaboration with key parties at the design phase to foreground undervalued talents, assets, knowledges, language, and voices of liberation. They emphasise that systems change is an ongoing process beyond decolonisation that requires ongoing dialogue and inquiry. In the spirit of inquiry, this chapter is not about blueprints.

Individualisation, community, and hybridity

White Mindfulness' foundational hyper-individualism embodies, I believe, an anti-community sentiment, making it difficult to simply slap community onto the existing model. Much has already been said about the discourse of individualism that drives whiteness and neoliberalism. My purpose here is to show how the construct of the individual, conceptualised through capitalism and White supremacy, creates the very illness White Mindfulness seeks to mend.

The Oxford dictionaries describe the individual as a single, separate, discrete, mortal entity, separate from a group. An individual can also be distinctive and original but is always singular. The Latin infinitive 'dividere' means to divide. When the noun 'dividuus' is attached to the prefix 'in', it means indivisible. It refers to the most discrete unit of human life that can thereafter only be further split into head and heart or separated from its wholeness. Ahmed presents a different notion of the individual as an appearance of borders and fixity created by the dominant ideas that circulate in society. She also acknowledges that individuals 'feel' emotion and is not denying that individuals exist, merely that they are not the isolated, sovereign entities we are trained to see. In a world of inequalities, individual and collective bodies carry the markings of society's polarities. Fragmentation manifests at every societal level leading to growing binaries, splits, and fractures, internally, externally, and interstitially.

In White Mindfulness, community is encouraged through claims of 'sameness' rather than understandings of what keeps us separate and fractured. To add to the problem, with its emphasis on inner mental states and behavioural adjustments, it sells the belief that unhappiness or dissatisfaction are internal psychological states that can be changed through acceptance, patience, and trust in the good. Even if this was not originally intended in its formulation and conceptualisation, this is how it currently plays out. Uncritical psychological and sociological approaches objectify either individuals or groups and tend to disregard social context and norms. They don't necessarily help us address the politics of social atomisation. Placing emphasis on individual feeling tone gives little if any appreciation for how norms and emotional artefacts reproduce structural power and the 'individual self'. These neglected systemic facets are what maintain and reproduce systems. When the Mindfulness Industry makes mindfulness exotic and disengages 'community building and social support networks', it loses 'caring communities' as a primary 'source of healing' (Said, 1978: 29). Through these underpinning precepts, it maintains rather than transforms society structurally and becomes further dislocated from liberation, whether inner, outer, or in-between. Being trapped in an ideology of hyper-individualism rather than community estranges White Mindfulness from social transformation.

The absence of a social model of mindfulness, coupled with scientific reductionism and edicts of universality, damage White Mindfulness in every respect. Ironically, it fails to see that communal values of truth, honesty, and a commitment to justice build safety and belonging, enabling marginalised groups to bring all of themselves to spaces of contemplation. Social forces of inequity – and White Mindfulness itself – necessitate identity-based groups in the first instance. Over time, safe spaces make it possible for people to transgress identity borders and queer spaces. I am not suggesting here that identity is a passing fad but that when it is perpetually reconstructed through discrimination and inequality, and people are not self-identifying, it will remain an important marker of difference and a basis for organising. As Lorde (2007a: 137) proclaims: 'If I didn't define myself for myself, I would be crunched into other people's fantasies for me and eaten alive.'

When spaces are forged collectively along the lines of shared, practised values, they become safe and allow for unsafe practices to be called in. Queer spaces are usually driven by a shared vision that doesn't require a blueprint of the future, but that seeks to create worlds of belonging. They entirely disrupt business as usual and foreground marginalised voices. Qualities of these communally forged spaces such as open-heartedness, trust, and safety may well be the qualities emphasised in early conceptualisations of what was to become White Mindfulness – Kabat-Zinn undoubtedly envisaged the dawn of a more just world. As noted, neoliberal postraciality and whiteness engulfed and destroyed any such sentiments, forging and carrying White Mindfulness along without protest.

The decolonial landscape

Diversity efforts that start with 'what do we say so as not to offend anyone?', which is typical of White institutions, signal a paucity of critical thinking. Typically, organisations act in two ways to bring about change. First, performative DEI/EDI approaches add diversity onto the end of already-constructed systems – the adjunctive model. Second, well-intentioned policies seek to correct problems by improving representation or changing the face of the organisation with little understanding of what keeps the organisation going.

Educating the captains and crew of the metaphorical White cruise ship is an important starting point to decoloniality and systems change. Their active engagement in processes of transformation is foundational to change. Equally importantly, leadership by People of the Global Majority (PGM) and minoritised groups is not simply about tapping their perspectives on race, gender, and other multiple characteristics of difference. PGM leadership, visioning, strategic thinking, and actioning widens the talent pool and brings new insights and approaches to institutions and projects in ways that enhance performance, impact, and innovation. But in order to shift the needle, White Mindfulness' current leaders have to 'unpack their knapsacks' and address their own whiteness, not as a navel-gazing exercise but as an awakening to the demands of the current political conjuncture.

A growing number of initiatives that foreground intersectional politics and multiple responses to critical opportunities for change are springing up. Concepts underpinning these include embodied and social justice, operable values, and collective leadership. Much of this work composts what is unearthed to embrace a much wider view of building forward with humanity entangled as a non-dominant collaborator with other life on this planet. Promoting this view while adopting an intersectional approach to correcting injustices is a tall but necessary order. It ties the decolonial agenda to a wider social strategy to build forward consciously in ways that put in place conditions for ongoing change.

Embodied liberation and leadership

Embodied justice and embodied leadership are gaining traction as new fields of practice. Drawing on ancient traditions, histories of political struggle, critical theory, critical race theory, and somatics, new approaches to navigating change are challenging conceptualisations of power, accountability, and change itself. Recreating the world from a place of power requires a critical appraisal of power itself to avoid recentring dominant views entrenched in the collective psyche. Without such a review, change remains limited to alterations of the status quo.

Embodied justice is intrinsically tied to social justice. It is as much about the decolonisation of bodies and minds as it is about decentring whiteness and shaping justice through fundamental transformation. If universality, authoritarianism, dominant measures of success, competency, and privilege are tied up with coloniality and whiteness, decolonisation is about undoing the ways in which these forces mar our very beings. It exposes normative constructs, blinkers, and blind spots that invisibilise whiteness and its links to coloniality. In the absence of safe spaces and Black joy, these are often internalised and inform images and standards of bodies, success, and freedom.

Bayo Akómoláfé (2021) talks of a post-activism that deconstructs concepts like power, trust, and activism to be clear about how we see the world and to check the extent to which our visions are shaped according to our socialisation so that we really do build anew. But more than this, he dismantles concepts such as justice by querying our perspectives of decolonisation itself. Who is asking the questions, he asks, and how do they help us attend to the cracks, not as places to be healed, but wounds that teach us about the larger milieu and cosmos? Rather than being an existential endeavour, Akómoláfé is pointing back to African Indigenous wisdom to sense how to harness opportunities differently. This approach decentres whiteness and power as we know it and embraces instead real emergent understandings of collaborative co-creation. It invites us to lay the path as we walk it.[2]

An emphasis on positionality and co-creating collective futures makes it clear that worlds of belonging for PGM and minoritised groups must be carved by these communities rather than a small group of cis-White men, however well intentioned. Collective leadership that directs active transformation must include and be guided by those who continue to be most marginalised and downtrodden. This practice of intersectionality to generate equity and belonging for all requires cultivating the kind of integral justice that transcends constructed borders (Ramsden, 2016). But more is called for. A focus on justice can become parochial and demands-driven. It can fail to gaze above the parapet or beyond the horizon.

While there are always actions for freedom wherever there are injustices, there is limited focus on inner liberation. Steve Biko wrote in the early 1970s of the need for Black people to liberate our minds, to affirm our humanity and sense of worthiness of freedom (Mangcu, 2014).[3] Biko was influenced by Frantz Fanon, Aimé Césaire, and Malcolm X, revolutionary thinkers and political activists who encouraged a knowledge of Black protest history and Black-owned institutions as well as radical curricula reform that 'nurtured a positive Black identity for young people' (Marable and Joseph, 2008: ix–x). A few years later, in 1979, Bob Marley

wrote 'Redemption Song' containing the lyrics 'none but ourselves can free our minds', speaking to the need to liberate ourselves from the impact that the devastation of oppression imprints
on the mind. Drawing on the 1937 works of Pan-Africanist orator
Marcus Garvey, Marley expressed the same sentiments as Biko,
emphasising inner alongside outer liberation. Neither of them pitted
these freedoms against one another, nor graded or sequenced them.

Shaping an understanding of the person as inseparable from communities, ecosystems, and power, Biko and Marley enable richer
contemplations and actions for transformation. Today their legacies
live on in efforts to remove the blinkers that constructs of colonialism and whiteness perpetuate both structurally and in relation to
the White gaze and persistent Othering. Their works reinforce an
understanding that discriminations practiced today are not simply
rooted in histories of oppression and structures of power; they are
interstitially embedded in daily social practices. On 30 November
2021, as Barbados became a Republic, Prime Minister Mia Motley
confirmed the currency of this problem, saying: 'we are still faced
with the insidious nature of a culture that is intended to dehu-
manise [B]lack people wherever [B]lack or [B]lackness is found ...
it is the mental emancipation that shall forever always matter' (Safi,
2021). Motley's statement bears testament to the enduring nature
of mental incarceration and the drive for decoloniality to consider
comprehensive emancipation.

Decolonising the body, mind, and whole being through co-
regulation, co-decolonisation, and co-creation is an ongoing process to deconstruct and liberate the mind. A liberated being opens
to grander prospects of imagining and world-making. Practices and
actions that advance embodied justice and social justice are designed
to correct such power imbalances. Mindfulness, when it emphasises
the whole being in context, could potentially support this.

A personal account

Increased understanding of how dominance recycles itself tells
us that the circulation of discriminatory ideologies reproduces
social power. Exclusions are emotionally induced and structurally embedded, creating the effects of nationalisms, racism, sexism,

classism, homophobia, transphobia, ableism, ageism, Islamophobia, and anti-Semitism. These divides exist as much in the division of the head from the heart and body as they do in society. They detract from traditional cosmologies in which humans are inseparable from a far grander macrocosm. Healing these divides and confusions must address, therefore, all these levels. But healing, of course, calls for processes sensitive to how multiple bodies with multiple identities are treated differently by society and experience spaces differently. In other words, the process has to itself be radical and appropriate and must engage all key players in the context of their communal, eco-, and social systems.

In 2021, I attended a three-month embodied justice programme designed with a sensitivity to minoritised voices and experiences. The programme emphasised social justice and radical change with a primary focus on foregrounding Black, trans, intersectional voices. The virtual community was 700 strong, all set on the same course of embodied liberation. While learning how to be in community with allied, White-bodied people who stumbled and fell into the usual holes of dominating the discussion and centring whiteness, we were guided by expert directors who created space for these missteps to be named, processed, and revisited. At the same time, they selected GM, especially Black trans voices, before those of White respondents and named these deliberate choices to break with cultures of whiteness.

Working through 24 two-hour modules, followed by group discussion designed to expose the global group to the material of embodied justice, we had the choice of entering either PGM, trans, LGBT, queer, white-bodied, or open group spaces. Using presentations interspersed with somatics, movement, sound, traditional wisdom, science, and meaningful mindfulness, we were collectively shepherded towards our own processes of decolonising ourselves. This too happened in community. I was fortunate to end up in a diverse group of five, straddling three continents and four countries, albeit all middle class with reliable digital access.

Despite our small number, we ranged from GM to queer, trans, and White-bodied and spanned two generations, including recent gen Zs, millennials, and boomers. Our purpose was to produce a joint group project. This collective experience dug deep into how to avoid plastering over the cracks of our colonisation and conditioning in whiteness by hiding behind cognitive understandings of decolonisation. We chose to become uncomfortable and messy.

Taking to crayons and paints, we captured our evolving processes and revelations in a graphic e-zine. Some of the themes that emerged through collaborative investigation of our lives were polarity; hiding behind academia, theory, and the cognitive realm to bypass our own pain and confusion; appeasement; being 'good', compliant, and self-regulated. Bifurcation and binaries were a big theme echoing the deep chasms in our societies. I name this process in some detail here to highlight the depths of colonisation and the many bypasses created to maintain its grip on the mind-body to avoid fundamental change. What stood out for us was the power of building trust and safety through mutual learning and shared experiences. Rather than reducing this to a navel-gazing exercise, we created safety and accountability consciously by walking through the fire together. For some of us, we were able to link this process to broader community projects, allowing the principles of decolonisation and embodied justice to inform our work.

The process revealed numerous transferrable lessons. The intersectional approach as the ground to this programme, foregrounding PGM, queer voices, habits of whiteness, social norms, and providing spaces for processing and moving beyond, was extremely powerful. Coming together intersectionally with the purpose of embodying the very justice we are seeking in the world required us to uncover our own stuckness and to be committed to liberating ourselves instead of waiting for justice to be handed to us. We knew we were on the right path when it was uncomfortable and unfamiliar. Offering our eyes, ears, and senses to one another's processes, making sanctuary, and being consistent in showing up as we were, moved mountains. Our process culminated in a co-created artefact that marks our mutual experience.

White Mindfulness spaces lack this clear commitment to dismantling constructs and decolonising society, and while such processes may not work for all communities, versions of it can help build broader understandings of ecosystems and stress. Using somatics, ritual, safety, and rapport built in the collective reflections with different people over a period of three months gave time to consolidate learnings and revelations and consider how to implement these in our lives. Collective dialogue, witnessing, and wise action supported stepping outside the confined frames of dominant ideologies. Standing together in power to decolonise the whole being generated change not only in the sense of something new, but of something emergent, different, and in the service of PGM and minorities. But there was more. The very ethos and content of the curriculum dismantled hyper-individualism and supported systemic inquiries, including many teachings around how to understand and disrupt whiteness and racial capitalism. The programme was explicitly framed around liberation. It required White-bodied people to show up and do their work.

Liberatory questions

Applying Lorde's master's tools teaching to White Mindfulness helps clarify what precisely its ethos, lived values, and mechanisms are and how it reproduces itself pedagogically. It exposes the underpinnings of an ahistorical, depoliticised, decontextualised mindfulness that collapses difference and reads participants only as sharing 'common humanity'. Perspectives derive from US-Eurocentric influences framed by divisive, racialised norms. Currently, a neoliberal, postracial context of whiteness fashions universalist thinking that claims co-creation but delivers a one-size-fits-all approach.

Trajectories like that of White Mindfulness can move in directions that gather momentum so quickly that they become irreversible or difficult to slow down. Lorde's framing suggests that changes to the current White Mindfulness monopoly will not come about through its institutions but that it requires movement and change on the outside. Like Hall, she acknowledges political conjunctures and the irregular nature of change, which can cement rather than alleviate injustices.

In contemplating White Mindfulness' decolonisation, it is prudent to distinguish programmes in hospitals that diminish stress and illness from commodities sold on Amazon. While framed by the limitations of the White Mindfulness model, the former, albeit uncritically, are intended to serve society. They are different to the mindless consumption of commodities that feed the commercialisation and eradication of ancient wisdom. However, it is important to recognise that interventions in hospitals, prisons, communities, and schools are encased in ideologies that don't question power structures, school-to-prison pipelines, and other societal features that reproduce racial capitalism. So while it is helpful to acknowledge the sentiments and successes of bringing coping skills or transitory relief to people, it is as important to acknowledge the mechanisms that reduce mindfulness to sedatives, band-aids, and palliative care.

Hyper-individualism that further atomises people already isolated is fundamentally stress generating. In addition, the patriarchal social milieu that circulates all the isms creates and reinforces discriminations; it shapes society, the look of leadership, as well as fears and priorities. These emotional objects are not peculiar to the White Mindfulness Industry. They are the very waters in which we swim. They shape our minds so that even those who are structurally privileged are emotionally and mentally captive. In efforts to resolve the uncomfortable polarities in our minds, we blunt differences among key parties and declare common ground and consensus about how to move forward and where to go. As many initiatives show, these are not the tools that bear repeating. The devastating impact of dominant social norms, fixity, perspectives, constructions, and deep-seated assumptions of authority remind us of the need for new tools, approaches, and radical change. These appear to come less in the form of resistance to a misguided ship, and more in the form of works emerging at the epicentre of change. These new approaches continue to flourish as more voices shape the instruments and technologies that serve revolution in the interests of all.

If justice truly is sought as the birthright of all, context, purpose, and communities are pertinent. Acknowledging not only an unlevel playing field but also the need to change the game to better navigate the potholes, potentially guides the way to greater freedom. Being close to the people being served is an essential component of new programmes. Their inputs, skills, talents, and knowledges matter in shaping curricula and pedagogies. Their ownership of programmes and processes and their ability to lead programmes are crucial considerations in breaking with dominant, authoritarian cultures.

The transformation of systems and norms is neither a question of morality nor commerce. It rights the wrongs of injustice in ways that allow for safety, dignity, expansion, emergence, play, and trust to name a few core values that allow us to embrace greater understandings of being. Breaking free of oppressive regimes creates pathways that embrace revolutionary thought. At this time of truth and reckoning, it forges a new planet based on belonging and becoming, one that necessarily involves all key players in community building and worldmaking.

Structurally, decolonisation entails not only a turning towards justice and interrogating what this means. It necessarily involves an undoing of the uncritical pedagogy that besets the field. Critical race theory, intersectional analyses, and an honest appraisal of the roots and undergirding of White Mindfulness are important components of new social justice-infused curricula. Understanding how norms function to maintain the status quo and how power and relationality can shape inclusive democracies are rich components of new approaches. These are important to understand not only for their external disruption but to liberate all communal beings. To bring about inclusive transformation, we must become clear about how to disrupt the exclusive mindfulness practices and spaces to which the Mindfulness Industry clings.

The following questions are intended to generate dialogue, discussion, and communal practice around what is to be done. They are divided into three sets: the first regards a socially purposed mindfulness, the second pertains to restorative and transformative justice, and the third focuses on liberating our very beings.

One of the primary considerations in this chapter is whether mindfulness can be assumed in hooks' terms as part of a means towards liberation. Is such a use of mindfulness appropriation or bastardisation, or is it allowed due to its liberatory purpose? Is there a mindfulness that is neither colonised nor reductive, that is respectful of the bearers of traditions, and that can serve a radical agenda of change? Is this the mindfulness already practiced at the East Bay Meditation Centre (EBMC), the Buddhist Peace Fellowship, and within the Radical Dharma movement? Can these models guide White Mindfulness models in their transformation? With transformation as the starting point, can mindfulness become one of many contemplative traditions found across the planet that nourishes agents of change and their agency? Is White Mindfulness keen to transform and grow beyond its current provision? What would such a mindfulness look like? Would it be defined? Will it have an architecture, model, or system? Would this still be mindfulness or simply a way of being contemplative and purposeful together?

Questions around restorative justice lean into matters of reconciliation. They assume that White Mindfulness leadership is incentivised to acknowledge and address the challenges from Asian Buddhists who are standing in their power. What are the implications for relationships with traditional institutions such as the Buddhist Peace Fellowship and other organisations that deliver mindfulness in the context of Buddhism? Is reconciliation required as part of the process moving forward? Is restorative justice possible in this field premised on Orientalism, cultural appropriation, and authoritarianism, and what might that look like?

Decolonising ourselves questions how deeply we are motivated to change and how keenly we are aware of the grip of coloniality and neoliberalism on our whole being. It builds on the notion that well-meaning people can also be racist and discriminatory. How do we encourage ourselves and one another to address the imprints that all dominant systems leave on our beings, especially those constructs that are normative and invisibilised? In what ways can teachers of White Mindfulness undertake these trainings as parts of collectives to transform and create different spaces? How can we step outside the hyper-individualised world of White Mindfulness to see ourselves as entangled with each other and our collectives to arrest the circulation of whiteness? More importantly, how can we become free enough to imagine, dream, and generate new worlds fashioned in the images of community and belonging?

These questions of decoloniality lean towards reconciliation and call forth a serious review of what helps, what can be expanded, and what must change. It foregrounds ethos, context, positionality, and content. It requires conversations that acknowledge the hurts caused to traditional Buddhists, which have been publicly named but that go unacknowledged. In considering how to approach reconciliation, truth commissions held in numerous countries provide some insight. South Africa's Truth and Reconciliation Commission (TRC), for instance, founded by its first democratically elected president, Nelson Mandela, and chaired by Archbishop Desmond Tutu, may provide some direction. The TRC set out to facilitate restorative justice in the *de jure* post-apartheid era overseeing a process of testimonial hearings from those who had experienced gross human rights violations, as well as from perpetrators of such violence. It allowed people to appear before the TRC to voice, be witnessed, seek clarity on what had happened to loved ones, and to seek justice. It also allowed bastions of apartheid and perpetrators of the violence to attend hearings to seek forgiveness. Regarded as generally successful, the TRC process also met with mixed opinion, including observations that it allowed some to render apologies for their murderous deeds without sufficient retribution. This was seen to fail the marginalised majority who never received justice for the crimes committed against them, their communities, and families. This TRC model of justice may offer an approach to healing the divides wrought through White Mindfulness. Other examples are found in Congo, Chile, Germany, and Australia.

While White Mindfulness is not consciously administering violent exclusions, its operations are nonetheless exclusive, and its reflexions must address histories and patterns of Orientalism and appropriation. Any decolonial agenda includes matters of power and transformation. As a collection of institutions thriving in an ecosystem of whiteness, White Mindfulness faces increasing scrutiny of its historical orientation, invisibilisation of whiteness, erasure of PGM, Othering, claims of universalism, postracialism, and exclusions. It currently stands at a crossroads regarding its now conscious direction of travel. In a context of speaking truth to power and in the spirit of reconciliation, there is growing pressure to reckon with its past. Added to this, the Mindfulness Industry is now so culturally enmeshed in late capitalist society that the pedagogies and underpinning technologies of White Mindfulness that support it are in question. To return to the cruise ship analogy, these technologies function as propellers that can either support its uncritical onward trajectory or reverse their thrust to slow the ship down or turn it around. The heavier the ship, and the greater the speed, the longer it will take to stop or reverse direction. Buoyed by cheerleaders unconcerned with justice, it is unlikely that its commodification will pause let alone cease. But open to the voices of liberation that abound, there is every chance that the captains and their crew may be swept up by the winds of change.

Just as Kabat-Zinn's vision for MBSR shaped four decades of an exploding Western mindfulness field, a new vision is required, perhaps collectively created to usher a sizeable movement into the

next era built on truth, reconciliation, and worldmaking. A range
of organisations are leading the way.

Models of social transformation

Socially minded mindfulness protagonists keen to transform the
sector and society identify a politically fraught context in which
mindfulness lacks a politically explicit agenda. Magee (2018), for
instance, in pointing out that White Mindfulness ignores the social
milieu of 'racism, sexism, and all the other isms', states that hyper-
individualism also serves to 'disconnect [and] denude our experience from its embeddedness in community and culture. So, that is
kind of hand and glove with racism, sexism, homophobia [and] is
to deny the relevance of culture, of community, of history.' White
Mindfulness' reductionism, she says, makes it 'not about sex or race.
It's really about you as an individual and whether or not you can
overcome.' Yet, despite her appraisal, Magee remains optimistic that
as a practice, mindfulness can be extricated from the racialised neoliberal cultures that shape it; that because it 'opens up our capacity
to see things through multiple lenses at once, [it] has a profound
ability to help us, and in that sense lead Western culture forward'.

Magee captures the flaws of a model that personalises systemic
injustices and privatises transformation. Instead of inviting a range
of experiences, perspectives, and insights into dismantling injustice,
the model reduces mindfulness to cultivating patience while
awaiting change. The agency that potentially comes from being
together and shaping transformation is trained to accept injustice
as 'how things are', rather than engage with what must be changed.
In this light, its postracial, individualised, universal paradigm and
models are incompatible with social justice agendas. The very ethos
and philosophy of seeing an individual in isolation from their social
context and ecosystem keeps it constrained. Can it change gear?

Angela Black's focus on identity politics aims to create spaces in
which PGM can practice together and be taught by Black teachers.
This design immediately departs from White spaces, creating
greater opportunities for safety and trust. Her work, like Magee's,
foregrounds broader social context as key to transformation. But
in both Black's and Magee's insightful critiques, Kabat-Zinn's

operational definition holds. This seems to overlook the ways in which the conceptualisation is tied in with broader ideologies that neglect a social model.

To shift the paradigm, a social model of mindfulness would have to consider how to decolonise bodies and free minds collectively. It would need to revisit its 'non-judgemental present moment awareness' directive, given the many ways in which these terms can be reductionist and exclusive. To cultivate connection, collaboration, and insight for specific purposes of liberation requires judgement, interrogation, and transformation of dominant forms and norms of power. The social model of somatics used to transform individual, collective, institutional, and social bodies serves as an example of what is possible. It understands shaping of the body and the very being as inseparable from the situations and conditions in which we live. Frozen, fixed, and stuck bodies may be protective shapes adopted in response to ongoing adversity. While bodies learn to open safely in safe contexts, to reduce over-reactivity or hyper-arousal, they also learn to address power-over that 'result[s] in patterns of emotion, beliefs, behaviours, and physical patterns that become embodied habits' (Haines, 2019: 413).

Through somatic practice, over time bodies start opening and finding new shapes to uncover and liberate greater agency for change. In this social model, safety is paramount, and as playwright and poet Yolanda Nieves tells us, and Angela Black intimates above, bodies feel safe with like-bodied people. Similar bodies naturally gravitate towards one another. I have experienced this countless times in White Mindfulness spaces. There is an uncanny magnetic pull that attracts people to one another as if the space is commonly known on some unsaid level. When the likeness of bodies is not present, it takes a lot longer to build the safety and trust between bodies that are marked differently by society.

The expansion of the social model to link with an economic model focused on community-owned institutions moves closer to opportunities for liberation as imagined by Biko, Marley, and Motley. adrienne maree brown, author of *Emergent Strategy* (2017), invites a dimension of creating and owning institutions to grow and live with different rules and norms. Drawing on the work of Octavia Butler, her invitation encourages a dreaming beyond current systems about worlds that nourish transformation and nurture innovation. Such a space liberates thought about possible futures. In encouraging such imagining, thought leader Gillian Marcelle (2017) breaks from naming innovation merely as novelty. Writing in the context of business and economic justice, for her, innovation is a knowledge and learning space that brings together numerous players and multiple forms of capital to acknowledge the complementary roles played by different actors in pioneering change. She names social, network, relational, knowledge capital, and others as the kinds of resources essential to transformation that marginalised groups have in abundance. Such understanding invites what she calls a 'widening of the solution space' to extend beyond a dependence only on financial capital. It sets the stage for vaster, different worldmaking rooted in the realities and histories of discrimination and exploitation as well as liberation and joy.

The social model assumes that mindfulness teachers are sufficiently schooled in understanding socio-political and economic contexts, that they have an appreciation of cosmological influences and somatics, and have an embodied justice practice. In keeping with brown's notion of emergence, we can move the needle further by embracing the notion of an embodied liberation practice: becoming free of the shackles of oppression and awake to the possibilities of thriving futures. Being of service as a mindfulness teacher in contexts of mounting trauma requires teachers to be aware of the patterns of coloniality and whiteness they embody.

The politics of intersectionality, invested in shifting concerns from the individual to the collective, is essentially about transformation. Race and intersecting characteristics of difference constitute 'coalition locations' or the basis of organisation. As catalysts for organisation, identity-based groups are what Crenshaw calls 'coalitions waiting to be formed' (Crenshaw, 1991: 1299). In organisational contexts, such groups, as Gajaweera discovered in her research, collectively identify the possibilities for meaningful change. The works of Black and Magee, for instance, are not simply about separate community organising; they have political agendas of transformation. Similarly, the work at the EBMC – one of the originators in identity-group gatherings and teachings in the Western world of Buddhism and mindfulness – lays the basis for coalition formation to advance change.

In 2006 the EBMC launched out of the prior work of the East Bay Dharma Centre, which originally formed in 2001 to reach a diverse community. EBMC uses a gift economy model to improve access and welcome all. Deliberately locating itself in the predominantly Black Oakland area, its mission was to create an inclusive space for marginalised communities. They offer 'safe space' classes for PGM, LGBTQI, disability, and chronic illness and chronic pain communities. These initiatives are now also supported financially by funders sensitive to the compulsory integration of wellbeing, justice, and PGM self-determination 'in the service of the collective liberation'. The Kataly Foundation, for instance, supports community-based projects that promote new understandings of liberation at the same time as they train people in whole-being-whole-world liberation. Their Mindfulness and Healing Justice programme supports mindfulness programmes, teacher training, and retreats designed and led by PGM. They centre 'the power of internal and external awareness in the service of collective transformation, social justice and racial equity'.[4]

Buddhist Global Relief (BGR) is a further example of a pro-justice model which, although not limited to mindfulness, encapsulates a Buddhist social model that redresses injustices. BGR actively engages community organisations with whom they co-produce programmes, embodying a social ethic that privileges community interests to build different futures. Their work highlights one of the ways in which White Mindfulness avoids this integration of mindfulness and justice by divorcing their purposes. A respondent ratifies this by identifying two discrete, sequential projects – the cultivation of mindfulness and the political agenda of social transformation, underlining their separation rather than their confluence: 'first get the mindfulness right, and then turn to the politics'. Even if by this it is suggested that teachers put mindfulness to work to decolonise themselves, this is a political process. Politics, society, social, environmental, and economic context are all personal. In contrast to bifurcations that extricate the individual from their context, the examples cited above appreciate that they are entangled and that social norms are personal.

The Radical Dharma community, which is growing globally, offers ways of working outside the frame of coloniality to transform society. They exemplify mutuality between Buddhism and social justice, harnessing difference to challenge inequalities and hegemonies in the pursuit of social justice. The project functions independently of the White Mindfulness field and indirectly, by virtue of its presence and growing popularity, contests some fundamental pillars such as whiteness, pathologisation, and psychologisation. This approach expands the remit of mindfulness saying that when we seek 'the embodiment of truths, giving ourselves permission to be honest, more healed, more whole, more complete ... neither the path of solely inward-looking liberation, nor the pursuit of an externalised social liberation prevails; rather a third space, as-yet-unknown, emerges' (williams *et al.*, 2016: xxxi–ii). In other words, this radical approach embraces emergence and the unknown as opportunities and imperatives in worldmaking. Taking form as trainings and offerings led primarily by the three authors of the book *Radical Dharma*, a growing movement is using mindfulness practices, dialogue, and inquiry to find liberation in community. Two of these teachers, Lama Rod Owens and Reverend angel Kyodo williams, are senior Buddhist teachers who focus their public teachings on social transformation and liberation. Operating mainly in the US, there are questions regarding the extent to which these programmes blend with Indigenous cultures to develop closer relations with the land and broader ecosystems. Whether this movement conveys a more sophisticated temporality than that of 'present-moment awareness' is unknown, although Lama Rod's work with ancestry and the circulation of emotional artefacts certainly suggests a more expansive, responsive, evolving outlook.

The examples cited here challenge the 'second Renaissance' aspiration of universality and underline the need for networked context-specific approaches to stress and trauma that invites new and different ways of building the world. It might be that one-size-fits-all models are no longer pertinent, that tailored, emergent solutions are more responsive and effective than anything imposed, that involving all key actors in co-creating numerous solutions that suit different circumstances and contexts is paramount in meaningful transformation, and that solutions are themselves living systems that continue to evolve.

Embracing decoloniality

When mindfulness is context-sensitive, it can play a role in rebuilding community, especially if it engages multiple solutions geared to create just and thriving societies. Stepping beyond the pre-occupation with universalism and a US-Eurocentric perspective of change allows mindfulness to open towards decoloniality, systems change, and building forward differently and agilely. Applications and models can become more explicit about pro-transformation agendas, as several of the programmes cited above demonstrate. As growing trans-disciplinary and cross-sectoral coalitions reveal, there is no single solution to change but multiple ways of building a different world. Collaboration and learning networks open opportunities for refining and evolving living innovations so that researchers can investigate agile, community-based, and climate-forward approaches for thriving.

A shared vision does not require a single pathway, just as shared solutions do not advocate uniformity in how wellness and agility are cultivated in different contexts. Embracing difference invites complexity and multiplicity in building collaboration and forging community, a factor to be encouraged to widen the solution space.

Notes

1 Prentis Hemphill's quote from the Radical Recovery Summit, 7–16 January 2022, found at https://bit.ly/3Lw55wy, pays homage to Martin Luther King Junior: 'Power without love is reckless and abusive, and love without power is sentimental and anaemic. Power at its best is love implementing the demands of justice, and justice at its best is power correcting everything that stands against love.'

2 This is a play on the cognitive scientist Fransisco Varela's quote: *to lay a path in walking.*

3 The South African Student Organisation (SASO), which Biko formed with comrades and to which he was elected the first president, promoted Black Consciousness, deliberately so named so as not to be framed in relation to whiteness, to advance 'Black is beautiful', and to cultivate a mental attitude of freedom. SASO encouraged Black people, a category they defined as including Indians and Coloureds (classified separately as part of apartheid's divide-and-rule strategy) to 'reject all value systems that seek to make him [sic] a foreigner in the country of his birth and reduce his basic human dignity' (Denis, 2010: 166).

4 East Bay Meditation Centre can be found at: https://eastbaymeditation.org. Kataly Foundation is at: www.katalyfoundation.org.

Conclusion: embodied liberation and worldmaking

Justice
is heartache
wrapped
in pretty paper
offered with
cheap sentiment
from friends
who own land.

Danai Mupotsa (2018: 58)

In 2015, at the Centre for Mindfulness (CfM) Conference, the previously cited group of Global Majority (GM) panellists spoke about their experiences of the world of White Mindfulness. Most of them had taught on CfM's Mindfulness-Based Stress Reduction (MBSR) programme and had experience of either the Insight Meditation Society in Barre or some other convert Buddhist space. They spoke of not belonging in the White spaces they navigated in order to do their jobs. One of the panellists spoke of the subtle patterns noticed when they passed White people in corridors. Handbags being shifted to hands that were safe from 'passers-by'; sideways, uncomfortable glances, or over-friendliness. This, they said, was happening at the mindfulness conference itself.

Within a year, as the UK started addressing issues of White Mindfulness, there was once again an outpouring of stories of microaggressions. These included PGM being told: 'but you're so educated!', 'but we're not really that different you know', and famously when directed at paler-skinned PGM, 'but look, we're the same shade', or 'my arms are darker than yours'. Another response to a critique of the whiteness of the convert mindfulness community from a senior teacher was: 'but you are practicing reverse-Othering. We are trying our best. Do you think this doesn't hurt us as much as it hurts you?'

These stories sound 'micro' until they are all pooled together to show the extent of the problem. Social norms of this nature are so commonplace that they are disregarded, isolated, and usually dismissed. Such events, of course, accord with what happens in wider society. People are publicly and privately harassed, abused, and threatened purely on account of their ethnicity and/or their gender or faith.

It is easy to call these experiences incidents, but of course systemic racism is inherent in White Mindfulness organisations. Reducing them to episodes or experiences is one of the ploys used to detract from their predominance. In White Mindfulness in both the US and UK, undressing whiteness is usually an add-on, featuring late on the agenda of a gathering, or as something additional to be dealt with. There is little appreciation that racism is at the heart of these organisations and that systems change and redress is their actual work.

To bring any hope to mindfulness contributing to a better world, these deep-set social norms must be consciously interrupted. Simply telling people that bigotry of any sort is wrong clearly doesn't change societies. Systems built on injustices that benefit some at the expense of others have their own subtle controls of power. The deeper work of social change makes it possible to wake up to what is being silently sponsored by an uncritical mindfulness. Clarity allows us to see that what is made out to be our insecurities, our illnesses, and our dis-ease is tied up with dominant power.

Poet Danai Mupotsa captures the reality that justice is being controlled and withheld daily not only by legislation but by what we culturally condone and let pass. The epigraph drops the heartbreak that comes with realisations of how power-over is wielded. Paternalistic cultures train an expectation of benevolent, peaceful change being freely given by a sovereign power that cares for people. And the same societies promote bigotry, greed, unfairness, injustice, and brutality.

But Mupotsa's poem also shows us that justice is ours, not something to be given to us. That, she intimates, is no justice. Millions of lives have been lost in efforts to create greater equilibrium in societies or because people are simply cast aside. Buying into the system and chasing the kinds of fantasies White supremacy encourages takes us way off track. Like Akómoláfé, Mupotsa is asking what our own sense of justice and freedom might be, given just how unequal our societies are. And then to determine how we get there without relying on whiteness, and without awaiting consensus. As history shows us, we cannot rely on people who wield undemocratic power to create the world we wish to live in.

Linking the different stories in this book, change sometimes comes about through pressuring authorities. It sometimes also comes by starting independent initiatives like East Bay Meditation Centre, the Kataly Foundation, and Radical Dharma. In all these situations, the message seems to be that we all play a role in the solution.

On its own, White Mindfulness cannot think outside the box. It only sees more space into which to spread its model. But in collaboration with people who see the world and create very differently, it can potentially transform to become part of something far larger and greater. It can open to the realisation that change is co-created and relies on different perspectives and outlooks. The starting point of inquiring into whiteness and neoliberalism cannot be the end point. Instead, the forces of change involved in purposeful worldmaking must guide this process.

Jaime Kucinskas (2019) outlines how the mindful elite sought social change through using their networks and access to power. Their conscious infusion of mindfulness into multiple social spheres including education, health, and business is evident in the uptake of programmes in schools, hospitals, the workplace, and prisons. They used the master's tools of marketisation, science and research, and education to popularise mindfulness and to change societies. And they've been successful, in that mindfulness is now well known in certain middle-class circles. However, their gains are limited by their perspectives as elites and their inability to bridge the deep chasms between their spheres of influence and most people's lives. Deep in the bedrock of late capitalism is hyper-individualism and consumerism. Deploying free-market strategies to popularise mindfulness seems to have spread it almost exclusively to middle and upper classes. Added to this, the inherent racialisation of the US and UK spreads individualised and therapised mindfulness mainly to White people.

White Mindfulness is premised on an appeal to behavioural change without addressing the systems that quietly sponsor those behaviours in the first instance. But social change cannot be brought about through personal behavioural change. The sum of individuals making incremental changes in their personal lives without addressing the broader social pillars that construct and maintain the status quo cannot result in social or systemic change. In contrast to behavioural solutions which are veiled forms of coercion, true democracies require ongoing inner, outer, and systemic change that supports communal agency to overturn precarity and social insecurity. When mindfulness teachers themselves self-govern as a form of obedience and then train their students to do the same, citing stress in pathologised rather than political terms, they participate in these surreptitious controls. Emphasis on behavioural change links them to a numbing of political agency. Such a focus, in which the individual is encouraged to change their behaviour to fit into the system, detracts from systemic transformation. This 'silent politics' or 'White noise' is once again projected as value-free, adding to mindfulness' 'uncritical' problem and its complicity in bolstering business as usual. Poor attention to what social justice means and how inequalities are perpetuated, not only through power structures but through normative Othering, means that we reproduce the master's tools.

This book set out to map the trajectory of White Mindfulness. Its starting point was to ask whether White Mindfulness could indeed support significant social change. The good intentions of elites and their access to power was regarded, by them, as a sufficient basis for skill-in-action to effect social change. Yet this inquiry has uncovered multiple tools and brick walls that stand in the way of social change. Much of what I've uncovered is a failure to turn 180 degrees to understand the ways in which the elite themselves and the organisations they create embody the very obstacles they seek to undo. Rather than a finger-pointing exercise, this is to acknowledge the ways in which we are all marked by social forces and norms that circulate to reproduce the status quo. Interrupting these requires thinking outside the frame of institutional power.

The simple map of internal and external change becomes much richer and cloudier when the interstitial comes into play. This is more than a vacuous gap between the inner and the outer. It points to the social norms and customs, the cultures and traditions, and the emotional artefacts that permeate societies and are constantly in circulation. Social norms are commonly implicit and deeply ingrained in societies as if they are the very air that we breathe. So strong is our conditioning that we believe we are individuals isolated from the influences and constructs that shape us. We are collectively unaware just how much we embody of the status quo or how much it eclipses our collective joy. It is also not always clear how much we need one another's eyes to see what it is that we embody, whether the joys of freedom or the cruelties of whiteness or apartheid.

This book has discussed mindfulness in relation to power. How the very process of selectively extracting knowledge from its root, or deracination, is imbued with Orientalism. The colonial power to appropriate knowledge capital, without acknowledging what such appropriation is linked to, highlights the extent of this power. The ability to not declare our social stature, and how this itself is linked to power and privilege, is a display of normative power from which other positions declare themselves. The underpinnings of Othering play themselves out not only in relation to the culling of traditional knowledges to adapt them for marketisation, but to the ways in which the bearers of these traditions are disregarded during such repositioning of their cultures. Othering also relates to the ways in which the significantly sized GM Buddhist community, especially in the US, continues to feel the brunt of being outsiders within predominantly White convert-Buddhist communities. Some significant studies shed further light on the histories of microaggressions and exclusions that Black Buddhists often experience in White spaces (Gajaweera, 2021; Hase *et al.*, 2019; Sasser, 2018).

Identifying the extremes of whiteness within Western Buddhism and White Mindfulness communities is not to question the measures underway at Spirit Rock and other Insight Meditation Centres to challenge their histories. And perhaps their focus extends an invitation to White Mindfulness to reveal their own cracks and to allow light to shine through the social wounds gaping in the US and UK. My point is that Spirit Rock and other Insight Meditation

Centres' attention to correcting injustices at these institutions is their actual work. It illuminates positionality or, put another way, how our power is tied up with one another and the systems we recycle or seed.

Social norms recycle in the ways we navigate and monopolise power. Having access to network capital to mobilise the resources that show the efficacy of a selective mindfulness is a significant demonstration of power. An even greater command of power is seen in the ability to start a secular movement based on the 'proven' model. Contained in dominant power are generations of privilege and the ability not to question that power or the lack thereof for others. Forming organisations without an awareness of how these social norms inevitably enter our lives and the spaces we occupy replicates power and privilege. Given the seas in which we swim, it is unsurprising that in White spaces contemplative traditions have not helped unearth the embodiment of social tenets like whiteness that permeate all of society. However, it is important to challenge these constructs of power by recognising the power in the new movements cited above, and emergent concepts like embodied liberation. In the broader context of intersecting social emergencies, these are now gaining traction and attention.

Closing remarks

Our positions in society define our explicit, external power. As hooks, powell, Biko, Vaid-Menon, and others have indicated, they do not – nor should they – dictate our inner and collective power. People with different values form different organisations. It is precisely the presence of a growing number of Black, traditional, and convert Buddhists interested in social justice that allows a more nuanced sense of how mindfulness can be used to address injustices and promote social change. And here, the work is about how to occupy, undress, and transform a distressed world to create the spaces we desire.

For many of us reading this book, White Mindfulness has no doubt made and continues to make a significant contribution to our lives. When we suffer loss, shock, devastation, or injustice – as all of us invariably do regardless of identity – and practices are accessible and possible, they usually calm an agitated nervous system. Thich Nhat Hanh's 15-second pause or reconnecting with the breath can, potentially, bring tremendous ease. Learning about our habits and how to improve our communication styles helps all relationships. When it is possible, developing a renewed relationship with the body – albeit via a Westernised spin on the body scan – and learning to care about ourselves and others can change our perspectives. It can give us the courage and support we need to take our next steps in life. And this, after all, was what White Mindfulness hoped to spread. But we are now living in a different world to the one over four decades ago when MBSR began. With hindsight, it is easier to know what we don't want to repeat, and to discern what is desirable.

This book is not about turning us all into political demonstrators who lobby authorities for change (although activism is never out of date and is often effective). It is interested in how we disrupt and decolonise our own lives and our worlds. How we might use the opportunities to train together to change the world by refusing the very social forces that generate power-over in the first place. This deeper work of creating worlds of belonging starts with innate wisdom, knowledge, education, networks, curiosity, and community. It taps into our own social capital and is, of course, ongoing and never done. Current crises present opportunities to nourish the forces that nurture dignity, respect, and social transformation. There is nothing stopping White Mindfulness from embracing the radical sea change underway other than its own uninterrogated embodiment of whiteness, and an incentive to change.

References

Ahmed, Sara. (2018). Rocking the Boat: Women of Colour as Diversity Workers. In *Dismantling Race in Higher Education: Racism, Whiteness and Decolonising the Academy*, edited by Jason Arday and Heidi Safia Mizra, 331–48. London: Palgrave Macmillan.

Ahmed, Sara. (2014). *The Cultural Politics of Emotion*. Edinburgh: Edinburgh University Press.

Ahmed, Sara. (2012). *On Being Included: Racism and Diversity in Institutional Life*. Durham, NC: Duke University Press.

Ahmed, Sara. (2007a). A Phenomenology of Whiteness. *Feminist Theory*, 8(2), 149–68.

Ahmed, Sara. (2007b). The Language of Diversity. *Ethnic and Racial Studies*, 30(2), 235–56.

Ahmed, Sara. (2004a). Declarations of Whiteness: The Non-Performativity of Anti-Racism. *Borderlands*, 3(2).

Ahmed, Sara. (2004b). The Non-Performativity of Anti-Racism. Text and Terrain. Legal Studies in Gender and Sexuality Colloquium, University of Kent, 29 September 2004.

Ahmed, Sara, Shona Hunter, Sevgi Kilic, Elaine Swan, and Lewis Turner. (2006). *Race, Diversity and Leadership in the Learning and Skills Sector, Final Report*. London: Centre for Excellence in Leadership.

Akómoláfé, Báyò. (2021). Báyò Akómoláfé. Accessed 19 December 2021. www.bayoakomolafe.net.

Alton, Nancy. (2017). Someone you Should Know: Angela Rose Black, PhD. *ParentMap*, 29 August. Accessed 13 September 2017. https://bit.ly/30Fym4I.

American Mindfulness Research Association (AMRA). (2018). *Mindfulness* journal article titles published by year: 1980–2021. Accessed 13 February 2022. https://bit.ly/3RDmrta.

Anderson, Elijah. (2015). The White Space. *Sociology of Race and Ethnicity*, 1(1), 10–21.

Apple, Michael. (2001). *Educating the Right Way: Markets, Standards, God, and Inequality: Schools and the Conservative Alliance*. London: Routledge.

Arday, Jason and Heidi Mirza. (2018). *Dismantling Race in Higher Education: Racism, Whiteness and Decolonising the Academy.* London: Palgrave Macmillan.

Armstrong, Margalynne and Stephanie Wildman. (2007). Teaching Race/ Teaching Whiteness: Transforming Colorblindness to Color Insight. *North Carolina Law Review, 86,* 635–72.

Arthington, Phil. (2016). Mindfulness: A Critical Perspective. *Community Psychology in Global Perspective, 2*(1), 87–104.

Asad, Talal. (2003). *Formations of the Secular: Christianity, Islam, Modernity (Cultural Memory in the Present).* Stanford, CA: Stanford University Press.

Associated Press. (2020). Explaining AP Style on Black and White. Accessed 21 September 2021. https://bit.ly/3qVD9sw.

Aung, Shwe Zan. (1910). Introductory Essay and Notes. In *Compendium of Philosophy: Being a Translation Now Made for the First Time from the Original Pāli of the Abhidhammattha-Sangaha,* translated by Shwe Zan Aung, revised and edited by C. A. F. Rhys Davids. London: H. Frowde for the Pāli Text Society.

Badat, Saleem. (2016). Difference, Diversity, and Inclusion: Critical Reflections on Post-1994 South African Higher Education. United Negro College Fund Summer Institute Address, Atlanta, Georgia, 20 June 2016.

Bailey, Alison. (2014). 'White Talk' as a Barrier to Understanding Whiteness. In *White Self-Criticality beyond Anti-racism: How Does It Feel to Be a White Problem?*, edited by George Yancy, 37–56. Lanham, MD: Lexington.

Barker, Kate. (2014). Mindfulness Meditation: Do-it-yourself Medicalization of Every Moment. *Social Science & Medicine, 106,* 168–76.

Barnard, Helen and Claire Turner. (2011). Poverty and Ethnicity: A Review of Evidence. Joseph Rowntree Foundation. Accessed 20 March 2017. https://bit.ly/3mhgHb8.

Barnett, Ronald. (1994). *The Limits of Competence: Knowledge, Higher Education and Society.* Buckingham: SHRE and Open University Press.

Batchelor, Stephen. (1994). *The Awakening of the West: The Encounter of Buddhism and Western Culture.* London: Aquarian Press.

Bécares, Laia. (2011). Which Ethnic Groups have the Poorest Health? Ethnic Health Inequalities 1991 to 2011. Dynamics of Diversity series. Centre on Dynamics of Ethnicity. Accessed 19 December 2021. https://bit.ly/3mikswS.

Bell, Karine. (2021). Ecologies of Trauma and Resilience. Embody Lab: Integrative Somatic Trauma Therapy Certificate: Module 20, 1 December.

Bell, Sandra. (2000). A Survey of Engaged Buddhism in Britain. In *Engaged Buddhism in the West,* edited by Christopher Queen, 397–422. Somerville: Wisdom.

Berila, Beth. (2016). *Integrating Mindfulness into Anti-Oppression Pedagogy: Social Justice in Higher Education.* New York: Routledge.

Bhabha, Homi. (1994/2004). *The Location of Culture*. London: Routledge.
Bhabha, Homi. (1985). Signs Taken for Wonders: Questions of Ambivalence and Authority under a Tree outside Delhi, May 1817. *Critical Inquiry*, 12(1), 144–65.
Bhambra, Gurminder. (2014). *Connected Sociologies*. London: Bloomsbury Academic.
Bhambra, Gurminder, Dalia Gebrial, and Kerem Nişancıoğlu (eds.). (2018). *Decolonising the University*. London: Pluto Press.
Bhanot, Kavita. (2015). Decolonise not Diversify. *Media Diversified*, 30 December.
Biko, Steve. (1978). *I Write What I Like*. London: Bowerdean.
Black, Angela. (2017). Mindfulness for the People: Radically Re-imagining the Mindfulness Movement. Accessed 17 November 2017. https://bit.ly/3QfKm0I.
Boal, Augusto, and Adrian Jackson (translator). (1994). *The Rainbow of Desire: The Boal Method of Theatre and Therapy*. London: Routledge.
Bodhi, Bikkhu. (2016). The Transformations of Mindfulness. In *Handbook of Mindfulness: Culture, Context, and Social Engagement*, edited by Ronald Purser, David Forbes, and Adam Burke, 3–14. Cham: Springer.
Bodhi, Bikkhu. (2013). In Conversation with Maia Duerr: Toward a Socially Responsible Mindfulness. Creating Space for Liberating Change. Accessed 19 December 2021. https://bit.ly/3qeBTj4.
Braun, Erik. (2013). *The Birth of Insight: Meditation, Modern Buddhism, and the Burmese Monk Ledi Sayadaw*. London: University of Chicago Press.
Brazier, David. (2016). Mindfulness: Traditional and Utilitarian. In *Handbook of Mindfulness: Culture, Context, and Social Engagement*, edited by Ronald Purser, David Forbes, and Adam Burke, 63–74. Cham: Springer.
Bristow, Jamie. (2016). *Building the Case for Mindfulness in the Workplace*. London: The Mindfulness Initiative. Accessed 10 December 2021. https://bit.ly/33HXyJ8.
Britton, Willoughby. (2014). Meditation Nation. *Tricyle*, 25 April.
brown, adrienne maree. (2017). *Emergent Strategy: Shaping Change, Changing Worlds*. Chico, CA: AK Press.
Brown, Austin Channing. (2018). *I'm Still Here: Black Dignity in a World made for Whiteness*. New York: Penguin Random House.
Brown, Candice. (2016). Can 'Secular' Mindfulness Be Separated from Religion? In *Handbook of Mindfulness: Culture, Context, and Social Engagement*, edited by Ronald Purser, David Forbes, and Adam Burke, 75–94. Cham: Springer.
Buchholz, Laura. (2015). Exploring the Promise of Mindfulness as Medicine. *Journal of American Medical Association*, 314(13), 1327–9.
Bulhan, Hussein. (1985). *Frantz Fanon and the Psychology of Oppression*. New York: Plenum.

Buswell, Robert and Donald Lopez. (2013). *The Princeton Dictionary of Buddhism*. Princeton, NJ: Princeton University Press.

Butler, Judith. (1993). *Bodies that Matter: On the Discursive Limits of 'Sex'*. New York: Routledge.

Butt, Jabeer, Samir Jeraj, Kat Clayton, Rebecca Neale, Zoe Gardner, Kathy Roberts, Katja Huijbers, Annie Whelan, Farah Islam-Barret, and Grace Wong. (2015). Better Practice in Mental Health for Black and Minority Ethnic Communities. Race Equality Foundation. Accessed 19 December 2021. https://bit.ly/3GXRZog.

Butterwick, Shauna and Jan Selman. (2012). Embodied Knowledge and Decolonisation: Walking with Theatre's Power and Risky Pedagogy. *New Directions for Adult and Continuing Education*, *134*, 61–9.

Caccavale, Joe. (2021). The Truth About Equality of Opportunity vs Equality of Outcome. *Applied*, 16 April. Accessed 19 December 2021. https://bit.ly/3q8fHas.

Cadge, Wendy. (2005). *Heartwood: The First Generation of Theravāda Buddhism in America*. Chicago: University of Chicago Press.

Campbell-Stephens, Rosemary. (2020). Global Majority: Decolonising the Language and Reframing the Conversation about Race. Leeds-Beckett University. Accessed 19 December 2021. https://bit.ly/3J0e7QN.

Cannon, Jennifer. (2016). Education as the Practice of Freedom: A Social Justice Proposal for Mindfulness Educators. In *Handbook of Mindfulness: Culture, Context, and Social Engagement*, edited by Ronald Purser, David Forbes, and Adam Burke, 397–410. Cham: Springer.

Caring-Lobel, Alex. (2016). Corporate Mindfulness and the Pathologization of Workplace Stress. In *Handbook of Mindfulness: Culture, Context, and Social Engagement*, edited by Ronald Purser, David Forbes, and Adam Burke, 195–214. Cham: Springer.

Carrette, Jeremy and Richard King. (2005). *Selling Spirituality: The Silent Takeover of Religion*. London: Routledge.

Cederström, Carl and Andre Spicer. (2015). *The Wellness Syndrome*. Cambridge: Polity.

Chapman, C. (1986). Pain, Perception and Illness. In *The Psychology of Pain*, edited by R. Sternbach, 153–79. New York: Raven.

Cheang, Kai Hang. (2020). Asian American Sociality after the Anti-relational Turn in Queer Theory. *Criticism*, 62(1), Article 8, 157–63.

Cho, Sumi. (2009). Post-racialism. *Iowa Law Review*, 94(5), 1589–649.

Clough, Patricia and Jean Halley. (2007). *The Affective Turn: Theorising the Social*. Durham, NC: Duke University Press.

Collins, Michael. (1991). *Adult Education as Vocation: A Critical Role for the Adult Educator*. London: Routledge.

Cook, Joanna. (2016). Mindful in Westminster: The Politics of Meditation and the Limits of Neoliberal Critique. *HAU: Journal of Ethnographic Theory*, 6(1), 141–61.

Coronado-Montoya, Stephanie, Alexander Levis, Linda Kwakkenbos, Russell Steele, Erick Turner, and Brett Thombs. (2016). Reporting of

Positive Results in Randomized Controlled Trials of Mindfulness-Based Mental Health Interventions. *PloS One, 11*(4), e0153220.

Crane, Catherine and Zindel Segal. (2016). MBCT for Recurrent Depression: What Do We Know? What Does it Mean? Where to Next? *Oxford Mindfulness Centre News.* Accessed 12 February 2018. http://oxfordmindfulness.org/news/mbct-recurrent-depression-know-mean-next/.

Crane, Rebecca, Judith Soulsby, Willem Kuyken, Mark Williams, and Catrin Eames. (2016). Mindfulness-based Interventions Teaching Assessment Criteria (MBI:TAC): Manual, Summary and Addendum. Accessed 19 December 2021. https://bit.ly/3J4Batr.

Crane, Rebecca, Steven Stanley, Michael Rooney, Trish Bartley, Lucinda Cooper, and Jody Mardula. (2014). Disciplined Improvisation: Characteristics of Inquiry in Mindfulness-Based Teaching. *Mindfulness,* 6(5), 1104–14.

Crane, Rebecca, Catrin Eames, Willem Kuyken, Richard Hastings, Mark Williams, Trish Bartley, Alison Evans, Sara Silverton, Judith G. Soulsby, and Christina Surawy. (2013). Development and Validation of the Mindfulness-Based Interventions – Teaching Assessment Criteria (MBI:TAC). *Assessment, 20*(6), 681–8.

Crane, Rebecca, Willem Kuyken, Mark Williams, Richard Hastings, Lucinda Cooper, and Melanie Fennell. (2012). Competence in Teaching Mindfulness-Based Courses: Concepts, Development and Assessment. *Mindfulness, 3,* 76–84.

Crane, Rebecca, Willem Kuyken, Richard Hastings, Neil Rothwell, and Mark Williams. (2010). Training Teachers to Deliver Mindfulness-Based Interventions: Learning from the UK Experience. *Mindfulness,* 1, 74–86.

Crawford, Robert. (1980). Healthism and the Medicalisation of Everyday Life. *International Journal of Health Services, 10*(3), 365–88.

Crenshaw, Kimberlé. (1991). Mapping the Margins: Intersectionality and Violence against Women of Colour. *Stanford Law Review, 43,* 1241–99.

Crenshaw, Kimberlé. (1989). Demarginalizing the Intersection of Race and Sex: A Black Feminist Critique of Antidiscrimination Doctrine, Feminist Theory and Antiracist Politics. *University of Chicago Legal Forum,* 1989(1), Article 8.

Daniel, Drew. (2010). Trading Futures: Queer Theory's Anti-Anti-Relational Turn. Reviewed Work: Cruising Utopia: The Then and There of Queer Futurity. *Criticism, 52*(2), 325–30.

Darder, Antonia, Marta Baltodano, and Rodolfo Torres (eds.). (2003). *The Critical Pedagogy Reader.* London: Routledge Falmer.

Davies, William. (2016). *The Happiness Industry: How the Government and Big Business Sold Us Well-being.* London: Verso.

Davis, Angela. (2017). Angela Davis in Conversation. Women of the World Festival, 11 March 2017, Southbank Centre. Accessed 16 December 2017. https://bit.ly/3q7pfm1.

Davis, Angela. (2016). *Freedom Is a Constant Struggle: Ferguson, Palestine, and the Foundations of a Movement*. Chicago: Haymarket.

Davis, Angela. (2012). *The Meaning of Freedom: And Other Difficult Dialogues*. San Francisco: City Light Books.

Davis, Angela and Jon Kabat-Zinn. (2015). An edited video of 'Mindfulness and the Possibility of Freedom: Angela Davis and Jon Kabat-Zinn in Dialogue', a benefit for the East Bay Meditation Center (EBMC), 15 January 2015.

Denis, Philippe. (2010). Seminary Networks and Black Consciousness in South Africa in the 1970s. *South African Historical Journal*, 62(1), 162–82.

Dhawan, Nikita. (2018). Colonial Repercussions. Planetary Utopias – Hope, Desire, Imaginaries in a Post-Colonial World, opening plenary, 23–24 June, Berlin. Accessed 30 June 2018. https://bit.ly/3E6DxZe.

DiAngelo, Robin. (2010). Why Can't We All Just Be Individuals?: Countering the Discourse of Individualism in Anti-racist Education. *InterActions: UCLA Journal of Education and Information Studies*, 6(1).

Dillon, Stephen. (2013). 'It's Here, It's That Time': Race, Queer Futurity, and the Temporality of Violence in *Born in Flames*. *Women & Performance: A Journal of Feminist Theory*, 23(1), 38–51.

Dimidjian, S. and Zindel Segal. (2015). Prospects for a Clinical Science of Mindfulness-Based Intervention. *American Psychologist*, 70(7), 593–620.

Doran, Peter. (2017). *A Political Economy of Attention, Mindfulness and Consumerism: Reclaiming the Mindful Commons*. London: Routledge.

Doran, Peter. (2018). Towards a Mindful Cultural Commons. *Cultural Matters*, 27 February. Accessed 1 March 2018. https://bit.ly/33wudkD.

Dorjee, Dusana. (2014). *Mind, Brain and the Path to Happiness: A Guide to Buddhist Mind Training and the Neuroscience of Meditation*. New York: Routledge.

Dreyfus, Hubert and Stuart Dreyfus. (1986). *Mind Over Machine: The Power of Human Intuition and Experience in the Age of Computers*. New York: Free Press.

Du Bois, W. E. B. (1984). *Dusk of Dawn: An Essay Toward an Autobiography of a Race Concept*. New York: Shocken.

Duerr, Maia. (2015). Toward a Socially Responsible Mindfulness. Creating Space for Liberating Change. Accessed 19 December 2021. https://bit.ly/3cOiV0i.

Eagleton, Terry. (2016). The Happiness Industry by William Davies Review: Why Capitalism has Turned us into Narcissists. *Guardian*, 3 August. Accessed 19 December 2021. https://bit.ly/3H07agq.

Eaton, Joshua. (2014). Gentrifying the Dharma: How the 1 Percent is Hijacking Mindfulness. *Salon*, 5 March.

Ehrenreich, Barbara. (1970). The Medical-Industrial Complex. *New York Review*, 17 December. Accessed 19 December 2021. https://bit.ly/3e6zsK8.

El Magd, Noha Abu. (2016). Why is My Curriculum so White? Accessed 19 December 2021. https://bit.ly/3paUBc9.

Equality and Human Rights Commission. (2018). Is Britain Fairer: The State of Equality and Human Rights 2018. Report, June 2018. Accessed December 2019. https://bit.ly/3QioZg0.

Equality and Human Rights Commission. (2016). Healing a Divided Britain: The Need for a Comprehensive Race Equality Strategy. Report, 18 August. Accessed 5 November 2016. https://bit.ly/32gLSwi.

Fanon, Frantz. (2001/1963). *The Wretched of the Earth*. London: Penguin.

Fleming, Crystal, Veronica Womack, and Jeffrey Proulx (eds.). (2022). *Beyond White Mindfulness: Critical Perspectives on Racism, Wellbeing, and Liberation*. New York: Routledge.

Forbes, David. (2016). Critical Integral Contemplative Education. In *Handbook of Mindfulness: Culture, Context, and Social Engagement*, edited by Ronald Purser, David Forbes, and Adam Burke, 355–67. Cham: Springer.

Freire, Paulo. (1993/1970). *Education, the Practice of Freedom*. London: Writers and Readers Publishing Cooperative.

Fronsdal, Gil. (1998). Insight Meditation in the United States: Life, Liberty, and the Pursuit of Happiness. In *The Faces of Buddhism in America*, edited by Charles Prebish and Kenneth Tanaka, 163–81. Berkeley: University of California Press.

Fronsdal, Gil. (1995). The Treasures of the *Theravāda*: Recovering the Riches of Our Tradition. *Inquiring Mind*, 12(1).

Gajaweera, Nalika. (2021). Sitting in the Fire Together: People of Color Cultivating Radical Resilience in North American Insight Meditation. *Journal of Global Buddhism*, 22(1), 121–39.

Gandhi, Shreena and Lillie Wolff. (2017). Yoga and the Roots of Cultural Appropriation. Praxis Centre, 19 December. Accessed 19 December 2021. https://bit.ly/324ukDT.

Gebrial, Dalia. (2018). Rhodes Must Fall: Oxford and Movements for Change. In *Decolonising the University*, edited by Gurminder Bhambra, Dalia Gebrial, and Kerem Nişancıoğlu, 19–36. London: Pluto.

Gilroy, Paul. (1990). The End of Anti-Racism. *Journal of Ethnic and Migration Studies*, 17(1), 71–83.

Giroux, Henry. (2012). *Neoliberalism's War on Higher Education*. Chicago: Haymarket.

Gleig, Ann. (2019). Undoing Whiteness in American Buddhist Modernism. In *Buddhism and Whiteness: Critical Reflections*, edited by George Yancy and Emily McRae, 1–22. Lanham, MD: Lexington.

Goenka, S. N. (2002). *Meditation Now: Inner Peace Through Inner Wisdom*. Washington: Vipassanā Research Publications.

Goldberg, Theo. (2015). *Are We All Postracial Yet? Debating Race*. Cambridge: Polity.

Goldberg, Theo. (2009). *The Threat of Race: Reflections on Racial Neoliberalism*. Oxford: Blackwell.

González-Calvo, Gustavo and Marta Arias-Carballal. (2018). Effects from Audit Culture and Neoliberalism on University Teaching: An Autoethnographic Perspective. *Ethnography and Education*, *13*(4), 413–27.

Gordon. Leah. (2015). *From Power to Prejudice: The Rise of Racial Individualism in Midcentury America*. London: University of Chicago Press.

Goyal, Madhav, Sonal Singh, Erica Sibinga, Neda Gould, Anastasia Rowland-Seymour, Ritu Sharma, Zackary Berger, Dana Sleicher, David Maron, Hasan Shihab, Padmini Ranasinghe, Shauna Linn, Shonali Saha, Eric Bass, and Jennifer Haythornthwaite. (2014). Meditation Programs for Psychological Stress and Well-being: A Systematic Review and Meta-analysis. *JAMA Internal Medicine*, *174*(3), 357–68.

Griffiths, Raza. (2018). A Call for Social Justice: Creating Fairer Policy and Practice for Mental Health Service Users from Black and Minority Ethnic Communities. A Report and Manifesto produced by service users from the BME community. Accessed 26 March 2019. https://bit.ly/3wWinwf.

Gritti, Paulo. (2017). The Bio-psycho-social Model Forty Years Later: A Critical Review. *JPS*, *1*(1), 36–41.

Grosfoguel, Ramón. (2013). The Structure of Knowledge in Westernized Universities: Epistemic Racism/Sexism and the Four Genocides/Epistemicides of the Long 16th Century. *Human Architecture: Journal of the Sociology of Self-Knowledge*, *11*(1), 73–90.

Guarino, Cassandra. (2017). Why Higher Education Needs to Get Rid of the Gender Gap for 'Academic Housekeeping'. *The Conversation*, 28 September. Accessed 29 September 2017. https://bit.ly/3EaEGPt.

Haines, Staci. (2019). *The Politics of Trauma*. Berkeley, CA: North Atlantic Books.

Hall, Stuart. (2011). The Neoliberal Revolution. *Cultural Studies*, *25*(6), 705–28.

Hall, Stuart. (1987). Minimal Selves. The Real Me: Postmodernism and the Question of Identity. ICA Documents 6, edited by Lisa Appignenesi, 44–6. London: The Institute of Contemporary Arts.

Hamilton, Peter. (1992). The Enlightenment and the Birth of Social Science. In *Formations of Modernity*, edited by Stuart Hall and Bram Gibbon, 17–70. Cambridge: Polity.

Harvey, David. (2005). *A Brief History of Neoliberalism*. Oxford: Oxford University Press.

Harvey, Lee. (2006). Impact of Quality Assurance: Overview of a Discussion Between Representatives of External Quality Assurance Agencies. *Quality in Higher Education*, *12*(3), 287–90.

Hase, Craig, James Meadows, and Stephanie Budge. (2019). Inclusion and Exclusion in the White Space: An Investigation of the Experiences of People of Color in a Primarily White American Meditation Community. *Journal of Global Buddhism*, 20, 1–18.

Healey, Kevin. (2015). Disrupting Wisdom 2.0: The Quest for 'Mindfulness' in Silicon Valley and Beyond. *Journal of Religion, Media and Digital Culture*, 4(1), 67–95.

Hemphill, Prentis. (2022). Radical Recovery Summit, 7–16 January 2022. https://bit.ly/3Lw55wy.

Henderson, Jan. (2010). The Politics Behind Personal Responsibility for Health. *The Health Culture*, 5 November. Accessed 7 July 2016. https://bit.ly/3GY0Rdm.

Hickey, Wakoh Shannon. (2010). Two Buddhisms, Three Buddhisms and Racism. *Journal of Global Buddhism*, 11(2010), 1–25.

Hill, Laura. (2019). Welltodo. *Global Wellness News*, 17 October 2019. Accessed 19 December 2021. https://bit.ly/323CQmF.

Hill Collins, Patricia. (1997). Comment on Hekman's 'Truth and Method: Feminist Standpoint Theory Revisited': Where's the Power? *Signs*, 22(21), 375–81.

Hill Collins, Patricia. (1986). Learning from the Outsider Within: The Sociological Significance of Black Feminist Thought. *Social Problems*, 33(6), S14–S32.

Hill Collins, Patricia and Sirma Bilge. (2016). *Intersectionality*. Cambridge: Polity.

Holden, Robert. (1994). The Happiness Project. Accessed 19 December 2021. https://bit.ly/3wTMPHm.

Holmwood, John. (2018). Race and the Neoliberal University: Lessons from the Public University. In *Decolonising the University*, edited by Gurminder Bhambra, Dalia Gebrial, and Kerem Nişancıoğlu, 37–52. London: Pluto.

Honey, L. (2014). Self-Help Groups in Post-Soviet Moscow: Neoliberal Discourses of the Self and their Social Critique. *Laboratorium: Russian Review of Social Research*, 6(1), 5–29.

hooks, bell. (2000). *Feminism Is for Everybody*. Cambridge: South End.

hooks, bell. (1995). *Art on My Mind*. New York: The New Press.

hooks, bell. (1994). *Teaching to Transgress: Education as the Practice of Freedom*. New York: Routledge.

hooks, bell. (1992). *Black Looks: Race and Representation*. Boston: South End.

hooks, bell. (1991). *Yearning: Race, Gender and Cultural Politics*. London: Turnaround.

Hsu, Funie. (2017). We've Been Here All Along. *Lion's Roar*, 17 May 2017.

Hsu, Funie. (2016). What Is the Sound of One Invisible Hand Clapping? Neoliberalism, the Invisibility of Asian and Asian American Buddhists, and Secular Mindfulness in Education. In *Handbook of Mindfulness: Culture, Context, and Social Engagement*, edited by Ronald Purser, David Forbes, and Adam Burke, 369–81. Cham: Springer.

Hsu, Funie. (2014). A Wake-up Call: The Suffering of Systemic Violence in Student Lives. Buddhist Peace Fellowship, 18 February.

Hubis, Peter. (2015). *Frantz Fanon: Philosopher of the Barricades*. London: Pluto.

Huijbers, Marloes, Rebecca Crane, Willem Kuyken, Lot Heijke, Ingrid van den Hout, A. Rogier, T. Donders, and Anne E. M. Speckens. (2017). Teacher Competence in Mindfulness-Based Cognitive Therapy for Depression and Its Relation to Treatment Outcome. *Mindfulness*, 8(4), 960–72.

Hunt, Vivian, Sundiatu Dixon-Fyle, Sara Prince, and Kevin Nolan. (2020). Diversity Wins: How Inclusion Matters. A McKinsey Report. Accessed 19 December 2021. https://mck.co/3GO6ISC.

Hunter, Jeremy. (2021). Achieving the Impossible: Embracing the Transformative Potential of Climate Change. The Great Leadership Reset Conference. https://bit.ly/3qW8mvl.

Hwang, Yoon-Suk and Patrick Kearney. (2015). A Genealogy of Mindfulness. In *A Mindfulness Intervention for Children with Autism Spectrum Disorders: New Directions in Research and Practice*, 5–21. Cham: Springer International.

Hyland, Terry. (1994). *Competence, Education and NVQs: Dissenting Perspectives*. London: Cassell.

Ige, Abiodun. (2006). The Cult of Ancestors in African Traditional Religion. *An Encyclopaedia of the Arts*, 10(1), 26–31.

Ileka, Kevin, Courtney McCluney, and Renã Robinson. (2020). White Coats, Black Scientists. *Harvard Business Review*, 23 September.

Jain, Andrea. (2020). *Peace Love Yoga: The Politics of Global Spirituality*. New York: Oxford University Press.

Johnson, Rae. (2017). *Embodied Social Justice*. London: Routledge.

Kabat-Zinn, Jon. (2017). Too Early to Tell: The Potential Impact and Challenges – Ethical and Otherwise – Inherent in the Mainstreaming of Dharma in an Increasingly Dystopian World. *Mindfulness*, 8, 1125–35.

Kabat-Zinn, Jon. (2016). What is the Fourth Industrial Revolution? Accessed 12 November 2016. https://bit.ly/3GOkcxI.

Kabat-Zinn, Jon. (2014). Interview by Ellen More. University of Massachusetts Medical School, Worcester, Massachusetts, 18 September. UMass Medical School Archives.

Kabat-Zinn, Jon. (2011). Some Reflections on the Origins of MBSR, Skilful Means, and the Trouble with Maps. *Contemporary Buddhism*, 12(1), 281–306.

Kabat-Zinn, Jon. (2010). Mindfulness and the Cessation of Suffering: An Exclusive New Interview with Mindfulness Pioneer Jon Kabat-Zinn by Danny Fisher. *Lion's Roar*, October 7.

Kabat-Zinn, Jon. (2005). *Coming to Our Senses: Healing Ourselves and the World Through Mindfulness*. New York: Hyperion.

Kabat-Zinn, Jon. (2000). Indra's Net at Work: The Mainstreaming of Dharma Practice in Society. In *The Psychology of Awakening: Buddhism, Science, and Our Day-to-Day Lives*, edited by Gay Watson, Stephen Batchelor, and Guy Claxton, 225–49. York Beach, ME: Samuel Weiser.

References   239

Kabat-Zinn, Jon. (1994a). Catalyzing Movement Towards a More Contemplative/ Sacred-Appreciating/Non-Dualistic Society. The Contemplative Mind in Society Meeting of the Working Group, 29 September–2 October. Pocantico, New York.

Kabat-Zinn, Jon. (1994b). *Wherever You Go, There You Are: Mindfulness Meditation for Everyday Life.* New York: Hyperion.

Kabat-Zinn, Jon. (1990/2013). *Full Catastrophe Living.* London: Piatkus.

Kabat-Zinn, Jon. (1982). An Outpatient Programme in Behavioural Medicine for Chronic Pain Patients Based on the Practice of Mindfulness Meditation: Theoretical Considerations and Preliminary Results. *General Hospital Psychiatry, 4,* 33–47.

Kabat-Zinn, Jon and A. Chapman-Waldrop. (1988). Compliance with an Outpatient Stress Reduction Program: Rates and Predictors of Completion. *Journal of Behavioural Medicine, 11,* 333–52.

Kabat-Zinn, Jon, L. Lipworth, and R. Burney. (1985). The Clinical Use of Mindfulness Meditation for the Self-Regulation of Chronic Pain. *Journal of Behavioural Medicine, 8,* 163–90.

Kabat-Zinn, Jon, L. Lipworth, R. Burney, and W. Sellers. (1986). Four-year Follow-Up of a Meditation-Based Program for the Self-Regulation of Chronic Pain: Treatment Outcomes and Compliance. *Clinical Journal of Pain, 2,* 159–73.

Kabat-Zinn, Jon, A. Massion, J. Kristeller, L. Peterson, K. Fletcher, L. Pbert, W. Linderking, and S. Santorelli. (1992). Effectiveness of a Meditation-Based Stress Reduction Program in the Treatment of Anxiety Disorders. *American Journal of Psychiatry, 149,* 936–43.

Kaleem, Jaweed. (2012). Buddhist People of Color Sanghas: Diversity Efforts Address Conflicts About Race Among Meditators. *HuffPost.* Updated 31 March 2015. Accessed 19 June 2018. https://bit.ly/3Qg9pBx.

Kankhwende, Kiri. (2018). The Mental Health System is Not Designed with Us in Mind. *Media Diversified,* 20 September.

Kerr, Catherine. (2014). Don't Believe the Hype: Neuroscientist Catherine Kerr is Concerned about How Mindfulness Meditation Research is Being Portrayed in the Media. *Tricycle,* 1 October.

Kerr, Malcolm H. (1980). Edward Said, Orientalism. *International Journal of Middle East Studies, 12,* 546–7.

Khoury, Bassam, Tania Lecomte, Guillaume Fortin, Marjolaine Masse, Phillip Therien, Vanessa Bouchard, Marie-Andrée Chapleau, Karine Paquin, and Stefan Hofmann. (2013). Mindfulness-Based Therapy: A Comprehensive Meta-Analysis. *Clinical Psychology Review, 33*(6), 763–71.

King, Richard. (2009). Philosophy of Religion as Border Control: Globalization and the Decolonization of the 'Love of Wisdom' (Philosophia). In *Postcolonial Philosophy of Religion,* edited by Purushottama Bilimoria and Andrew Irvine, 35–53. Dordrecht: Springer.

King, Richard. (2004). Cartographies of the Imagination, Legacies of Colonialism: The Discourse of Religion and the Mapping of Indic Traditions. *Evam: Forum on Indian Representations, 3*(1–2), 272–89.

King, Richard. (1999). *Orientalism and Religion: Postcolonial Theory, India and the Mystic East.* London: Routledge.

Klein, Naomi. (2008). *The Shock Doctrine: The Rise of Disaster Capitalism.* Oxford: Oxford University Press.

Kline, Roger. (2014). The 'Snowy White Peaks' of the NHS: A Survey of Discrimination in Governance and Leadership and the Potential Impact on Patient Care in London and England. Accessed 30 January 2017. https://bit.ly/3mijYXO.

Krznaric, Roman. (2017). How We Ruined Mindfulness. *Time,* 26 May. Accessed 19 December 2021. https://bit.ly/3Fg3I0P.

Kucinskas, Jaime. (2019). *The Mindful Elite.* New York: Oxford University Press.

Kundnani, Arun. (2020). What is Racial Capitalism? Havens Wright Centre for Social Justice, University of Wisconsin-Madison, 15 October. Accessed 15 November 2021. https://bit.ly/3TBf0nY.

Ladson-Billings, Gloria. (2007). Pushing Past the Achievement Gap: An Essay on the Language of Deficit. *Journal of Negro Education,* 76(3), 316–23.

Lange, Lis and Mala Singh. (2010). Equity Issues in Quality Assurance in South African Higher Education. In *Equity and Quality Assurance: A Marriage of Two Minds,* edited by Michaela Martin, 37–73. Paris: IIEP/UNESCO.

Lavelle, Brooke. (2016). Against One Method: Contemplation in Context. In *Handbook of Mindfulness: Culture, Context, and Social Engagement,* edited by Ronald Purser, David Forbes, and Adam Burke, 233–42. Cham: Springer.

Lee, Yo-An. (2007). Third Turn Position in Teacher Talk: Contingency and the Work of Teaching. *Journal of Pragmatics,* 39(6), 1204–30.

Levins Morales, Aurora. (2013). *Kindling: Writings on the Body.* Massachusetts: Palabrera Press.

Lewis, Amanda. (2004). 'What Group?' Studying Whites and Whiteness in the Era of 'Color-Blindness'. *Sociological Theory,* 22(4), 623–46.

Lewis, Bernard. (1982). The Question of Orientalism. *New York Review of Books,* 24 June, 49.

Lewis, David and Deborah Rozelle. (2016). Mindfulness-Based Interventions: Clinical Psychology, Buddhadharma, or Both? A Wisdom Perspective. In *Handbook of Mindfulness: Culture, Context, and Social Engagement,* edited by Ronald Purser, David Forbes, and Adam Burke, 243–68. Cham: Springer.

Linton, Samara and Rianna Walcott (eds.). (2018). *The Colour of Madness: Exploring BAME Mental Health in the UK.* Edinburgh: Skiddaw.

Lopez, Donald. (2002). *A Modern Buddhist Bible: Essential Readings from East and West.* Boston: Beacon.

Lorde, Audre. (2007a). Learning from the 60s. In *Sister Outsider: Essays and Speeches* (2nd ed.), 134–44. Berkeley, CA: Crossing.

Lorde, Audre. (2007b). The Master's Tools Will Never Dismantle the Master's House. In *Sister Outsider: Essays and Speeches* (2nd ed.), 110–13. Berkeley, CA: Crossing.

Lorde, Audre. (2007c). Age, Race, Class and Sex: Women Redefining Difference. In *Sister Outsider: Essays and Speeches* (2nd ed.), 114–23. Berkeley, CA: Crossing.

Lorey, Isabell. (2015). *State of Insecurity: Government of the Precarious.* London: Verso.

Love, Heather. (2009). *Feeling Backward: Loss and the Politics of Queer History.* Boston, MA: Harvard University Press.

Loy, David. (2016). The Challenge of Mindful Engagement. In *Handbook of Mindfulness: Culture, Context, and Social Engagement*, edited by Ronald Purser, David Forbes, and Adam Burke, 15–26. Cham: Springer.

Magee, Rhonda. (2018). When Mindfulness and Racism Intersect. *Mindful*, 21 March.

Magee, Rhonda. (2016). Community-Engaged Mindfulness and Social Justice: An Inquiry and Call to Action. In *Handbook of Mindfulness: Culture, Context, and Social Engagement*, edited by Ronald Purser, David Forbes, and Adam Burke, 425–39. Cham: Springer.

Mangcu, Xolela. (2014). *Biko: A Life.* London and New York: I. B. Tauris.

Marable, Manning and Joseph, Peniel. (2008). Series Editors' Preface: Steve Biko and the International Context of Black Consciousness. In *Biko Lives! Contesting the Legacies of Steve Biko*, edited by Andile Mngxitama, Amanda Alexander, and Nigel C. Gibson, vii–x. New York and Basingstoke: Palgrave Macmillan.

Marcelle, Gillian. (2017). Science, Technology and Innovation Policy that is Responsive to Innovation Performers. In *Research Handbook on Innovation Governance for Emerging Economies*, edited by Stefan Kuhlmann and Gonzalo Ordóñez-Matamoros, 59–86. Cheltenham: Edward Elgar.

Martin-Baro, Ignacio. (1996). *Writings for a Liberation Psychology* with Adrian Aon (ed.) and Shawn Corne (series ed.). Boston, MA: Harvard University Press.

Martinez, Elizabeth and Arnaldo Garcia. (1996). What is Neoliberalism? A Brief Definition for Activists. *Corp Watch*. Accessed 20 March 2017. https://bit.ly/3skgBDE.

Matilal, Bimal Krishna. (2002). *The Collected Essays of Bimal Krishna Matilal, Volume 1*, edited by Jonardon Ganeri. New Delhi: Oxford University Press.

McAvoy, Jean. (2014). Psy Disciplines. In *The Encyclopaedia of Critical Psychology*, edited by T. Teo, 1527–29. New York: Springer.

McCabe, Glen. (2008). Mind, Body, Emotions and Spirit: Reaching to the Ancestors for Healing. *Counselling Psychology Quarterly*, 21(2), 143–52.

McCown, Donald, Diane Reibel, and Mark Micozzi. (2011). *Teaching Mindfulness: A Practical Guide for Clinicians and Educators.* New York: Springer.

McGhee, Heather. (2021). *The Sum of Us: What Racism Costs Everyone and How We Can Prosper Together.* London: Profile.

McIntosh, Peggy. (1988). White Privilege and Male Privilege: A Personal Account of Coming to See Correspondences Through Work in Women's Studies. *Working Paper 189.* Wellesley College: Centre for Research on Women.

McMahan, David. (2017). Buddhism and Global Secularisms. *Journal of Global Buddhism, 18,* 112–28.

McMahan, David. (2012). *Buddhism in the Modern World.* New York: Routledge.

McMahan, David. (2008). *The Making of Buddhist Modernism.* Oxford: Oxford University Press.

McMahan, David and Eric Braun (eds.). (2017). *Meditation, Buddhism, and Science.* New York: Oxford University Press.

McPherson, William. (1999). The Stephen Lawrence Inquiry: Report of an inquiry by Sir William MacPherson of Cluny. Presented to Parliament by the Secretary of State for the Home Department by Command of Her Majesty. February 1999. Accessed 19 December 2021. https://bit.ly/3EdYu4z.

Michelson, Elana. (2015). *Gender, Experience, and Knowledge in Adult Education: Alisoun's Daughters.* New York: Routledge.

Mirza, Heidi Safia. (2017). Colloquium on Difference, Diversity, and Inclusion: International and Comparative Perspectives, 5 June 2017, Haarlem, The Netherlands. New York: Andrew Mellon Foundation.

Mirza, Heidi Safia. (2015). Decolonizing Higher Education: Black Feminism and the Intersectionality of Race and Gender. *Journal of Feminist Scholarship, 7/8,* 1–12.

Mitchell, Sherri. (2021). Embodying Ancestral Wisdom. Embody Lab: Integrative Somatic Trauma Therapy Certificate: Module 4, 6 October.

Mitra, Joy and Mark Greenberg. (2016). The Curriculum of Right Mindfulness: The Relational Self and the Capacity for Compassion. In *Handbook of Mindfulness: Culture, Context, and Social Engagement,* edited by Ronald Purser, David Forbes, and Adam Burke, 411–24. Cham: Springer.

Moeller, Carol. (2019). 'bell hooks Made Me a Buddhist': Liberatory Cross-cultural Learning – Or is This Just Another Case of How White People Steal Everything? In *Buddhism and White,* edited by George Yancy and Emily McRae, 181–206. London: Lexington.

Moloney, Paul. (2016). Mindfulness: The Bottled Water of the Therapy Industry. In *Handbook of Mindfulness: Culture, Context, and Social Engagement,* edited by Ronald Purser, David Forbes, and Adam Burke, 269–92. Cham: Springer.

Monteiro, Lynette, Frank Musten, and Jane Compson. (2015). Traditional and Contemporary Mindfulness: Finding the Middle Path in the Tangle of Concerns. *Mindfulness*, 6(1), 1–13.

moore, madison. (2018). *Fabulous: The Rise of the Beautiful Eccentric*. London: Yale University Press. Book Launch, Interviewed by Ruth Ramsden-Karelse, Blackwell's, Oxford, 18 June.

Morrison, Toni. (2001). How Can Values Be Taught in the University? *Michigan Quarterly Review*, *40*(2), 278.

Morrison, Toni. (1975). Public Dialogue on the American Dream Series. Accessed 19 December 2021. https://bit.ly/30FawpK.

Msimang, Sisonke. (2021). How Apartheid Endures: The Betrayal of SA. *Foreign Affairs*. Accessed 19 December 2021. https://fam.ag/3enBXrD.

Muñoz, José. (2009). *Cruising Utopia: The Then and There of Queer Futurity*. New York: New York University Press.

Mupotsa, Danai. (2018). *Feeling and Ugly*. South Africa: impepho.

Myers, Melissa. (2015). Improving Military Resilience through Mindfulness Training. *USAMRMC Public Affairs*, 1 June. Accessed 19 December 2021. https://bit.ly/3RgpHej.

Nathoo, Ayesha. (2016). From Therapeutic Relaxation to Mindfulness in the Twentieth Century. In *The Restless Companion: Interdisciplinary Investigations of Rest and Its Opposites*, edited by Felicity Collard, Kimberley Staines, and James Wilkes, 71–80. Cham: Palgrave Macmillan.

National Association of Black Journalists. (2020). NABJ Statement on Capitalizing Black and Other Racial Identifiers. Accessed 21 September 2021. https://bit.ly/2GUyCzR.

Naqvi, Habib, Saba Abid Razaq, and Johann Piper. (2016). NHS Workforce Race Equality Standard: 2015 Data Analysis Report for NHS Trusts. Accessed 30 January 2017. https://bit.ly/32bCeuX.

Ndefo, Nkem. (2021). Towards an Alchemical Resilience: Foundations and Inspirations. Embody Lab: Integrative Somatic Trauma Therapy Certificate: Module 3, 4 October.

Ng, Edwin. (2016a). The Critique of Mindfulness and the Mindfulness of Critique: Paying Attention to the Politics of Our Selves with Foucault's Analytic of Governmentality. In *Handbook of Mindfulness: Culture, Context, and Social Engagement*, edited by Ronald Purser, David Forbes, and Adam Burke, 135–52. Cham: Springer.

Ng, Edwin. (2016b). *Buddhism and Cultural Studies: A Profession of Faith*. London: Springer.

Ng, Edwin. (2014). Who Gets Buddhism 'Right'? Reflections of a Postcolonial 'Western Buddhist' Convert. *ABC Religion and Ethics*, 11 December.

Nieves, Yolanda. (2012). Embodying Women's Stories for Community Awareness and Social Action. *New Directions for Adult and Continuing Education*, *134*, 33–42.

Noah, Trevor and Heather McGhee. (2021). 'The Sum of Us' and the True Cost of Racism. *The Daily Social Distancing Show*, 18 February. Accessed 15 December 2021. https://bit.ly/3S8k9mA.

Noble, Safiya. (2018). *Algorithms of Oppression: How Search Engines Reinforce Racism*. New York: New York Press.

O'Brien, Hettie. (2019). How Mindfulness Privatised a Social Problem. *New Statesman*, 17 July. Accessed 19 December 2021. https://bit.ly/3mjOOPQ.

Ohanian, Alexis. (2020). Reddit Resignation Tweet, 5 June. Accessed 19 December 2021. https://bit.ly/3EcHMm6.

Olssen, Mark and Michael Peters. (2005). Neoliberalism, Higher Education and the Knowledge Economy: From the Free Market to Knowledge Capitalism. *Journal of Education Policy*, 20(3), 313–45.

Owen, Paul. (2012). 2011 Census Data: Key Points. *Guardian*, 11 December. Accessed 23 September 2019. https://bit.ly/3GZ1NhH.

Owens, Rod and Kate Johnson. (2020). A Conversation on Love and Rage: Lama Rod Owens and Kate Johnson. *Lion's Roar*, 16 June. Accessed 19 December 2021. https://bit.ly/3GXzKiB.

Painter, Nell Irvin. (2011). *The History of White People*. London: W. W. Norton.

Painter, Nell Irvin. (2020). Why White Should be Capitalised Too. *Washington Post*, 22 July. Accessed 19 December 2021. https://wapo.st/3mhVmyi.

Patricio, Marco. (2018). How Mindfulness Became a Billion-dollar Industry. *Medium*, 13 November. Accessed 19 December 2021. https://bit.ly/3slAZ75.

Payne, Richard. (2016). Mindfulness and the Moral Imperative for the Self to Improve the Self. In *Handbook of Mindfulness: Culture, Context, and Social Engagement*, edited by Ronald Purser, David Forbes, and Adam Burke, 121–34. Cham: Springer.

Payne, Richard. (2015). Sheep's Clothing? Marketing Mindfulness as Socially Transforming. Critical Reflections on Buddhist Thought: Contemporary and Classical. 27 October.

Pickert, Kate. (2014). The Mindful Revolution. *Time*, 23 January. Accessed 23 October 2016. https://bit.ly/3yJE1Dx.

Piyadassi, Thera. (1959/2008). *Dependent Origination*. Wheel Publication 15. Sri Lanka: Buddhist Publication Society Online.

powell, john. (2008). Post-Racialism or Targeted Universalism. *Denver University Law Review*, 86, 785–806.

Prakash, Gyan. (1995). Orientalism Now. *History and Theory*, 34(3), 199–212.

Purser, Ronald. (2019). *McMindfulness*. London: Repeater.

Purser, Ronald. (2015). The Myth of the Present Moment. *Mindfulness*, 6, 680–6.

Purser, Ronald and Edwin Ng. (2015). White Privilege and the Mindfulness Movement. Buddhist Fellowship Movement, 2 October.

Puwar, Nirmal. (2004). *Space Invaders: Race, Gender and Bodies Out of Place*. New York: Berg.

Race on the Agenda. (2017). ROTA Annual Report 2016–2017. Accessed 15 October 2018. https://bit.ly/3yHrH6z.

Raiche, Christopher. (2016). #BlackLivesMatter and Living the Bodhisattva Vow. *Harvard Divinity Bulletin*, 44(1–2) (Winter/Spring).

Ramsden, Ché. (2016). 'Showing up': Intersectionality 101. *openDemocracy*, 21 March. Accessed 30 January 2017. https://bit.ly/3yKIE0g.

Rashawn, Ray and Alexandra Gibbons. (2021). Why are States Banning Critical Race Theory. Brookings Institute, November. Accessed 14 June 2022. https://brook.gs/3CTQecV.

Reveley, James. (2016). Neoliberal Meditations: How Mindfulness Training Medicalizes Education and Responsibilizes Young People. *Policy Futures in Education*, 14(4), 497–511.

Rhys Davids, C. (1910). Preface. In *Compendium of Philosophy: Being a Translation Now Made for the First Time from the Original Pāli of the Abhidhammattha- Sangaha*, translated and with introductory essay and notes by Shwe Zan Aung, revised and edited by C. A. F. Rhys Davids. London: H. Frowde for the Pāli Text Society.

Riggins, Nash. (2018). Having Experienced the US and the UK Healthcare Systems, Here's the Truth About the Differences – and No, Donald Trump Isn't Right. *Independent*, 5 February. Accessed 30 March 2018. https://bit.ly/3slmMqX.

Riley, R. W. (1998). Our Teachers Should Be Excellent, and They Should Look Like America. *Education and Urban Society*, 31(1), 18–29.

Roithmayr, Daria. (2014). *Reproducing Racism: How Everyday Choices Lock in White Advantage*. New York: New York University Press.

Rose, Nikolas. (1999). *Powers of Freedom: Reframing Political Thought*. Cambridge: Cambridge University Press.

Rose, Nikolas. (1998). *Inventing Our Selves: Psychology, Power, and Personhood*. Cambridge: Cambridge University Press.

Runnymede Trust. (2021). England Civil Society Submission to the United Nations Committee on the Elimination of Racial Discrimination. Accessed 19 December 2021. https://bit.ly/3IWgG6a.

Safi, Michael. (2021). Mia Mottley: Barbados' First Female Leader on a Mission to Transform Island. *Guardian*, 3 December. Accessed 19 December 2021. https://bit.ly/3e7iVWk.

Saha, Anamik. (2017). Diversity Initiatives Don't Work, They Just Make Things Worse: The Ideological Function of Diversity in the Cultural Industries. *Media Diversified*, 16 February.

Said, Edward. (1978/2003). *Orientalism*. London: Pantheon.

Samudzi, Zoé. (2016). We Need a Decolonised, Not a 'Diverse' Education. *Harlot Media*, 29 March.

Samuel, Geoffrey. (2014). Between Buddhism and Science, Between Mind and Body. *Religions*, 5, 560–79.

Santorelli, Saki. (1999). *Heal Thyself*. New York: Random House.

Sasser, Sunara. (2018). Why Are There So Many Black Buddhists? *Tricycle*, 16 October.

Schwartz, G. E. and S. M. Weiss. (1978). Behavioral Medicine Revisited: An Amended Definition. *Journal of Behavioural Medicine*, 1(3), 249–51.

Scott, David. (2018). Colonial Repercussions. Planetary Utopias Conference, opening plenary, 23–24 June, Berlin. Accessed 30 June 2018. https://bit.ly/3e6LFhF.

Scott, David. (2017). *Stuart Hall's Voice: Intimations of an Ethics of Receptive Generosity*. London: Duke University Press.

Sebastiaan. (2018). How Judith Butler Overcame Foucault's Shortcomings. *Queer Europe*, 25 August. Accessed 19 December 2021. https://bit.ly/32fkuP5.

Sewell, Tony, Maggie Aderin-Pocock, Aftab Chughtai, Keith Fraser, Naureen Khalid, Dambisa Moyo, Mercy Muroki, Martyn Oliver, Samir Shah, Kunle Olulode, and Blondell Cluff. (2021). Commission on Race and Ethnic Disparities: The Report. Accessed 31 March 2021. https://bit.ly/3AOJOZT.

Sharf, Robert. (2017). Is Mindfulness Buddhist? (And Why It Matters). In *Meditation, Buddhism, Science*, edited by David McMahan and Eric Braun, 198–212. New York: Oxford University Press.

Sharf, Robert. (1998). The Rhetoric of Experience and the Study of Religion. *Journal of Consciousness Studies*, 7(11–12), 267–87.

Sharpless, Brian, and Jacques Barber. (2009). A Conceptual and Empirical Review of the Meaning, Measurement, Development, and Teaching of Intervention Competence in Clinical Psychology. *Clinical Psychology Review*, 29, 47–56.

Shaull, Richard. (1993). Foreword. In *Pedagogy of the Oppressed* by Paulo Freire. London: Penguin.

Shore, Cris and Susan Wright. (2015). Audit Culture Revisited: Rankings, Ratings and the Reassembling of Society. *Current Anthropology*, 56(3), 421–44.

Shore, Cris and Susan Wright. (1999). Audit Cultures and Anthropology: Neoliberalism in Higher Education. *Journal of the Royal Anthropological Institute*, 5(4), 557–75.

Singh, Mala. (2011). The Place of Social Justice in Higher Education and Social Change Discourses. *Compare: A Journal of Comparative and International Education*, 41(4), 481–94.

Singh, Mala. (2010). Quality Assurance in Higher Education: Which Pasts to Build on, What Futures to Contemplate? *Quality in Higher Education*, 16(2), 189–94.

Skrabanek, Petr. (1994). *The Death of Humane Medicine and the Rise of Coercive Healthism*. Suffolk: St Edmundsbury Press.

Smith, Linda Tuhiwai. (1999). *Decolonizing Methodologies: Research and Indigenous Peoples*. London: Zed.

Snodgrass, Judith. (2007). Defining Modern Buddhism: Mr. and Mrs. Rhys Davids and the Pali Text Society. *Comparative Studies of South Asia, Africa and the Middle East*, 27(1), 186–202.

Stahl, Bob. (n.d.). The Heart of the Dhamma. Posted to Centre for Mindfulness' Private Domain Teacher's Lounge, 15 February 2015.

Standing, Guy. (2011). *The Precariat: The New Dangerous Class*. London: Bloomsbury.

Stanley, Steven. (2012). Mindfulness: Towards A Critical Relational Perspective. *Social and Personality Psychology Compass, 6*(9), 631–41.

Stanley, Steven and Charlotte Longden. (2016). Constructing the Mindful Subject: Reformulating Experience Through Affective–Discursive Practice in Mindfulness-Based Stress Reduction. In *Handbook of Mindfulness: Culture, Context, and Social Engagement*, edited by Ronald Purser, David Forbes, and Adam Burke, 305–22. Cham: Springer.

Stevenson, Jacqui and Mala Rao. (2014). Explaining Levels of Wellbeing in BME Populations in England. University of East London. Accessed 20 March 2017. https://bit.ly/3en3B89.

Sullivan, Shannon. (2006). *Revealing Whiteness: The Unconscious Habits of Racial Privilege*. Bloomington: Indiana University Press.

Sun, Jessie. (2014). Mindfulness in Context: A Historical Discourse Analysis. *Contemporary Buddhism, 15*(2), 394–415.

Swarns, Rachel. (2016). Georgetown University Plans Steps to Atone for Slave Past. *New York Times*, 1 September. Accessed 19 December 2021. https://nyti.ms/3J344dD.

Sylvia, Dedunu. (2016). 5 Responses to the Awkwardly Titled 'New Face of Buddhism'. Buddhist Peace Fellowship, 27 January.

Thānissaro Bikkhu (trans.). (1997). *Sallatha Sutta: The Arrow*. Accessed 12 June 2017). https://bit.ly/3yIiwCZ.

The Mindfulness Initiative. (2015). Mindful Nation UK: Report by the Mindfulness All-Party Parliamentary Group (MAPPG). Accessed 3 November 2015. https://mindfulnessinschools.org/wp-content/uplo ads/2017/09/Mindfulness-APPG-Report_Mindful-Nation-UK_Oct2 015-1.pdf.

Thérien, Jean-Philippe. (1999). Beyond the North-South Divide: The Two Tales of World Poverty. *Third World Quarterly, 20*(4), 723–42.

Thompson, Becky. (2017). Domes of the Body: Yoga, Alignment, and Social Justice. *The Arrow, 4*(2), 70–92.

Thompson, Evan. (2016). What is Mindfulness? An Embodied Cognitive Science Perspective. Mind & Life Institute ISCS 2016 Keynote, 13 November 2016.

Thunberg, Greta. (2021). Keynote Speech at Youth4Climate Pre-COP26, 28 September 2021. Accessed 19 December 2021. https://bit.ly/3skzCpA.

Tomassini, Massimo. (2016). Mindfulness in the Working Life. Beyond the 'Corporate' View, in Search for New Spaces of Awareness and Equanimity. In *Handbook of Mindfulness: Culture, Context, and Social Engagement*, edited by Ronald Purser, David Forbes, and Adam Burke, 215–32. Cham: Springer.

Trilling, Daniel. (2020). Why is the UK Government Suddenly Targeting 'Critical Race Theory'? *Guardian*, 23 October. Accessed 14 May 2021. https://bit.ly/3QjuCJQ.

Tuxworth, E. (1989). Competence Based Education and Training: Background and Origins. In *Competency Based Education and Training*, edited by John Burke, 10–25. London: Falmer.

U.S. Census Bureau. (2021). US Department of Commerce. Accessed 3 July 2021. https://bit.ly/3e8Lsup.

Vaid-Menon, Alok. (2019). Fashion's Genderless Future. Accessed 10 December 2021. https://bit.ly/30Flr2H.

Wagner-Martin, Linda. (2014). *Toni Morrison and the Maternal: From 'The Bluest Eye' to 'Home'*. New York: Peter Lang.

Wallerstein, N. (2006). What is the Evidence on Effectiveness of Empowerment to Improve Health? Health Evidence Network Report. Copenhagen, WHO Regional Office for Europe. Accessed 12 March 2020. https://bit.ly/3RgCm0x.

Wallis, Glen. (2016). Criticism Matters. In *Handbook of Mindfulness: Culture, Context, and Social Engagement*, edited by Ronald Purser, David Forbes, and Adam Burke, 495–504. Cham: Springer.

Walsh, Zack. (2016). A Meta-Critique of Mindfulness Critiques: From McMindfulness to Critical Mindfulness. In *Handbook of Mindfulness: Culture, Context, and Social Engagement*, edited by Ronald Purser, David Forbes, and Adam Burke, 153–66. Cham: Springer.

Warner, Sara. (2011). Review. Cruising Utopia: The Then and There of Queer Futurity. *Modern Drama*, 54(2), 255–7.

Welwood, John. (1984). *Toward a Psychology of Awakening: Buddhism, Psychotherapy, and the Path of Personal and Spiritual Transformation*. Boston, MA: Shambhala.

Wiest, Amber, David Andrews, and Michael Giardina. (2015). Training the Body for Healthism: Reifying Vitality In and Through the Clinical Gaze of the Neoliberal Fitness Club. *Review of Education, Pedagogy, and Cultural Studies*, 37(1), 21–40.

williams, angel Kyodo, Rod Owens, and Jasmine Syedullah. (2016). *Radical Dharma: Talking Race, Love, and Liberation*. Berkeley, CA: North Atlantic Books.

Williams, Mark, Catherine Crane, Thorsten Barnhofer, Kate Brennan, Danielle Duggan, Melanie Fennell, Anne Hackmann, Adele Krusche, Kate Muse, Isabelle Rudolf von Rohr, Druvi Shah, Rebecca Crane, Catrin Earnes, Mariel Jones, Sholto Radford, Sarah Silverton, Yongzhong Sun, Elaine Weatherley-Jones, Christopher Whitaker, Daphne Russell, and Ian Russell. (2014). Mindfulness-based Cognitive Therapy for Preventing Relapse in Recurrent Depression: A Randomized Dismantling Trial. *Journal of Consulting and Clinical Psychology*, 82(2), 275–86.

Williams, Serena. (2020). Serena Williams interviews Alexis Ohanian. *Serena Saturday*, 7 June. Accessed 19 December 2021. https://bit.ly/33xW7g6.

Wilson, Jeff. (2016). Selling Mindfulness: Commodity Lineages and the Marketing of Mindful Products. In *Handbook of Mindfulness: Culture, Context, and Social Engagement*, edited by Ronald Purser, David Forbes, and Adam Burke, 109–20. Cham: Springer.

Wilson, Jeff. (2014). *Mindful America: The Mutual Transformation of Buddhist Meditation and American Culture.* Oxford: Oxford University Press.

Winder, Bayly. (1981). Review. Orientalism. *Middle East Journal, 35*(4), 615–17.

Wirth, A. (1991). Issues in the Vocational-Liberal Studies Controversy (1900–1917). In *Education for Work*, edited by David Corson, 55–64. Cleveland, OH: Multilingual Matters.

Woods, Susan. (2009). Training Professionals in Mindfulness: The Heart of Teaching. In *Clinical Handbook of Mindfulness*, edited by Fabrizio Didonna, 463–75. New York: Springer.

Yancy, George and Emily McRae. (2019). *Buddhism and Whiteness: Critical Reflections.* London: Lexington.

Yarnell, Thomas. (2003). Engaged Buddhism: New and Improved? Made in the USA of Asian Materials. In *Action Dharma: New Studies in Engaged Buddhism*, edited by Damien Keown, Charles Prebish, and Christopher Queen, 286–344. London: Routledge.

Zeilig, Leo. (2014). *Frantz Fanon: The Militant Philosopher of the Third World Revolution.* London: I. B. Tauris.

Zola, Irving. (1972). Medicine as an Institution of Social Control. *Sociological Review, 20*, 487–504.

Index